To Howard —

Nice to meet you in Colorado & on the phone. My son tells many wonderful things about you and that you are ~~not~~ a ~~beautiful~~ barrier buster and a bridge builder like my great grandmother Sarah —

Hope you enjoy reading it.

Sincerely,

Marlee Cockrell Medley

SARAH—THE BRIDGE BUILDER

Dowager of a Dallas Dynasty

Vivian Anderson Castleberry

Odenwald Press
Dallas

Published by Odenwald Press
Dallas, Texas / Panama City, Florida

Cover design by Boyd Brothers, Inc.

Printed in the United States of America

Library of Congress Cataloging-in-Publication Data

Castleberry, Vivian, 1922-
    Sarah—the bridge builder: dowager of a Dallas dynasty / Vivian Anderson Castleberry.
        p. cm.
    Includes index.
    ISBN 1-884363-19-9
1. Cockrell, Sarah Horton, 1819-1892. 2. Cockrell, Sarah Horton, 1819-1892-
Correspondence. 3. Dallas (Tex.)-Biography. 4. Widows-Texas-Dallas-
Biography. 5. Women-Texas-Dallas-Biography. 6. Women millionaires-
Texas-Dallas-Biography. 7. Dallas (Tex.)-History-19th century. 8. Dallas
(Tex.)-Social life and customs-19th century. I. Title.

    F394.D2153C63 2004
    976.4'04'092-dc22

                        2004011493

Dedication

For Mary Alice (Mackie) Cockrell Dealey
Who always kept the dream alive
And
For all descendants of Sarah Horton Cockrell
Whose cooperation made the writing of this book possible

Act well your part,

There all honour lies.

—Alexander Pope, 1688-1744

CONTENTS

PART II....LIKE A PHOENIX RISING

Acknowledgments

Like many stories, this one incubated in my brain for a long time and would not let me go. The book began with a telephone call I made to Mary Alice (Mackie) Cockrell Dealey who invited me to her home to talk about a possible book on her great grandmother. Satisfied that I was serious, but reluctant to continue the project without the support of Cockrell descendants, and only if no one in the family intended to tell Sarah's story, Mackie invited many of her relatives to join the two of us. The initial reluctance of some—("what does this woman want from us?")—faded away and, with few exceptions, Cockrell family descendants have been supportive. Clarence Cockrell, Mackie's brother, gave me a key to his office where over a two-year period I delved into the boxes of Sarah's memorabilia which had been salvaged, transported and stored at the insistence of Chris Mounts Cockrell, Clarence's son and Sarah's great-great grandson.

Provided with an office there, I opened boxes that had been stored for almost a hundred years and discovered a wealth of previously unpublished material, among it architectural drawings of the first bridge across the Trinity River, the wooden bridge Alexander Cockrell opened in 1855, and photographs of the Iron Bridge Sarah built in 1872. Also among the papers were letters and business documents in Sarah's handwriting: a will; a photograph album containing pictures of her four children—Aurelia Effie Cockrell (Gray), Robert Benjamin Cockrell, Frank Marion Cockrell and Alexander Cockrell II. There also were photographs of Dallas' founder, John Neely Bryan and Margaret Beeman Bryan, never before published, both of whom were treasured Cockrell friends. Also among the treasures was a log book containing registrants in Sarah's second hotel, the St. Charles, which included the names of prominent Dallas County early jurists who resided there when courts were in session.

Sarah's son, Frank Marion Cockrell, spent years researching and writing Dallas history based on his father's short-lived and his mother's long contributions to the city. His original manuscript was among the papers in those boxes. They are now at DeGolyer Library, Southern Methodist

University. Many of his articles appeared as columns in the *Dallas Morning News*. Parts of the manuscript were edited and 20 copies privately published by Sarah's grandson, Monroe F. Cockrell under the title, *Sarah Cockrell in Early Dallas*.

I am indebted to this grandson, Monroe Fulkerson Cockrell, eldest son of Alexander Cockrell II, for his recognition of the value of the Sarah papers, for rescuing them from the "little black leather trunk," that was her repository for valuable documents and donating them to the Dallas Historical Society at State Fair Park, Dallas. Monroe Cockrell also privately published other books, *History of Early Dallas* and *Civil War Letters of Col. George W. Guess*. He preserved documents and photographs, many of which are scattered among family members and/or were contributed to the Dallas Public Library, the Dallas Historical Society, Newberry Library in Chicago and Duke University.

Ruth Elinor Wilson Melton granted permission for the use of material from her father's unpublished manuscript, *Seven Generations in Dallas* by Joseph M. Wilson, Sarah's great grandson-in-law. Both George Jalonick and Barney Jones, descendants of the Cockrell family, lent their personal collection of papers and letters as did historian Frances James.

I am also deeply indebted to material previously published by a countless number of historians and writers. These include, but are not limited to books by Sam Acheson—*Dallas Yesterday* and *35,000 Days in Texas;* John Henry Brown's *History of Dallas County Texas from 1837-1887; Au Texas* by Victor Considerant; *Diaper Days of Dallas* by Ted Dealey; *Cannon Smoke* by Newton Fitzhugh; A. C. Greene's *Dallas: The Deciding Years—A Historical Portrait; Our City—Dallas* by Justin Kimball; *Greater Dallas and Vicinity* by Philip Lindsley; *Dallas Rediscovered: A Photographic Chronicle of Urban Expansion* by William McDonald; *Damn Proud People* by Mary Cullum Nash; *The Book of Dallas* by Evelyn Oppenheimer and Bill Porterfield; *Dallas An Illustrated History* by Darwin Payne; *Proud Heritage: Pioneer Families of Dallas County,* published by the Dallas County Pioneer Association; *The Lusty Texans of Dallas* by John William Rogers; *White Cliffs of Dallas* by George H. Santerre; and *Church at the Crossroads, a History of the First United Methodist Church Dallas.*

Two writers were especially helpful and I single them out: Shirley Seifert, author of *Destiny in Dallas,* based on the life of Alexander and Sarah Horton Cockrell, published in 1958 by J. B. Lippincott. Though billed as a novel, Ms. Seifert interviewed countless Cockrell family members and her book according to Monroe Cockrell is true in almost every detail. Florrie Wade is the second writer who deserves special credit. For years she researched and wrote about early Dallas citizens. Her article on Sarah, *Dallas' First Businesswoman* was published in the *Dallas Morning News* on March 9, 1941. The original manuscript, typed on onion-skin paper, was among papers left by Monroe Cockrell who commented on its accuracy.

Numerous resource books also helped—encyclopedias, *Timetables of History,* the *People's Chronology,* the *Almanac of American History, The World Almanac; Dallas City Directories from 1875 to 1890,* the *WPA Dallas Guide and History*—among them, from county court records, cemetery records (The Dallas Pioneer Park Cemetery, compiled and published by the Daughters of the Republic of Texas and from Greenhill Cemetery Records). Countless interviews with descendants proved immeasurably valuable. These included personal interviews with Mackie Dealey and her sister, Dr. Sarah Louise Cockrell Stevens and Dr. Stevens' daughter, Chari Stevens Singleton, Clarence Cockrell, Jr., Chris Cockrell, Ruth Elinor Wilson Melton, Noel Sever O'Reilly, Trudy O'Reilly, Marilyn Kay Cockrell Wadle, George Jalonick and Barney Jones. I appreciate the work of Elizabeth Enstam whose writings and lecture "Sarah Horton Cockrell, Builder of Dallas" on November 21, 1981, in the Hall of State auditorium confirmed and highlighted Sarah's life and contributions. At the Dallas Public Library, I am indebted to Carol Roark and to archivist Amy Truer for their help in locating elusive material. The Dallas Historical Society offered me sanctuary and support many times, and I am especially grateful to archives manager, Rachel Roberts. A note of special thanks goes to the unusually fine staff at SMU, Librarian Dr. Gillian McCombs and the DeGolyer staff, Russell Martin III, director; former director David Farmer and Kay Bost.

My gratitude to family and friends is deep and abiding. I thank my husband, Curtis W. Castleberry, for his faith in me and support of my work for more than half a century. His contributions to this work are limitless. His computer expertise made it possible to give birth to this work; otherwise it would still be on my mind and in my heart. Two daughters, Carol Castleberry Tate and Keeta Castleberry Rupp, contributed special skills. Carol's long-time work with her historian husband's several books gave her special proof-reading and editing talents and Keeta's expertise in transforming photographs and making them ready for publication is a great gift. I thank Steven Iu and his Filmless Photo for breathing new life into old pictures. Betty Birmingham Holcomb read the manuscript several times and found errors all of us had missed; I am so grateful. Stanley Dry caught errors in word use that would have been embarrassing had they been published; many thanks. And thanks to Mitch Gray Gilbert for finding and sharing the picture of Mitch Gray, his grandfather. I appreciate my publisher, Sylvia Odenwald, not only for her professional ability and her personal integrity but also for her patience with me. And I thank printers, Boyd Brothers, Inc., and their artist Louise Wright for their excellent skills.

And, finally, whatever errors and limitations remain are mine.

Preface

Dear Reader,

As I collected material for this book and learned about Sarah Horton Cockrell, she became my friend.

But I remained baffled about how best to tell her story. Then, as records surfaced—hand-written letters, ledgers, business papers, photographs with notes on the back, letters to and from her children and friends, among them the marriage proposal from the Methodist minister—it became clear to me that Sarah had to tell her own story. So, I have allowed her to do so.

While I have extended every effort to be true to her, I have taken liberties. It has been like weaving a tapestry, taking the many threads from personal interviews with her descendants, with checking existing documents, both published and unpublished, with looking at pages of microfilm, court records, cemetery records and other resources and backing them with their time in history. The thoughts and feelings, I hope, are hers; the words are often mine. Letter writing in the 1840s to 1900s was often flowery and repetitive. Though Sarah's writing style was usually crisp, she sometimes fell into the vernacular of her times. This is especially evident in her letters to her children where she let her feelings have free rein. I have also taken the liberty of adding reactions to some of life's more poignant moments that the protocol of her time probably would not have allowed her to express, interpreting in these places what must be women's universal reactions to the peaks and valleys of their lives.

The freedom I have allowed myself in bringing Sarah's story to you is now yours to evaluate. I trust that future historians will not allow this amazing woman to fade into oblivion but will continue to discover bits and pieces of her life that eluded me, or have been overlooked or misinterpreted. Her life and her contributions to the creation of a major city are of continuing value to future generations.

Most sincerely yours,

Vivian Anderson Castleberry

PART I: DESTINY AND DUTY

Prologue

January 1, 2001

My beloved Sarah Louise and Mary Alice,

I want to speak to you personally. And through you to the generations of our family and the generations of Dallas citizens who are . . . and who are yet to be.

I am your great grandmother—Sarah Louise Horton Cockrell, born on January 13, 1819, in Russell County, Virginia.

These memoirs are addressed to you, my Great Granddaughters, because both of you, in your individual ways, took up the gauntlet and caught the torch of my own special vision for our city and our world. You, Sarah Louise, my namesake, flaunted tradition, too, when you snubbed your nose at Society's expectations for women of your time and enrolled in medical school. And against the predictions of your venerable professors, you were among the top 10 of your 1936 graduating class, a class of 100 that included only one other woman. After interning, you married Dr. Richard Stevens, and the two of you set up practice together in West Virginia even while you birthed and cared for your seven children. Your pilgrimage has been so like my own when I picked up the pieces of my shattered life in 1858 at the untimely death of your great grandfather. For the next three decades, against the dictates for a woman of my time, I had a major share in the building and management, not only of my personal affairs, but also of our city.

And you, Mary Alice, came home to Dallas after having graduated from the University of Texas, aided your husband through seminary while you cared for your three sons. You helped him establish Churchill Way Presbyterian Church, so reminiscent of the Methodist sanctuary I helped to create back in the 1860s—and then courageously carried on with the rearing of your children after a devastating divorce.

Both of you—through my third son, Robert Benjamin Cockrell, and his only surviving child, Clarence Marion Cockrell—are "chips off the old block," exhibiting characteristics that motivated my own behavior and actions more than a century before you.

We never know what Destiny has in store for us.

Had I known what lay ahead on November 29, 1844, the day I arrived on Mountain Creek near the village of Dallas, I would have kept much better records. I would have outlined more accurately the dates, facts, places, events and people of the early beginnings of our family in Texas and of the growth of our city. As it is, I must rely on the many different versions of reality that have been preserved through written records and oral histories.

I am well aware that these are my own retrospections, that the people and places that occupy my view of history are subject to oversight, to flawed memory, incomplete information and honest error. I know that through the years many others have told bits and pieces of our story, of the tribulations and triumphs we encountered in the first decade of creating a city on the banks of the Trinity River deep in the heart of Texas. I am committed to rescuing us as real living, breathing, struggling human beings from the musty pages of facts and figures that too often comprise all that is known of the past. What follows is the best that I can do . . . and I am open to suggestions, to corrections and to interpretations, for none of us is Past Perfect.

I share what I remember, understand and believe, and leave the rest to you.

And to the generations that are yet to come.

I have called these memoirs *Sarah — The Bridge Builder* for two reasons, one literal and the other symbolic. In 1854, I helped my husband with the plans for building the first bridge across the Trinity River linking Dallas with Oak Cliff, at that time two separate towns. And almost two decades later, in 1872, I was responsible for constructing the first iron bridge that spanned the Trinity. But my symbolic contributions are even more important. The way I dared to live my own life for half a century, from the mid 1840s until my death in 1892, established a precedent and a tradition for women to be significant role players in developing a major city. The legacy left by my generation is the bridge that has spanned the nineteenth century through all of the twentieth century and now into the twenty-first.

With this, I step back in time and write letters to those who occupied my own years of living—my sister Jane, who remained in Virginia when I came with our family to Dallas, family members and friends I made through the years. Sometimes, when it pertains, I enclose clippings from newspapers and, occasionally, letters I received from others. A few of these letters are reproduced in whole or in part from correspondence written at the time they are dated. More often, they are letters I might have written. In all cases they are as true to the times in which they are dated as I can possibly make them.

Your loving great grandmother,

Sarah Horton Cockrell

December 10, 1844

Mrs. William Bradshaw
The Bradshaw Farm
Abington, Russell Co., Virginia

My beloved sister Jane,

We have arrived at our destination, and I hasten to pen these lines without knowing if, when or how they will reach you. Leaving you, my dear sister, was the hardest part of our move to Texas—harder than any of the frustrations and deprivations we encountered along the way during the four months it took our faithful oxen to pull our creaking wagons southward and westward to this place which Pa calls our Promised Land. I must tell you there have been many times during the past several weeks when that promise rang hollow. So many times during the journey, I secretly longed to be back in our dear old home in Virginia. I say secretly because I knew that Ma was suffering, too, and I did not want to say or do anything to make it harder for her.

You and your husband were generous to invite—even encourage— me to stay with you, but I knew you didn't need an extra person in your lives. You and Mr. Bradshaw have your own family. I could not think of intruding on your busy household, even though you tried so hard to convince me that I could be a help with the children. Oh, how I miss them— almost as much as I miss you. How tempted I was to accept your invitation. You and I have always shared a special bond that now has been temporarily severed.

And, of course, I had to come with the family. I could not leave Ma alone to cope with the cooking and with our younger sisters. I knew that much would be expected of each one of us as we settle into our new home. Our brothers, John, James, Enoch and Robert, are already hard at work with Pa cutting trees and smoothing planks to build our house. Mary and I bear much of the responsibility for looking after Ma and our younger sisters and brother. Nineteen-year-old Martha and Rachel, at 17, are both old enough to be a great deal of help, but you remember they are often daydreaming and not eager to be involved in the day-to-day housekeeping and cleaning. Lucy and Emmarine, both much younger, often squabble as sisters sometimes will and need constant attention.

I woke this morning to bitter cold. It is astonishing how fast the temperature changes here. When we arrived twelve days ago on November 29, it was a cool, crisp day of early autumn, not cold like the kind of cold we have this time of year back home. I could almost believe that we had reached the land of eternal springtime—just as the pamphlets put out by Peters' Colony promised. This morning frost blanketed the countryside, and we had to break a thin coat of ice in order to wash our hands and faces.

I first set eyes on our future home as our ox-drawn wagon creaked over unexplored hills and valleys, along virgin pathways through some of the most beautiful countryside we'd seen since we left Virginia. The trees—many of them strange to me—were resplendent in their autumn finery. Fiery reds and tarnished bronzes and brilliant yellows of all golden hues against backgrounds of pine and cedar greens painted a natural landscape far more wonderful than any artist could capture. The falling leaves sprayed a constant sprinkling over us as we made our way here. It was a visual paradise, but we were almost too tired to enjoy it.

We are settled on the 640-acre site our father secured through the Peters' Colony Land Grant. Imagine my surprise—and disappointment—when suddenly we stopped, not among the beauty of the hillsides, but in a level, plain terrain covered with shrubs and bushes almost too thick to hack our way through. We learned this was our destination, but my disappointment was assuaged somewhat by Father's promise that the land and the lake it overlooked was more amenable to farming. Since agriculture will provide our livelihood, it is imperative he said that we surround ourselves with land that can be cultivated as easily as possible with the few tools we have been able to bring with us. Tree-covered hillsides are not conducive to farming, but Pa says this location, fed by the nearby watersheds, will produce food and cash crops to sustain us in the days ahead. All we need to do is get through the winter before time for the spring planting.

I think we are the very first settlers in this part of the country. Our brothers have made a couple of forays into the adjoining countryside and have not come across anyone else. Every time they ride off on their horses to explore our surroundings, Ma is nervous, and I must admit I breathe a sigh of relief when I see them return. We just don't know what's out there. Rumors of marauding Indians keep us constantly vigilant. I would feel much safer if we had neighbors. Pa promises they will come—and soon. But you know our father—always a dreamer, always believing that his fortune lies just over the next hill. I so hope, this time, that he is right.

I keep very busy. Our campsite here is as comfortable as it can be under the circumstances, but I will be glad when we have a roof over our heads. The cold weather makes it very difficult to keep warm. So far our food supply is holding out fine. We still had flour, meal and coffee in reserve when we arrived here. The boys have killed and dressed a deer, and fresh meat adds greatly to our monotonous meals.

In addition to helping Ma with the cooking, cleaning, clearing and laundry—which entails hauling water from the nearby lake—I have tried to continue to teach our younger sisters. I think it is imperative that all of us know how to read and write. But providing a regular school routine is difficult. In addition to their resistance to attending class and doing homework, supplies are so scarce. I would give about anything for a new book, and I cherish these few pieces of paper to write to you.

Pa has just announced that he is leaving shortly to ride into the village for additional supplies. We need not only food and writing material, but also tools to assist with the cabin. We can only hope that he can find what we need in Dallas. I hear it is not much of a town.

The sun has come out and the weather is improved over earlier in the day when I first started to write. Pa says he must take advantage of this brief warm spell to go into town because we have been warned that the weather can turn bitterly cold this time of year and throughout the winter months. I will complete this brief message to let you know that we are all here, safe and in good health, and must get it ready for Pa to send through some courier when he goes into town. It appears that all four of our brothers plan to go into the village with Pa, but I feel sure he will insist that a couple of them stay here with us. I am not exactly frightened, but it does give me pause to consider what could happen if a band of roving Indians came upon us seven women here all alone.

Later, when we are more settled, I will write at greater length and in more detail about our trip and our surroundings here.

Much love,

Sarah

December 25, 1844

My dear sister Jane,

It's Christmas Day. To say that I am homesick for our dear home in Virginia is a gross understatement. What I would give to hear your voice and to have one of your enveloping hugs. It would be the most precious gift I can imagine.

But I hasten to say that all is well here. Ma and Emmarine, who insists on being called Emma these days, have been sick with catarrh. I was worried for a time that Ma might be coming down with pneumonia, but both seem to be a trifle better. Enoch fell from the highest part of the wall of our new cabin last week and hurt his wrist and hand pretty bad. We are so glad there was no breakage. You know how he is—something of a daredevil. And though none of the boys would admit it, I am convinced he was showing off a bit.

We are celebrating because Pa, John, James, Enoch and Robert finished one room of the cabin in time for us to move inside for the holidays. We are so crowded! But it's a great improvement over camping out under the stars, especially when there are no stars to be seen and the north wind almost turns us into blocks of ice. You can imagine how cramped we are—12 of us crowded into a space meant to hold two or three. Ma and I can't keep anything in order, and you know how Ma is— the world's best housekeeper. In fact, it is so crowded that our brothers usually go back to the outside camp to sleep. If we don't watch them, they "steal" all the covers!

For now, I have given up trying to be a teacher, too. There is simply no room for reading and writing. I try to teach some arithmetic to our sisters by having them measure the length and depth of the cabin and by measuring the ingredients for cooking. I've tried to lure Robert into my math games, but he laughs at my attempts. As soon as it is warm enough to set up a classroom outside or when we get another room of the cabin completed, I will become their ogre of a school marm again.

I hope you received the letter I wrote to you shortly after we arrived here. Pa took it into Dallas and was promised that it would be sent your way by the next courier, but nobody seemed to know when that would be. We have heard nothing from you at all, and I am sure you have written to us. I haven't been into the village—plan to go as soon as it's warm enough—but Pa says the mail is kept very harum-scarum. It arrives at Mr.

John Neely Bryan's place, which serves both as a residence, and the center from which all business in the area is conducted. Pa says there's only the Bryan cabin and another log cabin occupied by a Mr. Lundy and his family. Mr. Lundy is a blacksmith, something we are going to need right away since all our horses wore off their shoes on our trip here from Virginia. Mr. Lundy has opened a shop of sorts in a section of his log cabin, which serves both as his blacksmith shop and the family residence. His entire stock when Pa made the trip into town consisted of a barrel of whiskey and three bolts of calico. Pa bought enough yardage for each of us to have a new dress. How we do need it! Our clothes are really bedraggled after the four months we spent getting here.

I promised to give you a better idea of our trip from Virginia to Texas and since Pa was able to find additional writing paper when he made the trip into the village, I now indulge myself in sharing some of the trip with you.

As you know, we left Virginia very early on the morning of July 30, 1844. Our two wagons were packed to capacity. We started out with Pa driving one team of oxen and John herding the oxen on the other. Fortunately, for us, we had several men old enough to assist, but Pa was always in charge. John, James, Enoch and even Robert took their turns and, for the most part, everybody remained in good spirits.

And so, we inched forward! Mile by mile by mile.

As birds fly, it is something like 600 miles from our starting point in Virginia, but we did not travel as the birds fly. We took many a twist and turn, many a pause, many a stop to check maps and trails on our trek here. As best, we estimate we traveled a little less than 1,000 miles, probably around 900. I have had our sisters try to determine how long it would have taken if we had come the 20 miles a day that the Peters' Colony pamphlets projected.[1] I know you are good at math, so consider this: If we had traveled from July 30 for 900 miles at 20 miles a day, how long should it have taken us to arrive here? As you can see in a flash our journey lasted a lot longer.

Pa never seemed discouraged and that kept all of us ready, if sometimes not eager, to press forward. From time to time we joined other wagon trails headed west and made many new acquaintances along the way. But most of the time we followed Pa's map, trying to avoid the danger points and to travel through valleys rather than the highest peaks. We were always on the lookout for Indians because rumors were rampant, and we didn't want to take any chances. We had heard that many of the Indians were eager to steal unattended horses, so Pa and our brothers kept constant vigil, one of them

---

[1] The appendix page 277.

staying on guard every night. We could not afford to lose one of the horses. Worst of all, we had been warned that sometimes Indians stole women and took them away to their tribes. Ma was petrified that this could happen to one of her girls and constantly reminded us that we must not stray from the campsite. This was very hard on me because you know how much I treasure privacy and how heavenly it is to have a bit of silence in order to renew my soul. I didn't have a lot of either privacy or silence on my way here. And still don't!

I wish I had kept a journal so that I could tell you in more detail about the journey. All I remember now are the highlights. It is impossible to explain the times we spent hacking through the wilderness when the marked trails on our maps led us astray. Sometimes we made only a few miles a day, if that.

And, of course, we always rested on the Sabbath Day—of that Ma was immovable—as well you can imagine.

I wish I had words to explain to you the awesome experience of my first glimpse of the Mississippi River. We approached from the east, traveling westward at a point just above St. Louis, Missouri. It was early morning. We had camped the previous night in a forest of overhanging trees only a few miles away. In the night as I lay awake contemplating what the next day would bring, I thought I heard—or, at least I dreamed—that the mighty ripples of the majestic river ahead were impregnable. The next morning, a crisp, cool, sunny morning, we were up early and helped Ma make breakfast. The atmosphere was tense. Every one of us felt that we were approaching the point that divided us from the past into a new future. Nobody ate much. Almost in silence we assembled our possessions and stored them away. It was as if every family member knew what was expected. As we moved out, contrary to our normal lighthearted banter, there was only silence.

We topped a hill and looked down. And there it was! The mighty Mississippi! Endlessly long from north to south as far as my eyes could see, unfathomably wide—in my estimation miles across, though I knew in reality there were banks to the east and the west. We stopped to view the awesome sight before us. There are no words to describe my feelings. Only when you join us some day, My Dear Sister—and how I long for that day to be soon—will you, too, experience the breathtaking sweep, the mighty majesty of the Mississippi dividing our country from east to west.

Once you've crossed it, there comes a moment of reckoning. This is it! We have put the past behind us. The future lies in the distance.

But before that the crossing! We were very fortunate to have arrived early in the morning and to be first in line to move our wagons, oxen and ourselves onto the ferry, a wide floating barge-like contraption that looks for all the world like a floating house, only without walls! Just looking at it made me shudder, and Ma began right away cautioning everybody to take care. She was wasting her breath so far as I was concerned because I had no intention of staying near the edge and taking any chance of being thrown into the river. Our sisters felt the same way, and we all hovered as near the center of the ferry as possible. But our daredevil brothers were far more adventuresome. Robert asked a million questions. The crew in charge of loading the ferry was patient with him at first. But soon they were too busy to pay much attention, and he was left to explore and find answers for himself. We had only one bad moment when a frightened ox rebelled at setting foot on the ferry. The crew, accustomed to dealing with recalcitrant animals, soon outwitted him, and we pushed off and were on our way.

Landing on the west bank of the river, we left the ferry, assembled people and possessions and by noon were again on our way westward. It had taken about four hours from one bank to the other. It seemed like a lifetime.

Next time I write, I will explain a little better how we are situated here so that your vivid imagination will help you envision where we are and what we are doing.

In the meantime, on this Christmas, our first in a land that still seems alien to me, we will make this day as merry as possible. The boys went hunting yesterday and killed a wild turkey that we have dressed and threaded onto a spit. We'll roast it later on an open fire outside. Pa found oranges when he went into the village and bought one for each of us. We have saved them to savor this special day and my mouth waters just thinking about the taste of fresh fruit! Together with a pot of wild honey, some roasted sweet potatoes and some of Ma's wonderful bread this will be our Christmas dinner. Not bad for the wilderness!

Best of all, Pa brought me two books, *The Seraphim and Other Poems* by Elizabeth Barrett Browning and a new book, *The Pathfinder* by James Fenimore Cooper. I can hardly wait to find the time and a quiet spot to read! These two treasures together with this writing paper and a new quill are the best of all possible presents. Pa does know how to make a girl's heart glad! I treasure these things far more than the calico, but have no doubt I shall look grand when we have completed our new dresses.

I've been up before dawn and started this letter to you as soon as it was light enough to put pen to paper. I hear the boys moving around outside. Both Pa and Ma are up and dressed, and everybody is rousing except Rachel, our sleepy head.

In my imagination I am with you on this blessed holiday. Keep well. Keep us in your prayers, as you are always in ours. And let us hear from you as often as you can find the time to write—and a courier to deliver your messages.

All of my love,

Sarah

January 14, 1845

My dearest sister,

At last we have had a message from you! How wonderful to be in touch across these many miles. I despaired of ever hearing because Pa says that the delivery and reception of messages is really awful. It arrives—if at all—in Mr. John Neely Bryan's cabin which, as I've said before, serves as headquarters for everything that goes on in this tiny Texas hamlet. Since all of the men have better things to do—or so they think—than to take care of the mail, incoming letters and packets are strewn on a makeshift counter, and everybody who comes along simply rifles through them to see if and what they may have.

It is a joy to know that you, Mr. Bradshaw and the children are in good health. The same is true for us. Pa and the boys work every day to finish the second room of the cabin. I can hardly wait to have a little more space for this large and very busy family. I have tried to pick up my teaching duties again and am encouraging Martha, Rachel, Lucy and Emma to write to you as a part of their instruction. They promise, but so far I have seen no results.

I said I would tell you a bit more about our surroundings, and I shall try to paint you a word picture. To the west of where we live and continuing north to south for as far as I can see, we are semi-surrounded by a chain of hills, some of them high enough to be called mountains—though they are nowhere near as tall as the Appalachians we came through and some of the other mountains we skirted on our way here. As I mentioned in my last letter, our cabin is situated just east of a large lake. It seems really strange that we are in such an isolated part of the world since we grew up in Virginia, which is steeped in history as one of the original colonies of the United States. Texas is another world. In 1836, having recently won its independence from Mexico, this new land of ours became a separate country and elected Sam Houston, the military victor over Santa Anna, as its president. He served one term, was replaced by Mirabeau B. Lamar in 1838 but returned to office in 1841. He is officially still president of this, our new home, though annexation to the Union is imminent. As I understand it, Texas began negotiations to become a part of the United States even as it first became an independent nation and elected officers. Its first request was denied by Congress because of resistance to the spreading of slavery. Our new president, James Knox Polk, was elected to office largely because he favored the annexation of Texas to the Union. Pa says the news has reached here that a joint resolution of Congress approved annexation a few days after Christmas. Many people in this part of the world are fiercely independent and resistant to annexation, Pa says. But I think the idea is wonderful and can hardly wait for it to become a fact. Somehow I don't feel quite so cut off from you when I know we belong together in the same large and growing nation.

Geographically, we are located almost due west of the Dallas village and somewhat west of the Trinity River, which separates us from the village. I am enclosing a crude map of our possible location, though you are not to hold me to any exactness because I am using the Peters' Colony maps together with other guides we have received since we have been here—and all of them are subject to interpretation!

The landscape around here is bleak right now. All the beautiful trees that welcomed us when we arrived have shed their leaves and are bare. Only the cedars and an occasional pine show any sign of life. A couple of the bare trees are within a few yards of the cabin, but for the most part the surrounding terrain is flat and uninviting. It is covered in most places by a thick coating of underbrush—small bushes and dead weeds held together with brambles—which tear at our skirts and slow progress. On my way back from the lake the other day with a brimming pail of water in each hand, I stumbled into one of these treacherous patches and drenched myself. I thought I would become a block of ice before I reached the house to find something else to wear. My discomfort was aggravated because I'd lost two large pails of water after hauling them halfway up the incline. Also, we have such limited clothing. Ma and I have started to cut and sew a dress for each of our younger sisters from the material Pa bought that I told you about in the last letter, but the task goes slowly. We have not even touched new dresses for ourselves. Pa and our brothers need new shirts as soon as we can get the material and find the time to sew them. When Pa or one of the boys rides back into the village, they will need to buy needles and thread—if such is to be had in this part of the world.

Pa and the boys have marked off a large plot of ground to plant cotton and corn. When they are not working on the cabin or constructing furniture pieces, everybody pitches in to rid this portion of our acreage of underbrush. I often assist—when the weather is not too cold—because I greatly enjoy being outside. It is too early to put seeds into the ground. The soil here and the weather conditions are so different from what we had in Virginia that it's like having to learn a whole new way of doing things, and Pa listens carefully to what the men talk about when he rides into Dallas. He has learned that he can plant much earlier here than he did back home. But we can't afford to put precious seeds into the ground too early and take a chance on having a late freeze that would kill tender plants.

We still do not have close neighbors, but there is a thriving development across the Trinity River to the north. John, James and Enoch discovered it on one of their recent forays. It's called Cedar Springs, and though only a little more than a year old, is drawing a lot of attention.

James brought back the story: Its first settlers were Dr. John H. Cole and his family who came, as we did, in covered wagons, on horseback and on foot. They began their journey to Texas in Tennessee and upon arrival camped in a grove of cedars at Cedar Creek Springs. Our brothers describe the setting as pristine. Dr. Cole has opened a practice there; he is the only physician anywhere nearby. Though I sincerely hope that we never need his services, it is a comfort to know that a doctor is available—though really too far away to be any help in an emergency. He is also responsible for opening a pharmacy. One of his older sons has opened a blacksmith shop and another opened a store that features harnesses, saddles and other supplies needed by farmers. I am told that it is quickly becoming the hub of commercial activities for this part of our new territory, and I can hardly wait to make a trip there.

Since I am running out of both time and paper, I must close for now. All of our brothers chastise me for spending so much time reading—the few books and papers I have available—and writing at every chance I get. But what a comfort it is to be in touch with you across these miles!

Your loving sister,

Sarah

February 18, 1845

Dearest, dearest sister Jane,

This country is unbelievable! You cannot imagine the weather. Last weekend we had ice and a bit of sleet. Today the temperature feels like early summer. I am not even wearing a coat as I begin this epistle. I look out over the countryside and see a few patches of green. This morning as I walked back from the lake hauling water so that we can heat and wash a pile of dirty clothes, I saw a couple of tiny flowers! When the sun shines as it is doing at this moment, all of my homesickness disappears, and I can honestly believe that we have found the land of new opportunity. Well, almost. Except that I still long for you and for our many friends in old Virginny.

We have received only two letters from you. It is very upsetting to know that you are writing to us even as I continue to post messages to you and that it takes so long for these exchanges to reach each other. Please do not let that deter you from writing. Letters are the only connection we have with each other now that we are hundreds of miles apart.

The news here continues to be good. We are in excellent health—and that is the best of all news. When the weather is so warm as it is today, we are tempted to get out and begin planting. But Pa has been warned not to be too eager. We still may have a killing ice storm as late as mid-March. Mary and I—with some help from our younger sisters when they are in the mood—have dug flowerbeds outside the cabin. The task is difficult because the soil has so many roots and brambles. But when we get the debris dug out and the soil loosened, it should be a prime spot to grow flowers. I can just imagine how lovely things will be in a few months.

You should see our cabin! Pa and the boys completed the second room about a week ago. The first thing Ma did was to hold worship services in it. Our brothers protested all the way, but in the end, they and Pa joined Ma, Mary, Martha, Rachel, Emma and me to sing a hymn and read several verses from the Bible. It was a makeshift church service, but I think it lifted all our spirits. Even Pa said a brisk prayer of thanksgiving for the new room, our home and for you and our other loved ones that are so far away. Lucy sauntered in just as we were concluding the services. You know what a dreamer she can be, and she'd wandered off to find greenery to decorate the new room. Ma said we couldn't wait for her to get back—we didn't know when that would be—and the men were all getting restive.

Ma, Mary—with Martha's now-and-then assistance—got everything moved into the new part of the house right after the services of blessing while I prepared the noon meal. By the time we were ready to eat, we actually had a place to spread out a bit. It is still crowded, but nothing like it was when we were all crammed together in one room. Pa and James are now hard at work making a table. It's big enough for all twelve of us to crowd around and will completely fill the first room of the cabin. Even so it will be good to have a place where we can actually sit down and eat together. Until then, we are still doing makeshift. When the weather is warm enough, the boys usually take their plates outside to eat. Ma and our sisters and I, often joined by Pa, huddle around the fireplace. We make Ma take the one good rocking chair that came with us all the way from Virginia. We have two other chairs and several crude stools, so we manage.

More than anything else, I'll be glad to have a table so that I can insist on regular classes for our younger sisters. It is a constant challenge to keep them interested in studying—especially since we have so few books. Pa teases that all they need is the Bible! Though I agree this is a marvelous source, I long for books, newspapers and magazines. About a week ago when Pa came back from a trip into Dallas, he brought a newspaper, which had been published in Galveston. I've devoured every word. Galveston is on the coast far to the south of where we live, but seems to be the most advanced town in the entire area with the possible exception of San Antonio. All of these places are just names to me!

I was very much interested in a long article about a new treaty recently signed by President Sam Houston and nine Indian tribes. President Houston has always been a friend of the Red Man and has marvelous persuasive powers. He had issued an invitation to leaders of ten tribes—the Anadarkos, Biloxis, Chickashaws, Cherokees, Comanches, Delawares, Kichais, Hanais, Tawanokis and Wacos—last fall to meet him and several negotiators at Grapevine Springs in July to settle a territorial dispute. When he arrived from Austin on the designated day, only a handful of Indians were present. Indians have never kept times and dates the way we do in our world, so President Houston knew that they would wander in at their own pace. He waited several days and still only four or five of the tribes were represented. He had to return to the capitol to take care of pressing business, so he left General E. H. Tarrant and Gen. George W. Terrell in charge. Eventually delegates from nine of the ten invited tribes showed up, and by mutual agreement moved their meeting place to Bird's Fort (about which you will be told more later). And on September 29, 1843, all signed an agreement that the Indians would keep west of a line considerably to the west of our settlement. Later the Comanches also signed the pact.The Senate of the Republic of Texas ratified it on January 31, 1844, a little more than a year ago, and several months before we arrived to settle here. So far it seems to be holding pretty well and that's what the story was all about. I admit I would have been much more comfortable if I'd known about the treaty sooner. The ways of the Indian tribes differ so much from the way we live that I still fear reprisals. Even as I long to feel completely safe from danger, I cannot help think that we are intruding on a country that belonged to other people long before we entered it. I am glad to inform you that a joint resolution of Congress approved annexation of the Republic of Texas to the Union.We are now in a period of waiting for the business to be completed and for the Stars and Stripes to replace the Lone Star flag of Texas as an independent nation. It could happen any day—indeed, may already have happened as news travels so slowly.

Pa is more concerned about action to establish this area as a separate county in the state. If I have not already made it clear how vast this country is, I add this:There is no local legal entity anywhere near. Residents on the east side of the Trinity River—the village of Dallas and points to its east—are legally in Nacogdoches County and have to transact business in the town of Nacogdoches which is 200 miles to the east. Our part of the world, west of the Trinity River, is in Robertson County, which has as its capital Old Franklin, 150 miles south of us.Whatever legal papers have to be filed must be done at these headquarters. So far we have not been able to file papers to claim our parcel of land, though James and John plan to ride the distance on their horses as soon as the weather is more predictable.We understand that if a man is summoned to jury duty in the county seat, he is obliged to get there the best way he can. I can only hope that our lack of filing our claim other than with the official Peters' Colony agents will deter Pa and our older brothers from being called to serve on a jury until Dallas County is established.

Ma and I have completed making dresses for Martha and Rachel.We have cut garments for both Lucy and Emma but have not had a chance to put needle to fabric. Sewing goes very slowly when there is so much else to do. Mary is crocheting collars for all four of the dresses.

I long for an occasion to dress up and go to a party, though I must say I do not have appropriate clothes to make any kind of an impression. I don't think it would make a bit of difference—even if I had to attend in one of my faded old calicos. Neighbors are still non-existent, though we keep hearing that people are moving into the territory in record numbers. Enoch reported on his last trip into Dallas that six new families are scattered among us—the Webb family from Tennessee, a Cameron family state unknown, several Cox families from Illinois, the Harwood family from Tennessee, a Jenkins family state unknown and the Rawlins family from Illinois.

Every time Pa and one of our brothers returns from the village of Dallas, they tell stories about some of the original settlers, and I am eager to go into town to meet some of them. I especially would like to meet Margaret Bryan. She was a Beeman, the daughter of John and Emily Hunnicutt Beeman who came to this part of the world three years ahead of us and settled somewhat east of the village of Dallas. Margaret married the city's founder, John Neely Bryan, who is 15 years older than his wife. Though Margaret is six years younger than I am, she has been married for more than a year. From what little I hear, she and I seem to have a lot in common. Both of us are somewhat shy and do not need a lot of attention in order to feel important. I am looking forward to going into the village as soon as possible to meet her and other women. Even with Ma, Mary and our four younger sisters, I need to have an outlet to a wider world. Perhaps it will come soon.

Oh, how I miss you! When there were no friends with whom to share experiences I could always count on you, dear sister. You are very special to me and I miss you terribly.

All my love,

Sarah

July 4, 1845

Jane, my dearest sister,

Please forgive me for waiting so long to write to you. I feel as if I'm writing in a vacuum when we do not hear from you, but this should never excuse me from writing to you. We did not get your letter dated March 1 until a week ago, and much has happened since I last wrote. I have kept some notes in a *quasi* journal from time to time and will now update you, as best I can.

On February 29, Texas was officially admitted to the Union as its 28th state. I believe I wrote that the timing was imminent, but news travels so slowly that I didn't know the great switch had already occurred. On that date, the Lone Star flag of the Republic of Texas was lowered, and the

Stars and Stripes raised. I understand that there was great rejoicing in many quarters, but a few die-hards refused to celebrate. There is an abundance of resistance here to giving up any tiny bit of individual freedom—just as there is back home. As for the Hortons, all of us are delighted and grateful that the pact we made with a new land a little more than a year ago is turning out to be so good. Pa hasn't gloated openly, but his attitude tells us everything. "I told you so," you can almost hear him saying!

At last we have some neighbors—though they are far enough away that we almost never see each other. I did not know in February when I last wrote that almost a month prior to that, in January of 1845, the William H. Hord family arrived from North Carolina and settled on Cedar Creek, only several hours by wagon from our cottage. As soon as we knew they had time to settle in, Ma insisted on going to greet them. On a bright sunshiny day in early March, Pa hitched the oxen to the wagon, and we all set out to greet our new neighbors. We helped Ma pack a lunch for everybody and took a cake, meal, lard and a jar of our precious berry jelly as a welcoming present. We had no idea what kind of supplies they may have arrived with or what they might require to supplement their larder. We well remember what kind of hardships we endured on our trip here.

The Hords are a family of five headed by William H. Hord and his wife Mary J. Crockett Hord. Two sons and a daughter, Thomas, Ferdinand and Mattie, complete the family. They had arrived only a few weeks before our visit and were delighted to have company. We could not stay long enough to really get to know each other because, by the time we arrived, it was close to lunchtime. Mrs. Hord was already making their meal, so we spread ours along with theirs and sampled each other's victuals. It is truly amazing how different the same food is prepared in different parts of the world. By the time we had eaten and packed things away, it was time to start home. When we started out the day promised to be beautiful, but did not live up to the prophecy. By the time we were loaded in the wagon for the return trip, dark clouds coated the countryside to the north, and as we made our way back to our cabin, the north wind turned downright nasty. I was glad that I had thought to toss in a couple of quilts. At the time I put them in the wagon in the early morning, I thought we might use them to spread and sit on while we had our picnic lunch, and we did. But before we reached our domicile, Ma, Mary and I and all four younger sisters were huddled under both quilts to keep warm.

John and James have both laid claims to property to the north adjoining Pa's spread. As single men, they qualify for only 320 acres each. John's acreage is immediately to the north of ours and James's is to the north of John's. This makes it more convenient for the men to assist each other in the clearing, planting and harvesting of crops, but I cannot imagine how long it will take them to have all three pieces of property productive. There are so many brambles and bushes, roots and rocks that cultivating the soil is virtually impossible.

We have, however, made an excellent garden this year. Ma and our sisters and I planted and harvested tomatoes, potatoes, sweet potatoes, onions, turnip greens and turnips, collards, green beans, Lima and pinto beans and corn. We have watermelons and pumpkins just about ready to eat. We have dried the limas and pintos, stored the potatoes and sweet potatoes covering them with sand mixed with lime to preserve them. We pulled the onions as soon as the tops collapsed and hung them to dry before storing and have dried many ears of corn to grind for meal this winter. We have preserved several jars of green beans, tomatoes and greens and have made a ton of chow-chow and tomato sauce (well, not quite!). We have stored seeds to use for next year's garden and will depend on the boys' hunting prowess this winter for fresh meat.

Pa has managed to find us a cow. The day he drove her home from the village, all of us stood and cheered. It is absolutely wonderful to have fresh milk. Ma and I have a hard time keeping Pa and the others from drinking it all up before it has time to sour so that we can make buttermilk and butter. Bread is so much better tasting when made with buttermilk, and fresh butter on hot bread is a feast for the gods. We have also found and preserved wild berries. I long for apples and peaches but will have to postpone that desire until we can find and plant some trees and wait several years for them to become productive.

I am still waiting to make a trip into the village of Dallas. Pa and the boys have been there several times, but we—Ma and our sisters and I— can't seem to persuade them to take us along. We are told that the trip there and back consumes most of a whole day and that the crossing of the Trinity River is perilous. The men can ride their horses across (so could I if Pa would only allow it!), but our father would have to yoke up the oxen, hitch them to the wagon. And we'd have to take along food for a day's outing. I do not consider this a handicap, but Pa does, so we wait. They try to discourage us from wanting to make the trip by telling us that the river crossing is too dangerous. There are no bridges, only a rocky ford at the narrowest part of the river. And, even after you get across, they say, there is absolutely nothing of interest. The town consists of one crude building, mostly bare, which serves as the store, the post office and the residence of the town's founder, John Neely Bryan, who lives with his bride, Margaret. I am not discouraged—only frustrated—

that it is taking me so long to explore the wider area of this wilderness to which we have come.

I hear Ma calling, so I must hasten to go help her with supper. I have been writing while sitting under the tallest tree and leaning against its trunk. It is unbearably hot here. I brought my writing material, a book of poems and a quilt and escaped here for a nice visit with you. Please, please continue to write to us. I miss you so much.

Your loving sister,

Sarah

August 1845

Jane, my dearest sister,

I am going to keep a sort of diary-like letter for several days before mailing it to you. Other than the daily ups-and-downs of housekeeping, cooking, planting, harvesting and looking after the younger sisters, there is really no news from here. We are all well—and that is the best news of all. This is a very dull season because the crops—such as they are—are laid by. The garden peaked several weeks ago, and we have completed the canning and preserving for the year. Pa and the boys have made a small cotton crop, but harvest time for it is still weeks away. I can hardly wait to harvest the cotton so that we can make some better mattresses after we have sold the best of the crop for cash. The mattresses we brought from Virginia have been wet several times and need to be replaced. I especially want to get a new bed made for Ma and Pa; the rest of us can get by, but I admit it would be lovely to sleep on something soft and clean.

I have not yet tried to start school for our four younger sisters. It is simply too hot! I have warned them that when the first cool day arrives—I hope in September—we will be back to the classroom. I am still determined that each member of this family be able to read and write! Sometimes I think this is a losing battle. Pa does not give much verbal support to my efforts, but almost every time he goes into the village, he brings me writing material and whatever books or papers he can find. The last time he went into Dallas, he brought back a copy of *The Cincinnati Enquirer*. I don't know why it had reached Texas, and I don't know anybody who is mentioned in the paper or anything much that has been reported as going on in the world, but I have read every word of it several times! One thing I picked up: the U.S. population has reached 17 million! I can't think in terms that big. In our world here, there are still so few people.

Pa also brought me a copy of a poem, *Pippa Passes* by Robert Browning. The introduction says it is the first of a series that will be published in the next few years under the heading of *Bells and Pomegranates*. I love the poem because it is so hopeful. Are you familiar with it? The ending is "God's in His heaven. All's right with the world." I so enjoy literature that is affirming, makes me dream a little and helps to lighten the "dailyiness" of life. Browning's work is exactly opposite that of another recently published—and all the rage—poet, Edgar Allan Poe, whose work is dark and morbid. I am thinking of *The Raven* and its sinister line, "Quoth the raven, nevermore!"

In addition, I've been reading Alfred Lord Tennyson and am delighted by his poem, *Locksley Hall*. When I read, "in the spring a young man's fancy lightly turns to thoughts of love," I wonder if it will ever be so for me. I was 27 years old last January and am fast approaching my 28th birthday. I often dream of having a husband, a home and children of my own. I do not look forward to the traditional life of an old maid aunt who moves into the house with her married brother or sister and spends the rest of her life taking care of their children. I have seen several older women dry up like prunes when they become extra wheels in the homes of their sisters or brothers. I can just hear you denying that this would ever happen to our relationship—yours and mine—and if I am not fortunate enough to have a young man's fancy turn to thoughts of love when he looks at me, I would rather live in your home than with any other sister or brother and their spouses. All this makes me wonder why it is that men always get to do the asking!

I can only express these thoughts to you, and in a letter at that. Martha is stepping out with our cousin, William Horton, and I think it's serious. Lucy, at 18, is the family beauty and will have no trouble at all finding a suitable suitor. I worry about Rachel. She is so quiet, moody and withdrawn a lot of the time. Emma is your typical harum-scarum youngster, so full of life and so often the one in the family who makes everybody lighten up a bit.

Ma continues to keep most of her thoughts to herself. She is a devoted and loving mother and a good wife, but I ask myself often if she is really happy and if the move to this strange and barren land suits her. Pa is the gregarious member of the family and his namesake, Enoch, is so like him. Robert, too, is quiet. When the family is together, he is often a little outside the circle. Just now I looked up and he was standing down by the cow lot, his back to the house gazing into space. John and James, our two big brothers, are busy clearing and tilling the soil, planting and harvesting, and making the necessary trips into town for supplies. I wonder what kind of husbands they will turn out to be?

Never a day goes by that I don't think of you and wish we could be together. Has Mr. Bradshaw shown any inclination to want to move to Texas?

Two days later: Having just read over what I wrote earlier this week, I was inclined to tear it to shreds and toss it to the four winds but have decided to send it along anyway in hopes that you will respond in kind to some of my musings. Somehow it makes me feel closer to you when you relate what you are thinking and feeling as well as what you are doing.

Though the heat makes us lethargic, Ma, Mary and I have completed the dresses we started earlier this year. We had already made dresses for Martha, Rachel, Lucy and Emma and Ma, and have Mary's cut and ready to sew up. Mary makes the tiniest, most perfect stitches, and we all hold out for her to do most of the work on the garments. Mine is waiting to be cut. It is gray calico, not a dull miserable gray, but tending toward blue. I think it will enhance the gray of my eyes. But, then, who is there to notice?

This reminds me: I read in the *Enquirer* about a new machine invented by a Mr. Elias Howe that sews pieces of fabric together automatically—well, not quite automatically. You still have to push a pedal. The story says that the machine uses two threads to create an interlocking stitch and that the results are much faster and more exact than even the best of hand sewing. Can you imagine such a thing? But how I would love to see one in operation and even, perchance, some day own one! Since sewing is not my favorite occupation, I would certainly welcome anything to make it easier.

And speaking of inventions, have you heard about a new contraption called a plow that was invented by a Mr. John Deere? The story I read talked about how he created these instruments that turn the earth. Somehow, you attach a mule or an ox to the gadget and walk behind it guiding it to turn the soil where you want the seeds planted. The story said he created 100 of them, loaded them into his wagon and peddled them to friends in and around his home base of Grand Detour, Illinois. He sold all of them in less than a week! Now everybody in the vicinity turns out to watch farmers using their plows. When John and James came in for supper after I'd read that story, I told them about it and they don't believe it. But I do. The world is changing. We won't always have to do back-breaking work with our bare hands in order to eke out survival.

And one more story I read: A new kind of bridge opened in January of 1842, but I hadn't heard anything about it until recently. It's called a wire suspension bridge and spans the Schuylkill River at a town called Fairmount near Philadelphia. What this area couldn't do with a bridge like that! If we had a wire suspension bridge across the Trinity, I could make that long-delayed trip into Dallas.

A day later: I have just completed churning the sour milk to make a beautiful large pat of fresh butter which will melt in our mouths as soon as Ma cooks the yeast rolls. We have had nothing but hoecake and bread made from corn meal for days on end. But James discovered that yeast had just arrived when he was in town yesterday and brought some home to us. It is precious! Ma is such a good cook and all day I've been watching it rise, seeing her beat it down and knead it and form it into loaves. I do hope the covered pan in the hot coals cooks it well. It takes a lot of experience to know when to cover the pan with the hot coals and how long to let it stay there keeping the embers stoked all the time.

Three days later: Yes! The bread and butter turned out to be every savory bite the way I had longed for it to be. Sometimes I get so hungry for the food we enjoyed together back in Virginia.

But, I do not want to tarry talking about food! We have had a remarkable experience. A circuit rider for the Methodist Church came through shortly after I penned those last lines three days ago. We were all lazing around! Pa had come in from the fields. Ma, our sisters and I were trying to get up enough energy to continue with our sewing. Enoch and Robert were sitting around whittling, so they saw the rider approach from the north. As soon as the rider was within easy shouting distance, he let us know that he was a circuit rider representing the Kingdom of God, or as he put it, a lone Methodity Rider bringing the word of the Lord.

Ma was ecstatic. Not since we had left Virginia had we had a real Man of the Cloth in our midst. Not since we had attended the little church in which we were baptized and reared had we heard a real sermon. With the example of our parents, welcoming this bedraggled, hungry, lone rider into our home, all of us felt both cautious and reverent. After Ma had laid out the best of our larder for his sustenance, he was disappointed to learn that we were the only people within a wide area able to participate in such a real worship service. But after initially showing his disappointment, he rallied remarkably and preached a real hell fire and brimstone service fitting for a congregation at least quadrupled our size (there were eight of us—our brothers conveniently disappeared—later claiming to Ma that the cow, horses and oxen demanded attention). Taking his cue from Ma, Pa effusively welcomed the stranger and invited him to spend the night. Needless to add, the boys were most put out to be replaced in their bed with a visiting minister!

All I can say—and I wouldn't dare say it to Ma or even to Pa—I'm glad he's gone. He may be a real Man of the Cloth, a bonafide Minister of the Gospel for all I know. But his yellow teeth, terrible table manners and lack of proper use of the English language turned me off and when he began to sidle up to our younger sisters, ignoring me—after all, I am the Old Maid in this family—I could have gladly swatted him. Besides, I could have preached a far better sermon than he delivered in our living room. He took his biblical text out of context—ah, how often this happens—and he ranted on and on growing more and more flagrant in his delivery. It was all I could do to sit through the sermon, if such it could be called! There is no doubt in my mind that I could have greatly improved on his text and his delivery, but who would have listened to a mere woman?

How I long to have you near so that we could discuss these topics that disturb me.

With all my heart, I send you LOVE,

Sarah

September 17, 1845

Jane, my dear sister,

We have become quite friendly with our neighbors, the Wesley Cockrell family, who have moved onto a 640-acre land grant farm just east of us. Six hundred and forty acres is a lot of land, and we do not get to visit often with them. But what a joy it is to have neighbors who share so many things with us.

The Cockrells came from Missouri. I don't know exactly when. There's Mr. Cockrell and Mrs. Sarah Wilson Cockrell and several children. The Cockrells are much younger than Pa and Ma—more our ages—and because of that more inclined to entertaining. In fact, Mrs. Cockrell is only seven years older than I am, but she is already several times a mother. Their children are Bill, Amelia, Susan, Permelia, Morgan and Lee.

When I watch her with these children, it seems impossible that she would have the energy or the inclination to be so welcoming to visitors, but such is not the case. Mary, our older brothers and I have been to a couple of parties at their home and had a marvelous time.

Pa, our brothers and Mr. Cockrell with son Bill, who is just a kid, have been hunting several times lately, and we have wonderful fresh meat. They killed one buffalo recently and a bear not long before that. Prairie chickens are numerous, so we are not lacking for good food. We have tried to keep chickens so we could have fresh eggs, but something got into the hen house. James says it was probably a wolf; John thinks it was more likely a panther. In any event, about half of the hens were destroyed and the other half so disturbed that they are not laying very well.

I don't think I told you how important wheat is to this area. Enoch has contrived some sort of grinding apparatus that turns the wheat into a fine mist, much finer than the corn to which we are accustomed. It makes marvelous breads and pastries.

Pa says the entire area is growing at a rapid rate. There must be at least a hundred families now living, as we are, west of the Trinity River. If only we had a good passage into the village of Dallas. I have still not met the founder of our new area, Mr. John Neely Bryan and his wife, Margaret Beeman Bryan, who is younger than I am! The Horton men, Pa and our brothers, brought back the sad news that Mr. and Mrs. Bryan lost their baby son, Holland Coffee, in July shortly before his first birthday. I heard Pa whispering to Ma that the Bryans should soon have another child. This is wonderful, though I am certain that a mother's heart must break every time she loses a child and that the birth of a new one cannot ever replace the emptiness left by having to give up one—and so many children are lost in this uninhabited land. It makes me fearful to consider ever becoming a mother—though so far as I can see, there is no reason to think I ever might.

Everybody here is greatly concerned about a possible major war with Mexico. When Texas was admitted to the Union, Mexico severed diplomatic relations with the United States claiming that it still owned the State—even though Texas had been an independent country since 1836. Now there is increasing unrest with skirmishes along the Rio Grande River which divides Texas and Mexico.

All this is fresh on my mind because I am getting ready to resume classes for our younger sisters next week and have been exploring all resources for things that might hold their interest. My primary concern is that all of us are able to read and write, but I also want my "students" to be aware of what is happening in the world around them.

The Cockrells are not the only newcomers to our area. A widow, Mrs. Catherine Hunsaker Kimmel and her daughter, Anna Minerva, arrived recently and settled to the south and west of us. They are from Union County, Missouri. Not long after they moved into the area, Crawford Trees, a single man, also from Missouri, claimed property adjacent to them.

The village itself is expanding rapidly. Pa says it even has an exclusive-type neighborhood developing just to the south of John Neely and Margaret Bryan's cabin. And a woman is largely responsible! Her name is Lucy Jane Monroe Browder. Smart lady, she retains her maiden name of Monroe because she is doubtless very proud of it! She is a niece of President James Monroe, and there is every evidence that she is trying to create the comforts and something of the class she enjoyed back in Missouri. She's a widow who moved here with her two sons, Edward Cabell and Isham Bell Browder. All three are very enterprising, though there's no doubt that Mrs. Browder is in charge. She has named the area The Cedars and is promoting it as the most prestigious part of town in which to locate. While her sons—or son (Isham is away now; he has gone back to Missouri to get married but plans to bring his bride back to Dallas to live)—survey and lay out the area, it is she who sells the property.

Even more important than Mrs. Browder's development of an elite neighborhood to most of us is the contribution of another woman— Elizabeth Durgan. She has assumed the responsibilities for handling the mail! Her husband, Charles M. Durgan, has been named U.S. postmaster, but Pa says he is postmaster in name only. It is Mrs. Durgan who receives, sorts and delivers the letters and packages. How wonderful that is! I no longer worry about receiving your letters. If the mail arrives in Dallas, Mrs. Durgan will see that it gets to the proper person. Pa says she has personally stitched leather pouches and lettered them from A through Z. When a rider arrives with the mail, she receives and sorts it and takes care of it until the addressee or a member of that family arrives to claim it. No longer are the letters and packets strewn onto a table, which each person can sort through. That system really concerned me. Not only was there a great chance of misplacing something, but nobody had any privacy at all.

I will be glad when our furniture arrives. Did I tell you Ma selected several pieces—two bedsteads and bedsprings, a chifforobe, two tables and 12 chairs from the catalog—and Pa ordered them from St. Louis three months ago? They should be here any time. This will add greatly to the meager furnishings we brought with us from Virginia. We are going to turn this into a civilized place yet!

School is going quite well considering the meager books, papers and pens we have to work with. I so wish we were close enough that the girls could go to a new school in Dallas. Mrs. Mary Ann Ryland West, who recently arrived, with her husband from Tennessee, has opened a school in her home on the banks of the Trinity River. I am told that she is quite an artist, and students who do well are rewarded with hand-made certificates. These are so valuable! How I wish I could earn one. And how I wish that our sisters could make the trip into town to be in her classes. But the distance is too far—all of five miles, I wager. If this were not enough, crossing of the Trinity to be at her school would make it impossible even to consider.

I am glad, too, that Texas at last has a university. Baylor University, the first Baptist university in the south, was established recently after being supported by Supreme Court Justice Robert Emmet Bledsoe. I would just love to be able to go to a university, but women are strongly discouraged from developing their minds. I recall how significant it was when Mount Holyoke was established in Massachusetts nine years ago. I was so excited that women at last had a place where they could attend an institution of higher learning without being so discouraged. Mount Holyoke was The Promised Land for Women who wanted to hone their minds. I so longed to go, but of course it was impossible. The distance was prohibitive, and we didn't have the money, but I followed with eagerness every story about the school. The fact that Mary Lyon started with 80 students and the very next year had so many applications that she had to turn away 400 should tell everybody how eager women are for an education.

How I miss you! Never a day passes that I do not think of our time together as children and young girls in Virginia and wonder if we ever can be together again. In the meantime, I hope that Mr. Bradshaw is making plans to join us in Texas. I am almost certain that Pa will never want to move back to Virginia. Both of our parents are getting up in years. I must stay close to both of them, but I must never give up everything to be their total caretakers. Is this selfish? Every day, I wonder what the future has in store for me. Would that I could sit down over a cup of tea and talk it all over with you! Until that time comes, know that I send . . .

All my love,

Sarah

Monday, December 1, 1845

Jane, my dearest sister,

So much has happened since I last wrote to you in September. The days have flown by so fast that there's not even been time for me to bring you up to date. Now that Christmas is fast approaching—our second one in this new land—I must take the time to tell you what is going on.

In my last letter, I think I told you that Pa and Ma had ordered furniture, new cutlery and glassware from St. Louis and hoped that it would arrive any day.

It came, but even as I review what went on with its arrival and the days that followed, I cannot believe!

We had just had a week of unrelenting rains, cold and wet, but last Wednesday, the day before Thanksgiving, dawned crystal clear, the sun shining brightly, unseasonably warm and beautiful. The weather and the fact that it was the day before a holiday had lifted everybody's spirits. Our father and brothers had gone hunting, hoping to shoot a turkey for the Thanksgiving feast. Ma had decided to take our accumulated dirty clothes and linens down near the creek to do the laundry. James and Enoch have rigged up an outdoor laundry space there, and it's ever so much easier to haul our dirty clothes down and bring the clean folded ones back than it is to cart bucket after bucket of water uphill. Mary had gone with Ma down to start the laundry. Our younger sisters were lolling about, hoping to be ignored so that they could laze around in bed. As soon as I could get the housework in order, I'd join Mary and Ma to hasten the laundry so that we could begin to prepare the mince and sweet potato pies for tomorrow's feast. I had just finished washing the breakfast dishes and was at the front of the cabin cleaning and dusting when I heard the most awful commotion you can imagine. Somebody yelling and cussing in such a loud voice that I thought for sure a band of Indians had surrounded the house. But when I opened the cabin door a crack and peeked out, imagine my surprise when all I saw was one man sitting high up on a lone wagon pulled by two tired looking old oxen. I took everything in at a glance. The wheels of the wagon were so caked with mud that they would hardly turn. The wagon was loaded to capacity, and the oxen were straining at every breath to get to our front door. The deliveryman cracked his whip above his head and let go with a long string of profanity, the likes of which I'd never heard in my life.

I was of two minds! There was no doubt that the loaded wagon was filled with our new furniture, but who was this wild man making the delivery? I knew in an instant that he was not our kind. I would have to confront him because there was nobody else around to claim the freight. But I certainly didn't have to be cordial, and I must get rid of him as soon as possible. And who would help to unload the heavy pieces?

I opened the door, stepped out and stood waiting. The wagon came to a halt within inches of our front door. The wild man, upon seeing me, swept off his hat and with one swift, graceful movement was out of the wagon and on his feet. He bowed. I had no intention of accepting his apology for the disturbance he had just made, but then he didn't bother to apologize. He just said, "Ma'am, I do believe this load of stuff is intended for you." I allowed as to how it was. He stood straight and tall, hat in hand, his long black hair sweeping across his face. I do believe he has the most piercing blue eyes I've ever seen in my life.

I was as frosty cool as it was possible to be when you consider that a stranger had just arrived with furnishings we'd been longing for a fortnight to arrive.

By that time Martha and Lucy were hovering in the background, and I had to take my attention away from the unwelcome delivery man long enough to chastise them for coming to the door in their nightgowns! While we were still at this impasse—the man not able to unload the furniture by himself and I, wondering how we could accomplish the feat— Mary came hurrying up to see what was going on. And, fortunately, the clamor and noise had reached Robert and Enoch who were not far away.

I said my brothers would help with the furniture—and I closed the door. I would have slammed it if my manners had allowed! The very idea of having a stranger arrive at our home shouting such inappropriate language made me almost ill. Never in all the days of my life have I been so offended. I only wanted to escape his presence. Anyone using that kind of language was no gentleman! But, never mind. Robert would take over, and I'd never have to see the man again.

In no time at all they had the furniture unloaded and were trying to move it into the house. Even though Ma had arranged and rearranged the pieces many times in her mind and had pointed out to me how things were to be moved around and where the new pieces were to be placed, I was so rattled that I could not remember what she had said. Mary seemed to remember everything and immediately took charge. I was so upset that all I could do was hover and be a nuisance.

I had heard Robert introduce himself as soon as he rode up, but I could not hear the stranger give his name. When every piece was in place—or as nearly as could be done at the moment—Robert had the audacity to invite the man into the house for refreshments. I had left the coffeepot simmering on the back of the stove, and there was bread and butter and jam. From the other room, I could hear the goings on, but I was determined not to go back into that man's presence. Ma had come up by that time, and I heard everybody laughing and talking and enjoying the new furniture. Then Enoch pushed open the door and wanted to know why I had disappeared; I should come out and meet our guest properly, he said. With everybody looking on, there was nothing I could do but make my appearance.

Robert introduced us. "Alexander Cockrell," he said, "this is my sister, Sarah Horton. I believe you have already met her, but have not been properly introduced." I extended my hand. What else could I have done under the circumstances with several pairs of eyes boring into me? Nobody knew what I did about this uncouth stranger, so I played along. I could be both friendly and frosty, and I had every intention of doing just that.

I must admit that Alexander Cockrell had done a complete about face. He was every inch the gentleman as he sat at our dining table having coffee with our brothers. It turned out that he was a nephew of our friend, Wesley Cockrell who he was visiting. He'd ridden his horse into Dallas early that morning and was there when the freight wagon arrived with our furniture. He was having an early morning drink (I feel certain whiskey!) with the men when the agent approached and asked if anybody would deliver the furniture to the Hortons out on Mountain Creek. When he found out that a delivery fee would be paid, Mr. Cockrell said he jumped at the chance to make a few dollars. He had nothing better to do. He was only spending a few days with his relatives before riding down south to be a soldier in the Texas/Mexican war.

I was vastly relieved!

We were invited to a party on Saturday at the Cockrell home, and all of us were looking forward to attending. I could not imagine having to be in the presence socially of such a foul-mouthed man as Alexander Cockrell, so I was pleased to hear that he would be riding out as soon as tomorrow's Thanksgiving repast was over.

I thought he would never take his leave on Wednesday. He kept hovering, laughing and talking to the boys. Ma and all five of our sisters had joined the festivities. By the way everybody was behaving, you'd have thought we were having a party! Only I held back, but then I was the only one who recognized what an unsavory character we were entertaining. Finally, he left. By that time I had to get our noonday meal on the table.

Mary and Ma went back to complete the laundry, Rachel and Lucy reluctantly joining them, leaving Emma and Martha to help me.

We are enjoying our new things so much. The new cutlery and a complete set of dishes that match are so pretty! I am thrilled that we will have everything rearranged into its proper place by morning and will be able to set a lovely Thanksgiving table. I sometimes think that the worst part of being out here in the wilderness is leaving behind so many of the "nice" things, which made our lives so much more comfortable back home. I'm sure you've noticed that I often refer to Virginia as home—but more and more I am becoming acclimated and aware that this new land is my destiny. I would like to think that I can contribute something to the future, but I cannot imagine what it would be.

Do you remember the article in the New Haven, Connecticut *Columbian Register* several years ago (Feb. 15, 1840) that we clipped and giggled about? I came across it last week folded and tucked at the bottom of my handkerchief box. It's called "Glorious chance for Girls" and tells about the Government of Texas encouraging young women to emigrate from the United States promising that they will be offered a bounty of land if they will marry a citizen of Texas. It talks about the quality of the land, but the stress is on the large number of bachelors who are looking for suitable wives. It says that Texas is well adapted for raising soldiers, cabbages, lawyers, potatoes, pumpkins, cotton, sugar, dandies, babies, pigs and chickens! It adds, "Girls, Texas is the place. Pack up your duds, take your knitting work and be off!" I got another good laugh when I read the clipping again . . . don't know why I kept it, except to prove that whoever wrote it is wrong! There may be bachelors aplenty floating around, but I haven't met any of them. The only men who have come into my life are either married, too young, or people like that Alexander Cockrell. I guess I'm doomed to be an old maid!

Now, I am meandering, daydreaming, as it were. Enough! I must put pen and paper away and begin to think about how I can help Ma prepare for the morrow . . . with Christmas just around the corner. How I wish that you were here to celebrate with us.

Your loving sister,

Sarah

Wednesday, December 31
(last day of 1845)

Dear precious sister Jane,

Oh, what a week has wrought! So much has happened since I wrote to you on the day before Thanksgiving that I hardly know where to begin.

Thanksgiving has come and gone. Christmas has come and gone. But that's not the half of it. I have seen Mr. Cockrell again, and there is no way I can tell you what a difference a few days has made in his appearance and in his behavior.

To keep you up-to-date, I relate that our Thanksgiving dinner was a feast for the gods. The boys brought home a wild turkey that, when dressed and baked in Ma's huge pot among the coals, was absolutely delicious. We had turnips, onions and potatoes supplemented with canned greens and peas from last Spring's garden. Ma made some more of the delicious yeast rolls. None of us knew she had cached away enough yeast to make a holiday meal, and we were all surprised and pleased. The pies— sweet potato and mincemeat—were marvelous. Only Ma can make a crust so light and flaky from whatever lard she has available.

But I am putting off the best part. On Saturday after the Thanksgiving feast, we all got dressed up in our finest and set out in the wagon around four o'clock in the afternoon for the Wesley Cockrell house. We knew we would have fun. We always do when we visit with that family, but I had no idea what was in store. Ma had packed a picnic dinner, and we stopped shortly before sundown and spread our evening meal on a sunny spot. It was cold, but not frigid and our spirits kept us warm. Along the way, James played the harmonica and Robert the ukulele, and we all sang. We arrived at the Cockrell house just before dark. It does get dark early in this country. Other neighbors were pulling up in their wagons, and we could hear music from the candlelit interior.

The first person I saw was Alexander Cockrell. I must tell you he looked like a dream come true—tall, very handsome, that black hair perfectly groomed and the piercing blue eyes literally drilling into me. I had to pinch myself to remind me that he was a scoundrel, given to taking the Lord's name in vain, a wild man not fitting for pleasant society. He certainly didn't seem so that night. He was grace personified. I did my best to avoid him, but he returned again and again, asking me to dance, cutting in when I was waltzing with someone else, and squeezing my hand when we passed each other in the square dances. He made himself omnipresent and an absolute nuisance. He did not say very much, but his constant attention was, if I tell the truth, very flattering. I cannot recall ever having any man pay me such courtliness.

Only once he alluded to our first meeting, saying "Miss Sarah, I hope you will see fit to forgive me for my indiscretions at our last encounter." I pretended I did not know what he was talking about.

Several of the other girls present, including two of our own sisters, were shameless in their attention to Alexander Cockrell! I was embarrassed for them, and I did my very best to avoid his consistent attention.

Toward the end of the evening, he cut in when I was dancing with James and told me that he would be leaving on the morrow for the Texas border. He had postponed leaving earlier in the week because he did not want to miss the party when he heard that I would be coming. This made me very flustered. I did not know how to respond. He asked if I were promised to anyone back home in Virginia or if I were walking out with anyone since arriving in Texas. I had to be truthful and admit that there was no other suitor in the picture, but it embarrassed me tremendously. It was as if he were asking whether, or not, I would be willing to be his girl though he never came right out and said that!

The boys hitched up our oxen shortly after 10 and we all said our good-byes. Mr. Cockrell hovered around with the rest of the Cockrell family and all of the other guests who were staying the night. Once he even brushed my arm! Then, at the last moment, when I had no idea how to say good-by properly, he held out his hand first and held mine just a bit longer than necessary. His eyes held mine in an intimacy that was both thrilling and embarrassing. All the way home, I held that handclasp to my heart wondering what on earth was happening to me.

The next day I learned he had, indeed, saddled up early the next morning and headed south. I don't know what to think! But I can tell you I have had an earful from the rest of the family.

You would think from the way everybody is behaving that I am about to become engaged! Our brothers are teasing me unmercifully. Martha and Rachel both say they are jealous! I can take their teasing just fine, but it's Ma and Pa who have me baffled. After everybody had gone to bed last night and Pa was heaping ashes on the sparks for the night, I came back into the front room of the cabin for a glass of water, and Pa very seriously asked me to sit down for a moment. He acted very nervous. You know Pa has never been one to give us advice head-on, but always talks to Ma about his thoughts and expects her to tell us. Finally, he cleared his throat and began to talk, very haltingly, about Alexander Cockrell. It turned out that he had been checking up on the man! Your first impression was right, Pa said, the man is not our kind. He is a rover. Since he was a kid, he's lived at one place and another across the country. He's an opportunist. He grabs whatever work he can get—not all of it honest—wherever he happens to land, and then he moves on. He is not to be trusted. Then Pa wound up saying, "And I would not give my approval for any serious relationship to develop between him and any one of my daughters." With that, he turned beet red and went off to bed.

He left me baffled. I was literally shaking as I filled a glass with water and found my bed. Then, I could not go to sleep. I lay there and lay there going over every one of my actions that might have led anyone to think I would ever consider becoming seriously attached to such an individual. Finally, some long time after the middle of the night I fell into a confused sleep and dreamed about a man with piercing blue eyes who had taken my hand in both of his in a gesture ever so gentle, but possessive. I honestly don't think the man in my dream had anything to do with Alexander Cockrell. But how can I be sure?

And that wasn't the end of it! After breakfast this morning, Ma sent all four of our younger sisters down to the branch to fetch water for drinking and bathing. They were hardly out of the house when she started in on me. She hinted rather than approached the subject directly. She started out telling me how she and Pa had grown up on adjacent farms whose families had known each other all of their lives. She said how important it is for a man and a woman who contemplate marriage to have similar backgrounds and common interests. She added that it is even advisable for them to be of the same religious faith or at the very least to share similar values. She said it is hard enough for a married couple to be compatible when they have known each other for a long time. And it is rarely possible for any couple to find happiness unless they have gone through a ritual of walking out together, being in each other's company under many different circumstances. They should attend not only social events but also religious services together, know each other's families and talk together about how they will resolve the inevitable conflicts that arise. She even brought you into it! She said you and Mr. Bradshaw are the ideal couple because you experienced all of the important things she had just mentioned. And even though she misses you terribly, she had no reservations about leaving you in Virginia when we came to Texas because she knew your husband would be good to you.

All the time she was talking, I was speechless. Mary never uttered a word, just kept on stacking the breakfast dishes, but when I glanced in her direction, she winked at me! It was all I could do to keep from bursting out laughing.

I cannot believe that our parents have me all but promised to this man I find utterly appalling—at least most of the time.

You must think that I am obsessed with these concerns. Other things are going on in our lives!

For the past two weeks a tribe of Indians has been camped near us. John says they are Delawares, and he estimates there are more than a thousand of them, probably as many as 1,500. The Delawares are reputed to be friendly. Even so, we keep an all-night vigil with our livestock. We are told that the buffalo are becoming very scarce in the area, and most Indians have hunted buffalo for years to provide their major source of meat. I wish it were possible to expand our farms and enhance our own livelihood and not disturb the lives of people who occupied this land long before we ever arrived. I see some of the tribe only from a great distance and have no desire to see any of them at close range, but Pa says we are not to be afraid. Some may come to our door asking for food, but nobody will harm us. I guess I have been so preoccupied with concerns over my family's reaction to Alexander Cockrell that I haven't given as much thought to Delaware Indians as I would under different circumstances.

I am gravely concerned about what looks almost certainly like a new war with Mexico. The official annexation of Texas to the Union continues to rile the officials in Mexico, and though sane voices are struggling to find a peaceful settlement to the disagreement, many men led by President Polk seem determined to shoot it out. Why is it that men are so quick to settle their arguments with their fists? Or with guns? If mothers had their way, there would be no more war, I wager. Who wants to give birth to a child only to have him grow up to be fodder for annihilation in battle?

I continue to hold school, even if only now and then, for our younger sisters. Sometimes Mary helps, though she does not seem to be as determined as I am. The men in the family mostly raise their eyebrows at my efforts, as they did recently when I asked Pa if he would order me a copy of author Margaret Fuller's *Woman in the Nineteenth Century*. When I read an item about her work in one of the papers Pa brought me, I felt that my own convictions would be strengthened by her writings. In the item I read, she was called a "feminist," a term that was not meant to flatter! I find it appalling that women do most of the hard work that keeps body and soul together—like giving birth, caring for children, keeping the home clean, planning and cooking meals, looking after the sick and laying out the deceased for burial—and yet are not allowed to speak out in public places about the policies that shape their lives and the lives of their children. It seems to me that it is time women had the same vote and voice and the same responsibilities in the public sphere that they have in their homes. Until women have a legal voice, we will just have to continue to manipulate our husbands and brothers and, yes, even fathers, to gain our proper place in the scheme of things. No wonder I heard James say to John that their sister is something of a rebel!

James, by the way, is beginning to seriously develop the property he claimed to the north of us. John's plot lies between ours and his. He has begun slowly to build a cabin on his piece of land, and I am sure is courting one of the neighbors, though I have not been privy to finding out who she is.

Tomorrow begins a whole new year! I wonder what joys and sorrows lie ahead, and I continue to pray that you and your family will join us in Dallas, Texas!

Your loving sister,

Sarah

April 12, 1846

Mrs. John Neely Bryan
The Bryan Cabin
Dallas, Texas

My dear Mrs. Margaret Beeman Bryan,

Thank you for your hospitality on Tuesday, last. My mother, my sisters and I very much enjoyed our visit with you and the opportunity to see for ourselves the vast growth of the village.

For a long time we have wanted to come into town. The distance from our home here on Mountain Creek has been but one of the deterrents to our making the trip. My father and our brothers discouraged us because of the hazardous crossing of the Trinity River. You certainly have first-hand knowledge of what can happen when rains flood the area and the river rises. Your story about losing your first home to flooding while you and Mr. Bryan were away at Coffee's Landing on the Red River for supplies two years ago was very sad. Your resilience to that catastrophe—having to live in a tent while the cabin was being rebuilt—is a testament to your endurance and is so typical of the hardships that women face while surviving in this part of the world. I am sure that your life back in Illinois was much more comfortable, as was ours in Virginia. But progress comes only through hardship, I suppose.

We so very much enjoyed shopping in the Smith & Patterson Emporium. Everything was so fresh that we could still smell the newness! The wares, though limited, were the best we can expect for an establishment that had been open for business less than a month. It will take Ma and my sisters and me some time to fashion dresses from the fabrics we brought home.

The new store is a testament to the tenacity of your husband and other town leaders. I was amazed to learn that 53 families now reside in the general area though they are scattered throughout the countryside. As you pointed out, there are only four small residential cabins in town, including yours. So those of us who live west of the Trinity River and your own family which lives a distance to the east, are all a part of the total.

We were most excited to hear that a Dallas County has been created by the new Texas State Legislature and to see with our own eyes the beginning of the cabin that will house Dallas County offices. Our men have been loathe to ride horseback the long distance to Old Franklin in Robertson County to take care of official business. I have wondered if we even had legal claim to the land on which we live because I was not certain that our deeds were properly registered.

Most of all we were overjoyed to see your new baby. At two months of age (didn't you say he was born on January 9?) he is a healthy, happy child and I am so pleased for you. Pa had told us about the loss of your first son last year. You must have already known that a new child was expected when Holland Coffee died last July. One baby can never replace another, but it must be a great comfort that John Neely Jr. is so healthy. When I think of you, which is often, I see you cuddling the child in your arms as you waved us adieu when we were stepping into the canoe on our way home. It took three trips across the Trinity to transport all eight of the Hortons and our wares back to the west bank of the river where we were met by John and Robert with the wagon.

Thank you again for a marvelous day in Dallas. I can hardly wait to make a return trip to the town, and I hope you will be able to visit us soon here in our cabin on Mountain Creek. Even though we have just met, I feel that I have known you forever.

Most sincerely yours,

Sarah

June 12, 1846

Mrs. William Bradshaw
The Bradshaw Farm
Abington, Virginia

My beloved sister, Jane,

Two of your letters arrived in the same post yesterday. It was good to hear from you. I can tell by some of the questions you asked and the comments you made that you have not been receiving all of my letters. It is just as well. I have no idea which ones you received and which ones were lost en route, but I can only wish that some of my babbling went astray. My face turns red when I think how I must have sounded like a lovesick school girl in some of the things I wrote. If you, perchance, did receive those two letters telling you about my meeting with Mr. Alexander Cockrell, please know that I have come to my senses and no longer give him a thought.

We are having a beautiful spring. The crops are all in and looking great. Harvest time is just around the corner. For now, I have dispensed with school. I can only hope that encouraging our sisters to read, to write to you and to take advantage of every opportunity for learning is turning them into young ladies who will have a modicum of education along with their charm and beauty. Our sisters are beautiful! I look at them and wonder how I could have turned out so plain—nondescript brown hair, and not a lot of it—to their ravishing locks that fall halfway down their backs and are chestnut, bronze and golden wheat. Our three sisters with blue eyes all are framed in black lashes as are Martha's lovely brown—almost black—eyes while I managed to get deep-set gray eyes with little to recommend them! There is no doubt that of all of my sisters—you, Mary, Martha, Rachel, Lucy and Emma—I am the most forgettable of all!

During the second week of April, Pa finally gave way to our wheedling and took us into town. It was an all-day affair with only a couple of hours to spend in the village before we had to begin our trip back home. The boys hitched the oxen to the wagon and took us to the banks of the Trinity River. Pa rode across on his horse and rented Mr. Bryan's canoe, then returned for us. The little boat is so small that only four of us, at best, could make the trip across. Pa took Ma, Mary and Emma across, then returned for Martha, Lucy and me. It took only a short time to row across the river, but I felt that time was wasting for my own adventures to begin. I learned later that Ma, Mary and Emma were welcomed by Mrs. John Neely Bryan as soon as they arrived, as were we when we got to her cabin on the east bank of the Trinity.

Mrs. Bryan is such a tiny thing and so young! I am sure she has not yet reached her twenties, but she is twice a mother already. I felt such a kinship with Mrs. Bryan, whose name is Margaret. She was a Beeman, the daughter of the second family to arrive in the area to join Mr. Bryan in the founding of the town. The Bryans live in the largest cabin in the town; it is their third. Mrs. Bryan said that her husband brought her as a bride to his first home right on the banks of the Trinity, a one-room tiny cabin where she prepared their meals on the open hearth. Shortly after their wedding, Mr. Bryan started another house for them, a larger cabin that was washed away when the river overflowed not long after they moved into it. Then, he build a third cabin, the one in which they now live, which was completed shortly before John Neely Bryan, Jr. was born. It is a fine home, located far enough away from the river where Commerce and Broadway streets (more on this later) intersect. Made of cedar logs, it has two big rooms under one roof. The room on the east with doors and a window facing the rising sun is for cooking and dining. The one on the west, its outlets facing the river, is the family space that is used for a living room and for sleeping. We were royally entertained in the family room but were shown the rest of the house. The second room has a walkway between it and the first so that cooking odors and heat will not permeate the other part of the house. Both are floored with puncheons, wide planks smoothed on top but still uneven. Mrs. Bryan is working on a rag rug for the "front" room. She said it is going slowly because fabric is so hard to get, and she must use what she can find. When we cut our dresses from the fabric we bought in town at the new Smith & Patterson general merchandise store, I hope to have some scraps to give to Mrs. Bryan for her rug. I am tempted to start one of our own. Perhaps some day in the future I may even have a house where I could use such a thing!

We were told that the first census has been completed and that 53 "men" now live in the area. I take it that means families! There is such a tendency in these parts to count the men and dismiss all the rest of us as irrelevant. The "First" families include: the Bryans, of course; the John Andersons; the Beemans (brothers John and James Beeman with their wives Emily Hunnicutt and Sarah Crawford, later joined by Samuel, a third brother); the Cochrans (William M. and his wife, Nancy Hughes Cochran) three of Nancy's sisters with their husbands (Mary Hughes Webb and her husband Isaac Blackmon Webb, Sarah Matilda Hughes Williams and her husband Thomas Carroll Williams and Serena Caroline Hughes Knight and her husband, Obadiah Woodson Knight); the Rawlins family; and, of course, I include our own family—the Hortons on Mountain Creek, plus the Wesley Cockrells, our neighbors to the north and the Hords, our neighbors to the south. There are others, many which this first census missed. The one thing that most upsets, even angers me, is that the "men" are counted. Many, like my own father, is "head" of a large family that includes Ma, our four brothers, five sisters and me! What is this? That only the married men count and nobody else is to be noted in the census?

In February Texas formally installed a state government in Austin. Several men from Dallas are among the new officers. Even more important to us than having a state government is that we now have a COUNTY! One of the state legislature's first acts was to create Dallas County, carving it from portions of Nacogdoches County on the east and Robertson County on the west. Dallas has been named the first seat of county government simply because Mr. Bryan designated space in his cabin for county records and immediately, with the help of three or four other men, began to construct a separate building to seat the officials and house the records. We witnessed the start of the cabin, some 15 by 16 feet in size, which is located on the northwest corner of what Mr. Bryan designates to be the "square" of his town. It is being made of four-foot boards, has puncheon floors and a large fireplace with a chimney of split wood daubed with clay. For furnishings, at least temporarily, split logs will be put in for seating. Mr. Bryan is a real visionary, never lets an opportunity pass without taking advantage of it. Mrs. Bryan seems to take everything he does calmly. She is several years younger than he, and I suppose looks on him as the founding father he claims to be.

Not everybody is pleased with the town of Dallas as a seat of government. We are a part of a community west of the Trinity River now known as Hord's Ridge. To the north of the village of Dallas is a settlement called Cedar Springs. For now, as of May 12, Mr. Bryan has been designated as the official to select managers who are to name temporary officers and select a date, time and place for an election that will determine where the county government will be permanently located and who will serve as its officers.

Mr. Bryan was also concerned with setting up a city government. He has already laid out the "city" of Dallas and named its streets. When J. P. Dumas, a surveyor, and Mrs. Dumas arrived two and a half years ago, Mr. Bryan hired him to survey the area in 200 by 200 foot blocks. As it was laid out, it extended eight blocks west to east from the Trinity to Poydras Street and 10 blocks north and south from McKinney to Young Street. Mr. Bryan proudly showed Pa and James the plat provided by Mr. Dumas. Neatly laid out in squares, it included from the north to the south, McKinney,

Columbia, Polk, Wood, Jackson, Commerce, Main, Elm, Burleson, Carondelet, Walnut and Calhoun streets and from the Trinity River on the west eastward, Water, Broadway, Houston, Jefferson, Market, Austin, Lamar and Poydras. Mr. Bryan says he is selling city lots on these streets, and he hopes to have at least a hundred families living in the "city" soon. But now, as I said, there are only four cabins! There is no doubt he was hinting that Pa should purchase one of the lots, but none of us has any desire to live in town.

Everybody is talking about the Mexican War. The men, of course, discuss it and the women are supposed to play dumb and have no clue about what is going on. I listen but do not voice an opinion. That way I learn a lot! There is a great deal of disagreement over whether we should be fighting this war at all. In April when President Polk asked Congress to declare a state of war with Mexico, there seemed to be no way to settle the dispute between that country and ours over the borders of Texas, portions of California and New Mexico. But then, as General Zachary Taylor was ordered to post troops on the left bank of the Rio Grande River, across from Matamoros, Mexican authorities began to seek a face-saving way to avoid conflict. By that time, I understand, President Polk was spoiling for a fight and in mid-May had his way when Congress approved a resolution that "a state of war exists between the Government of Mexico and the United States Government." Congress then authorized the recruitment of 50,000 soldiers and agreed to $10 million to fight the war. There is a growing feeling that the real issue has to do with the disagreement between the North and South over whether, or not, slavery will continue. For me, this war has a face—that of Mr. Alexander Cockrell. I think of him often and wonder what role he is playing. He told me that he was not in the regular Army, only a volunteer, and I wonder if this means he can walk away if he wants to. Please don't misunderstand; I have absolutely no romantic feelings toward this man. I would feel the same way toward anyone who faced danger in battle. I think women do this. The government can glibly talk about an Army of 50,000, but each of those is an individual, some mother's son, some woman's husband or sweetheart or friend, some sister's brother. I think of how I would feel if any one of our brothers was recruited into the Army. I lie awake at night and ponder these things . . . and all the while continue to miss you so very much.

Much love,

Sarah

December 1846

My beloved sister, Jane,

The year is winding down. My long silence is due to three things—laziness, lack of new information to share and that all of us have been busy harvesting the crops, preserving the garden foods, rendering lard, making soap and candles, sewing clothing and the thousand and one other small things that must be done daily. I had Martha and Rachel, as an exercise in practical mathematics, keep a record for one week of the time required to plan and prepare meals for this large family. They could not believe the results—and neither could Pa and the boys, who scoff at the amount of time required to keep them fed. Why is it that men think they are doing the real work in the family? They may be primarily responsible for the economic survival, but they usually discount the contributions of wives and daughters who make it possible for them to function. Oh well, here I go on another tirade! I can tell you one thing—when (and if) I ever have a husband and a home of my own, I am going to know where the money comes from and where it goes! That seems to be the only value that men understand. I do not discount the economic status of the family as imperative, but I know it is not the whole story.

But back to our exercise in financial reality. According to Martha's figures (I had each sister keep her own records for comparison), it took a combined five hours a day to prepare meals. According to Rachel's figures, it took almost six. She counted in the time it took to set the table and clear it afterward, just as she should. This time was calculated on an ordinary day. During the holiday seasons—Thanksgiving and Christmas and on birthdays—we spend a lot more time in the kitchen. I wish I really enjoyed meal planning and preparation. There are so many other things I'd rather do. But I listen and learn from Ma because I know that women spend so much time feeding themselves and others, and I want to do the best job I can in the shortest time!

There is still a squabble over where the Dallas County seat will be located: the town of Dallas where it is now temporarily located, Hord's Ridge where we live or Cedar Springs. But we have our first elected county officials. The chief justice is a man named John Thomas. Pa says he doesn't know Judge Thomas but has learned that he has lived in the area about the same time we have, coming here from Missouri with his wife and six children. The two oldest boys, John and Alex both signed up for active duty at the start of the Mexican War, and John recently was killed in battle. There are four younger children—Ellis, Elizabeth, Eliza and Sarah.

Elizabeth, incidentally, is married to Charles Durgan and is the young woman I mentioned who now handles the mail in Dallas—though it's her husband who has the title of postmaster.

The other county officials are John C. McCoy, district clerk; William M. Cochran, county clerk; John Huitt, sheriff; Anson McCrackin, coroner and Benjamin Merrill, tax assessor. I've mentioned Mr. Cochran to you before, but you may not remember that he is among the first settlers, having arrived here from Missouri three years ago. His wife is Nancy Jane Hughes Cochran. There are seven Hughes sisters, natives of Tennessee, who, with their husbands, moved here. I don't know anything about Mr. Huitt or Mr. Merrill, but Mr. McCoy is a very popular newcomer to the area. An attorney with Peters' Colony, he came late last year or earlier this year. He, like most people who came because of flagrant promises of Peters' Colony officials, soon became disenchanted, resigned his position and has gone into private practice in general law. Mr. McCoy is widely traveled. He grew up in Indiana but practiced law in both Kansas and Missouri. He is single and cuts quite a swath with the ladies. I have not had the privilege of meeting him.

The county was not long in business before deeds were filed, documents legalized and licenses granted. The start-up of any organization is an exhilarating experience, and I sometimes wish I were a man so that I could enjoy the changes first-hand rather than having everything come through Pa and our brothers. Enoch is the most garrulous of the group. He never rides off anywhere that he does not come home full of stories and always shares with me. I am so curious, eager to listen.

The first marriage license issued by the county happened on July 20. Crawford Trees and Anna Minerva Kimmel, our neighbors to the southwest, applied for a license to wed. They were married two days later and set up housekeeping on his property, which adjoins her mother's grant. Mr. Trees is 22 and the bride only 15. Both families lived in the same general area in Illinois before they moved to Texas. They did not know each other until they came here and established residence on adjoining farms.

Recently the courts presided over the first civil suit in the county, Dalton *v.* Dalton, a divorce suit brought by Mrs. Charlotte Hewitt Dalton against her husband, Charles B. Dalton. An ironic twist of the whole thing was that Henderson Couch was foreman of the jury, which granted the divorce. And before the sun went down Mr. Couch and the former Mrs. Dalton were married!

Mr. Bryan and William Baker were granted permission by the court to establish a ferry across the Trinity River and immediately put one into service. Until this time, people have crossed the river in canoes, or at low tide ridden horseback or even walked across. The court established ferry rates—$1.25 for large wagons, up to $1.50 for the same when the river is out of its banks. Two-horse wagons and pleasure carriages can cross at low tide for 75 cents; when the water is high, the cost is $1.00. A man riding a horse can cross for twenty cents. (There is no designation about what it will cost a lady on horseback to take the ferry!) Single loose horses and footmen are charged ten cents to cross and live stock is ticketed at five cents each.

Talk of the Mexican War reaches us every time neighbors meet or when we can get newspapers. I hear that the *Boston Courier* recently published a diatribe, "The Bigelow Papers" by James Russell Lowell, setting out his opposition to the war. My own conflicted views are brought home every time I hear about a young man killed in action—such as the young Mr. Thomas. And, also, every time I think of Mr. Cockrell. To me the war has names.

To look at Mr. Bryan's map of Dallas with its neatly drawn streets and cross streets, its walks and its location of stores and houses, one would think it is a thriving metropolis. And he continues to promote it as such, but it's pretty sad looking. Winding paths and wagon roads run through tangles of weeds, avoiding small stumps and drawfed trees. Dirt "roads" make travel all but impossible in the hot weather, when the dust boils with every passing wagon, and entirely impassible when it rains. Only four families live in close proximity to "downtown." There are two stores—the new emporium run by J. W. Smith and James M. Patterson and another by Charles Durgan and a Mr. Stanley. The post office moved from Mr. Bryan's cabin to the latter facility to make it simpler for Mrs. Durgan to sort and distribute the mail.

All of us are looking forward to Christmas when several parties with music and dancing are planned for the holidays. It is the one time of the year when Pa doesn't complain about hitching the oxen to the wagon and setting out for the neighbors' houses. We celebrate from Christmas Eve through New Year's Day just as we did back in Virginia. And even though our friends and neighbors from different states have brought slightly different customs and expectations with them, everything blends perfectly here. All of us will have new dresses, and we have made new shirts for all of the men. I am both looking forward to the next few weeks and dreading it—for it is always a great deal of work. I am hoping for a new book, perhaps a copy of John Greenleaf Whittier's *Voices of Freedom*, which I've read about.

With fondest wishes that the holiday be your brightest yet and that, somehow, in the next year we meet again, I am,

Your loving sister,

Sarah

Spring, 1847

My dearest sister,

Your letter of Christmas Day arrived here in late February. How we all cherish news from you. Family members, friends and acquaintances from our old home in Virginny come alive as you describe people and events of our past. I have read your letter over and over, am being more careful with it now because it is about to come apart. It is ever so much more difficult to write to you because you do not know the people, events and surroundings that now comprise our lives here. I know this is no excuse for my long delay in writing, and I shall strive to do better!

Every time the "boys" ride into the village (and they go far more often these days than Pa), they return with stories about new families moving into the area. Two Miller families have settled a distance from us. William Brown and Minerva Barnes Miller came from Missouri with six children, the oldest 17 and the youngest only two. He had made a prior trip to this area last year and bought property on a beautiful hillside about six miles east of us. Where we are south and a bit west of the downtown village of Dallas, they are south and slightly east. We are on a pretty lake, but as I've explained before, except for the lake, our surroundings are not pretty unless you look to the distant hills. Enoch tells me that from their higher location, on a clear day, Mr. and Mrs. Miller can almost see our house.

I understand that the oldest Miller child, the 17-year-old called Crill (what kind of a name is that?), is Mr. Miller's by a prior marriage. He and his wife have an eight-year-old son, Alonzo and four little girls—Mattie 6, Mary Brown 4, Virginia 2, and Susan only a few months old. I get these details from Enoch who humors me by learning the tiniest information about new residents. Knowing how chagrined I can be because we women are not privy to running about like the men, he comes home with all kinds of marvelous stories even though he sometimes loses patience when I probe for more details than he has.

The second Millers to settle in our area are the Madison Moultrie Miller family. They are in an area to the south in what is known as Pleasant Run. This Mr. Miller may have first arrived in Dallas with William Brown Miller. We are told that the men are friends, not related, but I wonder about that because the Pleasant Run area Miller is considerably older than William Brown Miller. In any event, Mr. Madison Miller is from Alabama where his wife, Isabell McClusky Miller, had died leaving him with two children, Mary Cordelia and William. On the scouting trip to this area before it was designated as a county, he met Mary Parks Rawlins, the 18-year-old daughter of R.A. and Mildred Rawlins, apparently courted her and proposed before going back to Alabama to collect his children. Upon his return to Texas, the two were married on May 25—a year ago—so at age 19, Polly, as she is known, is the mother of a five-year-old son and a seven-year-old daughter. Her husband is almost 13 years older. Such a difference in ages would not matter a great deal to me, I think, because you and I grew up in a family with older brothers. But I cannot imagine it would be easy for a girl described as an older daughter both high-spirited and a bit spoiled!

I mentioned a bit back that Pa does not ride off on scouting expeditions nearly as often as he used to and that concerns me. He seems to be aging before my eyes. Neither he nor Ma has the energy that you remember. Both need to rest oftener, though Pa can still out-plow and out-harvest any of our brothers. Both Mary and I try to take as much of the family chores off Ma as possible. It sometimes gets a little touchy because she needs to be—and we want her to be—in charge. But it's very easy to find new and shorter ways to do the chores she has always done, and she finds it sometimes hard to let go of her way of doing things. Our younger sisters are coming along. I find myself trying to spare them of the most difficult tasks, which isn't fair because eventually they are all going to have husbands and families of their own and must know how to take care of themselves under all conditions. And, I must admit, I sometimes resort to bribery. I will prepare a meal or do their share of the laundry, especially the ironing, if they will study lessons, which I have outlined for them or if they even will read! Last week after I had agreed to fetch the water for the next day's laundry—a chore I hate because it requires emptying bucket after bucket of water into the huge black wash pot—if Lucy and Emma would complete writing an essay I had assigned them. I arrived back at the house to hear them giggling in the loft upstairs and climbed up to see their unfinished project on the bed beside them while they chatted and laughed about a couple of boys they had met the last time we attended a party at the Wesley Cockrell home. I scolded them severely, but on reflection, should have not been so hard on them. Just because I'm old beyond my years—and heaven knows, I have enough years!—I should not judge other young women by my standards.

Speaking of the Wesley Cockrells, our family and theirs continue to see a lot of each other. They are our closest neighbors, and it's such a pleasure to have people near enough that we can visit back and forth. I am especially glad that they like to entertain. Our place is not quite big enough for musicals and dancing and theirs is. Besides, Ma and Pa—dear as they are—do not enjoy partying as much as most of us would like. I have not heard one word from Mr. Cockrell's cousin, Alexander, since he left to ride off to the Mexican War in South Texas. I follow the fighting there as much as possible, but am aware that most of the "news" is but hearsay and propaganda. Even the newspapers fall into that category because they play up our victories and give little real information about what is taking place. Besides, the last newspaper I have is almost a year old, May 30, 1846. It was published in New York and called the *New-York Weekly Tribune*. I've kept it because it has a good outline map called "The Seat of War" which shows South Texas with Louisiana from New Orleans on westward to its right and top and Mexico to its bottom and south. One of its headlines is entitled, "The American Army Victorious!!" but the headline just underneath it in smaller type reads, "Death of Major Ringgold." Then, there's the next headline, "Vega, the Mexican General, Taken Prisoner," and underneath it, again in smaller type, "American Consul and Residents at Matamoros Imprisoned."

See what I mean? The good news is headlined in large letters. The bad news, if such is reported at all, is relegated in smaller type as if it is insignificant. Again, I say as I have so often been heard to utter before— for women, every man killed in battle is the name of a son, husband, brother, fiancé or friend. There are no such things as anonymous deaths.

But back to a more pleasant topic. I was telling you about some of the newcomers to these parts. To many people, especially to Ma, the most welcome newcomers are the Smith family—the Rev. James Anderson and Anne Killen Smith who came here from Mississippi but really are from Alabama. Other than occasional circuit riders, he is the first Methodist minister to come to these parts. He and Mrs. Smith, with their five children, her mother and 19 slaves arrived in January. They were lured, as have been so many families, by the outrageous promises of Peters' Colony agents. And like others found very soon that the dream of a modern utopia was non-existent and already have moved out to settle on a large farm about five miles north of town on a much traveled artery called Preston Road which originates at the Red River and extends into the village of Dallas.

The good reverend manages his farm by day—with, of course, a huge contingent of servants to do his bidding—and preaches somewhere in the area every Sunday. He is very popular, as is his wife, and conducts most of the weddings and funerals here. He told Pa that he had been licensed to preach for only the past three years and that he and his family were delighted to find other Methodist families already in the area when they arrived.

Isaac Webb had built Webb's Chapel Methodist Church on his property northwest of the town where services were regularly held, sometimes conducted by lay-people of the community or by visiting circuit riders. All of the Webbs and their family members—the Hughes, Cochran, Williams and Knight families—are Methodists. The first Methodist sermon ever preached in the Dallas area was in the living room of Nancy and William Cochran.

It is no wonder that the Rev. Smith was thrilled! He found a ready-made—if not huge—audience to listen to his sermons, which I find more inspiring than any I have heard recently from a pulpit.

The Rev. Smith is an inspired preacher. He is reed tall and thin, very straight and erect, topped with a mop of reddish blond hair that has earned him the nickname "carrot top." He is both intelligent and fiery (though, I must add, a bit too explosive for me: I prefer my sermons Bible-based but with current interpretations).

I must say it was a glorious outing and renewed my enthusiasm for Methodism. I vowed that sooner or later, I would help to create a Methodist church nearer to us. It is my hope that before we lose her, Ma can worship in a church of her faith as she did back when she was a girl.

So, it goes here! Whatever happened to the idea that you and Mr. Bradshaw would join us in the Land of Promise eventually? Believe me, it is that! On the days when I grow "weary in well doing," I am reminded that we have been prosperous here. We have our health, even when the ravages of time diminish the energy and enthusiasm of our parents. We have financial security, which was the vision of our father for bringing us here. We have each other—while missing you, the link in our family chain still in Virginia. And we have the promise of an unlimited future. What more could we ask?

Except, for me, a home, husband, children of my own? Ah, well! Before I grow maudlin and write what I might regret later, know that I am. . . .

Your loving sister,

Sarah

June 20, 1847

Dearest sister Jane,

So much has happened so very fast since I last wrote a few weeks back that I hardly know where to begin.

And if this doesn't make sense, it's because I am brimming over with happiness!

I am getting married!

But let me begin at the beginning.

It was the first Saturday in June—June 6 to be exact—and there was a party at the Wesley Cockrell house. Ma and Pa had decided not to go, and I was not looking forward to it. In fact, I would have stayed home with them if Mary had not insisted that I go. She has been stepping out with a young man whose name is Marlin Thompson and had admitted to me that she was seriously considering his proposal of marriage. She convinced me that if I did not get myself ready and go with her to the Cockrell's, she would stay at home, too.

I'll admit I was feeling a bit sorry for myself. All of our brothers and sisters—even Lucy and Emma (and she's only 15, remember!)—had girl friends or boy friends. Martha and Rachel are such beautiful girls, and Mary has become radiant since she has fallen in love. And what did I have to offer? On that Saturday, my answer would have been "nothing." I saw myself as one gray blob—nondescript brown hair, deep-set gray eyes, olive complexion. Oh well, I said to myself, at least I am slender, if not at all shapely. And I stand tall for my five feet four inches. I am neat and clean. When I smile, which I admit is not often enough (or wasn't!), my face comes alive. And most of the time I have a nice disposition. All of these things were chasing each other through my brain as I pressed my newest calico dress (it's blue) and laid out ribbons. I did the best I could and then helped our younger sisters get ready.

We left home around 4:30. I took a butter pound cake that I'd made earlier in the day. I knew there would be music and singing and dancing, but I had resigned myself mainly to helping out in the kitchen, serving refreshments and keeping the dishes washed up.

When we arrived, there was the usual crowd, all of whom we'd met in the past and mostly at the Cockrell home. Musicians took their places, and couples paired up to begin the first dance. There was much laughter, lots of innocent flirting, a crescendo of bantering—happy people having a good time.

There is no loneliness so devastating as being the outsider in a joy-filled room.

I slipped out to the kitchen, determined that I would not impose my misery on anybody else and convinced that the only way to survive the evening was to stay as busy as possible. My hands were almost elbow-deep in sudsy dishwater when I felt, rather than saw, a presence behind me. I did not want company and was about to say so when I was interrupted by a deep and resonant voice.

"So, here you are! I was about to give up hope, saddle up and go in search of you."

I turned to meet the steady gaze of Alexander Cockrell!

Before I could catch my breath and before I could say a word, he had picked up a towel, pulled my hands out of the water and dried them. I was still speechless. I cannot remember what, if anything I finally said. I only know that I was still in shock when he put one arm around my waist and whisked me out the back door. He did not stop until we were standing under a giant oak at the outer reaches of the Cockrell yard.

There, his words literally tumbled out. He had been in the midst of the fighting, he said, but the war was winding down and most of the volunteers had already left when he took off a week ago. "I came to my senses," as he put it, "reined in my horse and headed back to Cousin Wesley's house on Cedar Creek. It hit me like a thunder bolt," he said, "that my mind and my heart had been filled every moment with a beautiful girl in Texas, my cousin's neighbor, a girl named Sarah and that I could not have a moment's peace anywhere in the world until I had seen her again . . . ."

He did not stop talking. It was as if the cork had flown off an over-filled bottle! He said that in all his wanderings he had never encountered a girl he couldn't dismiss from his thoughts in a day or so after meeting her. But that he had carried a vision of me with him since the first day he arrived at our house to deliver the furniture. He said that my face had been with him on long, lonely weary rides through the blazing heat and the frigid winter.

And that he had come home to ask me to be his wife!

I don't remember what happened next, but I must have said yes because the next thing I knew, I was being lifted off my feet, swung around and soundly kissed. Ah, what bliss!

I have waited all my life to feel this way. I never thought it would happen.

And that wasn't the end of it. His lonely hours had been filled with making plans for our future. He started pouring out some of what he had been thinking, when he suddenly grew quiet. He took my hand, encircled me in a loving embrace and marched me back into the living room where he interrupted the dancing and announced to one and all.

"Miss Sarah Horton has just done me the inestimable honor of agreeing to become my wife!"

Bedlam broke loose. There was shouting and the pounding of backs and hugs and kisses and finally the music began again and I was led by my fiancé—**fiancé**—into the center of the floor where we moved together in a waltz. I'm not sure my feet ever touched the floor. Alexander Cockrell is a masterful dancer.

Only Mary seemed reserved.

Later—much later—on our way home she expressed her reservations. It wasn't that she disapproved, she said, but she wished that Alexander had not told the world about our plans before we told Ma and Pa.

How should I handle this? What should I say?

I need not have worried about relating the news. When I came down the next morning, Rachel was already there, and it took only one look at Ma and Pa to know that the secret was out. Neither of them said a word. I stammered an apology for not telling them first. I said I knew that Mr. Cockrell should have talked things over with Pa and asked for my hand. (I don't really believe this! I don't think any woman should have two men deciding her future, even for the sake of protocol. It's like bartering for her favors.) But I do understand that I should have dampened his enthusiasm until we'd told my parents. I explained that everything had happened so fast that my head was still reeling, and then I ended up, quite lamely, I think, by admitting that I was on that morning an ecstatic bride-to-be.

Ma hugged me and then Pa, too, but they still didn't say anything. Not then.

When breakfast was over everybody disappeared from the kitchen as if it were pre-arranged leaving Ma and me to do the dishes. In her very quiet way, she began quite hesitantly, to express her thoughts. She began by saying she had never seen me so happy and for that she was glad, but I was rushing into a lifetime commitment without thinking. She said that not many men were as good as Pa, and that I knew nothing at all about this man to whom I had pledged my future. She reminded me that I had found him uncouth and insulting the first time I had seen him and that nothing I had said or done since then led her to think I felt any differently about him.

Blushing deeply, she said that marriage entailed physical as well as emotional responsibilities and that I was both inexperienced in the ways of men and naive about what would be expected of me. She ended up by saying she wanted me to think deeply and prayerfully about the promises I had made and that there was lots of time to change my mind.

I listened quietly and assured her that I would take her counsel into consideration, but that I was not likely to change my mind.

In the middle of the afternoon it was Pa's turn to have his say. I was sitting under a tree with a book of poetry in my lap, daydreaming more than reading, when Pa woke from his nap and sought me out. He began by reminding me how special each of us, his children, were to him and that he had always felt extra protective toward his daughters. He assured me that my place in the family was secure and that I would always be surrounded with appreciation and love even if I never married. Then he warned me about the "vagaries" of many men. He said that so far as he had been able to determine Mr. Cockrell was a wanderer who had never settled down anywhere for very long. He said he was afraid the man I had accepted as my future mate was a bit of a scoundrel. I protested, quite gently I thought, that Mr. Cockrell was orphaned at an early age, had never had any reason for commitment to anyone. And that he had promised me he would settle down and live near his cousin, the only family he had ever known, and near my family. Pa said that promises came easily to some people and that, at the very least, I should insist upon a long engagement and give myself time to get to know this man.

When I put myself in their place, I understand why Ma and Pa are so nervous about my engagement, but I have never felt so certain about anything. I know that we will have things to work out, but I know how I feel and what I think and am confident about my decision—even though I admit I cannot remember making a decision!

I have been swept off my feet, both literally and figuratively, and am not the same person I was even a week ago.

And now for practical considerations: Mr. Cockrell has come calling every day since that whirlwind proposal. To say that I am being courted is the understatement of all times. On Monday morning following his proposal, he rode into town and registered a claim to a 640-acre plot that he had explored during his initial visit to his cousin's. There is no reason why he will not qualify for the property. Even if his promises to live on the land and build a house on it were not sufficient to certify the claim, the fact that he is a military man with an honorable discharge would cinch it. In order to justify the claim, he must be married—single men get only half of the land grant—but he said that would be no problem at all because by the time records came back from Austin for signing, he would certainly be a married man. I didn't say a word! With his exuberance, his enthusiasm and his constant expansiveness of plans for our future, I have not been able to tell him that our parents have counseled me to postpone the wedding until the two of us know each other better. And in all honesty, I don't want to put it off.

While my usual dependable and sensible self warns that there will be problems we will have to address and work through, I am convinced that I can do so. In our family, as the middle child, I have lots of experience in negotiating and mediating. And, I must admit, I look forward to being a stabilizer in the life of this mercurial and dynamic man who has never known stability.

Mr. Cockrell plans to come by later this afternoon so that he can show me the land he has chosen. I would like to ride out together, just the two of us, but Pa has made it clear that one or more of my brothers will accompany us.

As soon as we can manage some time alone, I think we will set a wedding date. My fiancé thinks we already have. I have a strong conviction that when I show how determined I am to be married, that Ma and Pa will give us their blessings and might even embrace Mr. Cockrell as the newest member of the family. I hope so.

How I wish you were here. I need someone for a special confidante, a role that you and I shared until you married and we moved away. Mary is a loving sister, but there's not the same closeness that you and I enjoy. But then, maybe if we were together I wouldn't dare pour out my deepest thoughts to you. As things develop, I promise to find the time to keep you updated. Until then, I am . . . .

Your loving sister,

Sarah

Sunday, July 11, 1847

My dearest sister Jane,

I have only a small bit of time to begin this letter to you before Mr. Cockrell is scheduled to arrive. We have a "date" at four this afternoon, but

I can never be sure exactly the time he will arrive because of the distance between his cousin's house and ours. He's almost always early which annoys Pa!

Our parents are still behaving as if my future husband is an intruder, though I can see softening signs. Pa asked him out to the barn the other evening to see a new horse he had brought home, and Ma has invited him to join us for dinner. Since the arrival of the Rev. and Mrs. Smith—the Methodist minister I told you about—in our area in January, Ma has wanted to have him and his family visit us. Next Saturday is her chance! Rev. Smith will be here at Mountain Creek to preach on Sunday at a new little church that we are trying to get started. Ma wrote asking him to bring Mrs. Smith and the rest of the family with him as our weekend guests, and a letter came day before yesterday saying they accepted. Now Ma is in a flurry, and I will be very busy helping to see that the food is planned and everything goes well. I was somewhat amazed that she asked Mr. Cockrell to join us, but she did! He arrived shortly after Pa came home with the letter. Ma handed it to me to read aloud, and I suppose she would have felt guilty not to include my fiancé for the event. I suspect she also has an ulterior motive. She probably thinks the good preacher will talk some sense into my head. Little does she know what the evening is going to be like. I am looking forward to the meeting because the men—Rev. Smith and Mr. Cockrell—are a match for each other. Both are candid, articulate and utterly charming. Wish you were here to witness what projects to be one of the highlights in this family.

None of our brothers has made a single comment about my impending marriage, but then they have rarely had anything to say about what goes on in the lives of the female side of the family. Only Enoch is expansive and expressive about his thoughts, and our parents, with their reservations, have probably intimidated him. I think all of them have adopted a wait-and-see attitude. Mary is quietly helpful with my plans, preoccupied as she is with her own slowly developing romance. Our younger sisters behave as if it were they who were in love and about to be married.

July 18—a week later. It is not possible that I have let an entire week go by without completing this letter and getting it off to you.

First, I want to tell you about my future home. It is unbelievable! About two miles south and a little west of where we are, the property is absolutely beautiful, even in this miserable summer heat. It is exactly what I dreamed about when Pa first told the family that he and Ma were moving us to Texas. I have told you about my disappointment when we arrived here, and I learned that we would be living on a flat piece of property cluttered with brush and undergrowth without many big trees. Pa was right, of course. A hilly, tree-covered area is not suited to farming.

So, when Mr. Cockrell and I rode uphill to the highest point in the entire countryside and he told me that this was to be ours, I had a moment of great concern. How were we going to make a living if we could not plow, plant and harvest food for ourselves and the livestock and grow a crop to bring in some money? Fortunately, I kept my misgivings to myself.

Standing at the very apex of the property on which he has filed a claim, with his arms waving in all directions, Mr. Cockrell began to paint a word picture of our future! He said he did not intend to farm the land, that he would cultivate only a small plot near the house for a garden. And he had found sufficient fertile ground near the back of the plot that would be ideal for growing grain to feed the livestock. He said the only experience he'd had at farming was as a helper on his cousin Wesley's place, but he was experienced in raising livestock.

Pacing around, he pointed out the exact location where he would build our house and showed me a cleared area with lines marked for the house. I had noticed the markings, but assumed the clearing had been done by the wind sweeping across the top of the hill. With his enthusiasm, I joined my fiancé in imagining a herd of cows grazing as far as our eyes could see from the front of our future home.

We had a wonderful time! I had packed a picnic. James and Robert, who had ridden out with us, very discreetly took off to explore the outer reaches of the property leaving the two of us to dream aloud of our future. . . .

And to set a wedding date!

Mr. Cockrell said he could have the house completed in a month and urged me to agree that we would be wed in August. I convinced him that I needed a little more time, and we compromised on Thursday, *September 9*. That is less than nine weeks away—53 days to be exact!

We ended our outing at dusk after the boys returned from their ride around our property. I had warned Mr. Cockrell to keep our agreed-upon date to ourselves until I had time to tell Ma and Pa. (I did not want a repeat of what had happened when we became engaged.) He readily agreed but in his exuberance let it slip while showing James and Robert the outline of our future home. He said he would have less than two months to complete the house before our wedding and that he would welcome any help the boys wanted to provide! They naturally wanted to know what wedding date we had set. With an apologetic glance at me, Mr. Cockrell hemmed and hawed—and I felt compelled to tell them, begging them to keep our secret until I had told our parents. It worked out fine. The boys are much more reliable at keeping mum than are our sisters.

I don't think I have ever told you very much about my future husband.

He is handsome! He has very dark, almost black hair that tends to fly about when he is excited, which is most of the time. He has a small, very dark mustache and luminous blue eyes. When I stop to ponder his appearance, which I am trying to do for you, I don't suppose there is a lot about him that would seem extraordinarily good looking to the average person. But I see him as beautiful, perhaps most of all because he sees me in the same light. Can you imagine that anyone would ever consider me beautiful? Come on, be honest now! Mr. Cockrell is not tall, only a few inches taller than I, but he stands tall.

I love his self-assurance, which has not come about lightly. He was born in Kentucky on June 8, 1820, which makes him a year and a half younger than me. But his life experiences make him seem a great deal older. He has been making his own way in the world since he was a young boy. His mother died when he was four. He says he barely remembers her and that he does not even know her name. His father, Joseph Cockrell, was born in Virginia but moved to Kentucky before he married. The elder Mr. Cockrell remarried soon after the death of Alexander's mother, and the little boy never felt loved or even wanted by his stepmother. Soon there were other children in the family. Alexander, by his own account, became a loner. He says he is sick of being all by himself, of having no one to whom he matters and no one who matters to him and that I am the first person in his life that has made him feel valued. I understand that I have my work cut out for me on this score, but I am looking forward to convincing him that he is, indeed, a wonderful person.

At age 14, Alexander left home riding off on his horse, taking with him his first suit of "store boughten" clothes, his gun and enough food to last a week if he was frugal. For the next four years he lived, as he explains it, "from pillar to post," working his way across country heading south and west. He learned to live on what the land produced, honing his hunting prowess to a fine art so that he had meat. He worked for food and lodging wherever he could find someone who would hire him. Six weeks was the longest he ever stayed in one place for the next four years. When he was 18, he made his way into the Cherokee Tribe in Indian Nation where for the first time in his life he felt he belonged.

Mr. Cockrell loves his Indian friends. He says they taught him so much, and he will be forever grateful. Together they hunted and trapped along the Red River, which separates Indian Territory from Texas. He has assured me that the Red Man is both peaceful and patient unless and until his very existence is threatened. He says that we—our government and its leaders—have treated the Indians who are native to this land abominably. He has assured me that the Indians are our friends and that he will teach me to trade with them. He says he has no reservation whatsoever about leaving me alone in our home because his Indian friends not only will never harm me but they will protect me from others. This is a whole new way of thinking to me. I wish I could say that I am completely convinced he is right, but I'm not and doubtless will be somewhat shaky when I am left alone atop that high hill in a house that is visible throughout the entire countryside. I do trust my husband-to-be and shall try hard to learn from him. He says he will teach me a few words of the language so that I will be more comfortable when our Indian friends come calling.

For some time before the Texas-Mexican War broke out, Mr. Cockrell said, he had the urge to move on. He had heard of great opportunities as settlers pushed westward toward the Pacific Ocean, and he had a yen to explore for himself. The fighting on the southern tip of Texas and across the Rio Grande into Mexico gave him the opportunity he had been putting off. So, he signed up to fight the Mexicans. On his way to the Gulf Coast, he decided to visit his Cousin Wesley, one of the only relatives his father had ever mentioned. When he arrived at their place on Mountain Creek, he had no intention of staying more than a couple of days at the most, but found that he was enthusiastically welcomed by all members of the family and urged to extend his visit.

Although Wesley Cockrell was several years older, Alexander felt an immediate connection and for the first time in his life enjoyed being a part of a family—his own family. He had gone with Wesley into Dallas to buy supplies on the day that the furniture our parents ordered arrived. The freighter who brought it had orders only to get it to Dallas. Nobody had accounted how it was to be delivered to us, some 10 miles away and across the Trinity River. I am certain Pa and our brothers had planned to go into town and fetch it. But the freighter didn't know what to do, had no time to make a side trip out to our place and made it known that he needed a deliveryman. Alexander Cockrell, with time on his hands and, he admits, seeing an opportunity to earn a little money, agreed to rent a conveyance and a team of oxen and make the delivery. His cousin assured him that his neighbor, Enoch Horton, would be grateful.

So it was that Alexander Cockrell made his first appearance at our front door. The rest is history!

Mr. Cockrell is brilliant, but he is not a man of letters. His life experiences have prepared him to be an arbitrator and a mediator. He has all of the native credentials to be a lawyer, which, he said, he sometimes passes himself off to be. But his formal education is virtually non-existent and he can neither read nor write. That I plan to remedy! It will take all of the diplomacy I can muster and all of the persuasion I have mastered while tutoring our younger sisters for Mr. Cockrell is a very proud man and will resist being taught by a mere woman. Even though he says he is determined to teach me to be entirely independent and to take care of any contingency, I know that he enjoys the masculine role of protector. More than once he has hinted that he looks forward to the time when he is my primary defender. I will never, as you know, be the submissive little woman, but I won't let him know this. I am also aware that Mr. Cockrell has a temper, evident from our very first meeting. Since then he has rarely allowed me to see even a hint of his being out of control. Once when Ma and Pa let it be known they thought our relationship was developing too fast, I thought for a moment he was going to flair up, but he backed off. Already I am aware of the kinds of situations that provoke him, and I shall tread softly around his vulnerable points, understanding fully that he has had to be a scrapper in order to survive. I also know that he enjoys his whiskey and probably drinks more than is good for either him—or me!

It will take time to smooth over the rough spots that my future husband has spent more than a quarter of a century developing, but I have every confidence that we will be a good match. I know I have a lot to learn; Mr. Cockrell doesn't know yet that he also does. I will be a good and patient teacher. But I have every intention of being a full working partner in my marriage. Just watch me!

The best I have saved for last. When I wrote last week at the start of this letter that we were entertaining the Rev. and Mrs. Smith over this weekend and that Ma had asked Mr. Cockrell to dinner with us on Saturday night, I couldn't have been more correct in the prophecy that the two men—the Reverend and my fiancé—would attempt to outdo each other. The dinner was last night. The Smiths, together with Mrs. Smith's mother and two of the Smith children, arrived early in the afternoon. We had spent the entire week moving the house about, preparing beds for everybody, planning and replanning the meal, cooking, cleaning and re-arranging furniture, even borrowing chairs from our neighbors, the Hords.

The dinner last night was—at least from my view—an overwhelming success. Mr. Cockrell arrived around five. He was splendidly attired and showed not one iota of deference to anybody. He greeted Ma, Mrs. Smith and her mother with a slight bow and even kissed the hand of our eldest guest. He shook hands with Pa, each of my brothers, then turned his full attention to Mr. Smith, reminding him that they had met briefly in town shortly after the Smith's arrival, but had not been properly introduced. He continued that he had been very much looking forward to spending some time with the one person who was the talk of the entire community and that—and here he turned to me and bowed—he hoped that the reverend would be available to conduct our forthcoming wedding. I was astounded and our parents were speechless. Before anyone else said a word, Mr. Smith agreed that he would be honored to officiate at the nuptials of two such outstanding young people. Also, he added that the community would surely grow and prosper with the establishment of outstanding young families such as ours was destined to be.

From that moment on throughout the evening, the dinner conversation sparkled with even Ma opening up to join the discussion. We talked about the community's growth, spoke of new neighbors moving in to the south and west of us, the upcoming election of county officers, the growth of the Methodist Church, the winding down of the war on the Texas Coast and the fact that Mr. Cockrell had served well. We even talked a bit about books and ideas! Mr. Smith told us that he had received a copy of the *Philadelphia Public Ledger* from his sister. The paper has been in existence only since April. Naturally, I am eager to secure a copy. Upon learning of my interest in reading, Mr. Smith offered to lend me books from his library.

Alexander Cockrell contributed greatly to the evening's success. He did not intrude into the conversation, but several times when talking lagged, he discreetly introduced a new topic. He was very flattering to all of the ladies without once fawning. He talked hunting, scouting and fishing with the men and food and recipes with the ladies. When he said good night around 10 p.m. and rode off, I tarried by myself outside for a few moments to savor the evening and say a private prayer of gratitude for all my blessings.

Oh, Jane, it's going to be a good marriage!

Everybody was in a flurry this morning to have breakfast and get off to the services. Mr. Smith's sermon was, I am sure, brilliant, but I barely heard a word because as soon as we were seated, Mr. Cockrell slipped in and sat beside me. He had told me he wasn't coming!

The Smiths left about four this afternoon to return to their home in the downtown village. Mr. Cockrell left soon afterward for our place on the hill where he is having lumber delivered tomorrow to begin our house.

I have much to do! Mary and I were discussing my wedding dress, and I told her I had recently read that Butterick Patterns had introduced paper dressmaking patterns and that I would very much like to have one as a model for my most important dress. Pa overheard our conversation and has promised to see if such a thing is available in our town. I doubt it. Nor can I imagine any paper pattern that would suffice for women of all different sizes. I will be perfectly happy with a new piece of calico, in bluebonnet blue if it can be found. The only thing: I need it soon. I plan to make every stitch of my wedding dress by myself and am eager to get started.

I am sitting up quite late to finish this letter because James says he is going into town in the morning and will post it for me. Mr. Smith told us last night that the government has introduced a new postage stamp that has adhesive on the back. You simply dampen it and attach it to your letters. Benjamin Franklin's picture is on the five-cent stamp and George Washington's on the 10-cent stamp. Will wonders never cease? My only wish is that this new stamp will hasten the delivery of our letters to each other.

Write soon!

With all my love,

Sarah

September 15, 1847

To: Mrs. William Bradshaw
     The Bradshaw Farm
     Abingdon, Virginia

From: Mrs. Alexander (Sarah Horton) Cockrell
     Mountain Creek, Texas

My dearest sister Jane,

I wrote our names above because I have not yet decided who I am in this new life, and the very idea of being who I've been in the past plus this new married lady is so wonderful and yet so strange!

Perhaps I owe you an apology for delaying so long in updating you on our lives here, but there has been so much to do. And I have been so happy doing it that I won't bother to waste words telling you that I am sorry for not having written. Your last letter that came the day before my wedding added the perfect final touch to a time and an occasion that I will always hold dear.

The wedding was perfect.

When Pa and Ma finally understood that I would not be dissuaded from getting married, they became supportive. Ma and all of our sisters pitched in to help me complete my wedding dress. I wanted something both pretty and practical—nice enough that I would always remember it as being special, but something I could continue to wear and enjoy. Pa made a special occasion of helping me choose the fabric. He would not, of course, apologize for the reluctance he had formerly shown at my choice for a mate, but he did the next best thing. He took me into town to pick out the fabric for my dress. I knew at first glance that I had found exactly what I had in mind—a light blue calico cotton with a subdued white stripe—all very subtle and pretty. We bought ten yards because I wanted a very full skirt. I did not even look for one of the new Butterick patterns because I knew exactly how I wanted the dress to look and, in fact, had drawn it several times. The bodice is very simple, fitted and but-toned in front to the waistline. The sleeves are long, full at the shoulders and fitted at the cuffs. Mary insisted on a lace collar and had, in fact, cro-cheted one that she wanted me to use, but I was determined this one time to have my own ideas, so I chose a collar in the same fabric as the dress, wide enough to appear almost as a brief shawl and edged with a double ruching of fine white lace, a compromise that pleased me and made Mary happy! (The crocheted collar was her wedding present to me, and I will probably wear it with the dress later, or use it on another garment.) The skirt is very full, floor length, gathered to the fitted waist-line and with a layered overskirt that falls just below my fingertips. Over a hoop and two petticoats, I felt very dressed up and special. At the last minute Ma suggested I wear her cameo at the throat—and I did, not only to please her but also to have something "old" as a part of my attire. Our sisters insisted on doing my hair. They tried all kinds of arrangements, but I settled on something very simple. We parted my hair in the middle, let it lie somewhat loose around my face and turned it under at the edges around my shoulders.

Rachel and Lucy had fretted for days that I had chosen a fall month to be married, and there would be no flowers available. But the girls for-aged the surrounding area and found some beautiful leaves and a few fall blossoms to decorate the house. The real decor was in the food! Such a table I had never seen before—not even at Christmas. Our sisters had been cooking a full week ahead of time, each preparing her own specialty. The boys were lucky at the fishing hole, so we had both fish and roasted beef as the main courses. Ma opened almost every kind of vegetable we had canned during the spring and early summer. There were cakes and pies of every variety.

Mr. Cockrell arrived on his horse ahead of the Wesley Cockrell family in their wagon. I was not allowed to see the bridegroom until the moment I came into the parlor on Pa's arm. Alexander looked absolutely resplendent! I had no idea that he would be wearing his army uniform, washed and pressed to perfection. I had not seen him in it since the night he proposed to me. And at a glance I was transformed back into that special evening when he first asked me to become his wife. It was a very special moment.

We had only the two families, ours and Mr. Cockrell's, present for the ceremony. The Rev. Smith brought his wife along, so I suppose you could say we had three families represented. To me it seemed like a large crowd—eight of the Wesley Cockrell family, the Rev. and Mrs. Smith and 13 of us (I had asked Mary if she would like to ask Mr. Thompson. She was reluctant at first lest he think she was rushing him into a proposal, but I could tell she was pleased. She did invite him, and he seemed very happy to be included).

I do not remember much about the actual ceremony. I know that Mr. Smith delivered a short homily in addition to the traditional rites in which he admonished the two of us to "cleave only to each other" as we began our new life together. I don't know whether Mr. Cockrell had confided that my parents were initially reluctant to give their blessings to our union, whether Pa had expressed their reservations to him or whether he was sufficiently perceptive to see that there was some disapproval by my family. In any event, I treasure his admonition, both for Alexander's sake and for mine. I know Ma especially dotes on the reverend and that this addition to our routine vows will go a long way to win her over completely.

Before I knew what was happening, I was Mrs. Alexander Cockrell. My wedding ring, like yours, is a plain gold band. I love it!

There were hugs and kisses all around, though the bridegroom, for the first time since I have known him, seemed almost shy.

Within thirty minutes after we had repeated our vows, our house was a beehive of activity. Neighbors began to arrive for the wedding feast.

Several brought instruments with them. Amid all the feasting, they assembled outside on the porch (there was not room in the house for them!) and began to play. Friends pushed back the table in the big room and made space for dancing. The day flew by.

Around five in the afternoon, I caught Mr. Cockrell's eye. We nodded almost simultaneously. It was time to go! I am amazed that we had been wed only a matter of hours, and we are already catching each other's thoughts across a crowded room. James and Robert brought the horses around, saddled and ready. I could not believe that our friends had decorated the saddles with white ribbons and that a tiny bell was attached to each rein.

I had changed into a dress more suitable for riding, one with a much simpler skirt, my wedding dress folded and left behind until another day. My husband still wore his army uniform. He all but lifted me into the saddle and then quickly hoisted himself into his own saddle. With shouts of good wishes from our friends and the music playing in the background, we left the home of my parents, a house that had been my home for a little less than three years. (To be honest, I still thought of Virginia as my home! But not anymore!)

I am now at home! We rode south and a trifle west into the setting sun. I do not honestly know whether it was the most beautiful sunset in history or if I only saw it that way because I had a sense of deep and abiding joy. I knew I had done the right thing. I knew that being Mrs. Alexander Cockrell was what I had waited for all of my life. There was not one moment of regret or hesitation as my new husband and I rode together, mostly in silence, into our future.

And, ah, the house! My new home! Alexander Cockrell had told me about what he was doing and had taken me over a couple of times since he started the building. He had sketched the plans on paper. Our brothers had helped him from time to time with some of the heavy lifting. Pa had even been over to help a few times, but he had sworn them all to secrecy about the big surprise. The house is bigger than our own home, one very large room that will be the living and dining room, with a smaller room to the side that is our bedroom and with a large loft overhead stretching the entire length of the house. It is still unfinished, but will be a great place for storage. Facing east, the house catches the first rays of the morning sunshine. The fireplace, which for now I will use as a kitchen, is on the south wall. Our furnishings are sparse. Ma gave me one small skillet and a larger pot. We will need to accumulate a few more things, but that will come. As a bachelor, Mr. Cockrell had no idea what to purchase in household wares, but is so eager for me to make a trip with him into Dallas to select other things we need. I am so unaccustomed to having a choice about what I want that it is exhilarating. And I have to be careful not to indulge myself too much, even when I admit it feels wonderful to have my wishes recognized and fulfilled.

But I am digressing! Our house sits on the top of the tallest rise in the entire area and can be seen for miles around when the trees shed their leaves in the winter. For now, in the autumn, a forest interspersed with leaves just beginning to turn red and amber, shields it from view. As we approached, I was astonished. There it sits atop the hill, PAINTED WHITE! I had never seen a painted house. I could not believe it. You cannot believe it. It was Mr. Cockrell's surprise and the most glorious wedding present imaginable. Nobody else in the entire countryside has a white house. I will always remember viewing it for the first time—glowing pristine white against a setting sun that had painted a rainbow of colors—streaks of blue and gold and mauve and magenta and pink. No artist could possibly capture the beauty my eyes feasted on. And Mr. Cockrell in all of his wishes for our future happiness and his promises of prosperity could not have given me a rarer gift than viewing my new home against that palette of beauty.

We did not need supper, though I offered to prepare a meal for us. We had been feasting all day, though I admit that neither of us had consumed much food. Laughingly, we admitted to each other that the excitement of the day had satiated our appetites. I knew I would cook tomorrow and a host of tomorrows into the future, but on my wedding day I was content that neither of us wanted to eat.

My new husband insisted that I rest in the house, relaxing in the one rocking chair in our front room, while he unsaddled, groomed and fed the horses and milked the one cow he has bought. This is a whole new idea for me, resting while someone else works! I must understand that I am not to become accustomed to such pleasures.

Even I, who know you so well and who has grown up sharing everything with you, would blush to write of our first intimate relationship. So I leave it to your imagination and hope it suffices when I say that every dream I ever had of my future was more than fulfilled in the night that followed our wedding. None of the brashness, lack of tenderness, lack of control that I had been warned about happened in the next few hours. I have not made a mistake!

Alexander Cockrell and Sarah Horton are truly one.

The only regret I have is that you were not here to share these precious moments with me.

My love always,

Sarah Horton Cockrell

December 27, 1847

Dearest Jane, my beloved sister,

One third of a year has passed since I became a wife and my entire life has changed. I am married to a brilliant, charismatic, energetic and totally devoted man who keeps me in awe of what he will do next. His fertile mind is continually inventing new ideas for our future.

I cannot say I have been too busy to write. I can say that I have been so involved in listening, learning and sharing, and sometimes in putting a damper on the steady flow of creations that have come to me that I sometimes have to take a deep breath. I never knew such people existed—someone in constant pursuit of a new vision.

If Alexander Cockrell has his way, we will own half this county before he is finished! I have my reservations, of course. While I try to both support his enthusiasms and keep us rooted in reality, he goes off to Dallas and comes back with a whole new scheme for our future.

I have told you previously a little about the house. It is bigger than the one we built when we first came here. I cannot get over the fact that it is painted white. Mr. Cockrell colored it with a new invention, called whitewash. It sits high on a hill and can be seen for miles around and everybody, including me, calls it the White House. Where the Horton house overflowed with people, ours has only two adults, and sometimes I think it isn't big enough to hold us!

I wish I could convey to you what our lives are really like. My husband is a buyer, a freighter, a builder, but most of all a dreamer. He says that our village will grow to become one of the most significant settlements in the country, that one day it will be a huge city, and that he plans to be a major part of its building and its future. He is talking about establishing a sawmill and a lumberyard to accommodate what he foresees as a major building boom. He is also talking about opening a ferry across the Trinity River. This latter makes good sense to me because, in the rainy seasons, we are sometimes isolated from the center for supplies and for filing legal papers for several days. There is, as I have told you, little access from our community into the downtown village, which makes it almost impossible for women and children ever to leave this little area. Mr. Cockrell talks of taking me with him on one of his buying trips to the Red River or even down to Galveston. I am not sure this can happen, but it sounds exciting.

He has told me that he will, as soon as the cold weather lets up a bit, make a cross-country trip to Shreveport in Louisiana for supplies. I am not looking forward to being alone here but must admit that so far I have never been lonely. The luxury of having my own home to do with as I please, the quiet times that I can sit and read a book of poetry or, when he thinks to bring a newspaper, enriches my life immeasurably.

We have had a wonderful Christmas. Mr. Cockrell and I spent the day before Christmas together here and early the next morning saddled up and rode over to our family's home where we had a lovely visit and a bountiful dinner. Ma wanted us to spend the night, but as the evening began to close, I knew my husband had rather be at home and comfortable in our own bed. So he and Robert saddled the horses, and we rode back together. We needed to be at home anyway because the cow had to be milked, and that would have meant an extra trip back and forth had we remained overnight.

As you know, cooking has never been a favorite of mine, but I love doing the simple meals that the two of us require. We have a bountiful larder—almost as much for the two of us as I was accustomed to having on hand before I married. Ma has been generous, encouraging me to take some of the vegetables, fruits and jellies we preserved last summer. Mr. Cockrell is a fine marksman and several times has brought in fresh meat—squirrel and rabbit and once a deer. We got our brothers to help with the latter and shared the meat with them and other neighbors. When it is cold, as it is now, the meat will keep for some time, but we have to be careful when the weather is hot not to keep any food too long. I cook over the wood fireplace, though Mr. Cockrell says he is going to see that we have a kitchen removed from the house and a better way for food preparation before another year passes. I have no doubt that he will do it unless his enthusiasms for something new and different absorb the time before he completes the project.

Mr. Cockrell has been teaching me a few words of the Cherokee Indian language. He lived with the Indians in the Oklahoma Territory for some years off and on before coming here and is quite fluent in the language. He says just a few words will be indispensable to me when, and if, we have Cherokee visitors when he is not at home. I refuse to think that this could happen but am not a reluctant language student. He also speaks passable Spanish, having spent time on the Texas border and across the Rio Grande into Mexico during the time he was in service.

In addition to the many laudable qualities of my husband, I have learned some things that help me understand why Ma and Pa reacted to my planned marriage with such resistance. Mr. Cockrell is not an easy man. His effervescence is sometimes overwhelming. He likes his liquor when he goes into town and has come home twice almost tipsy. I can understand how this is so easy because I am told that every establishment in the village has a barrel of whiskey with a cup attached that is open to any and all who want to partake. Most men do! My very tee-totaling background makes this difficult for me to understand or even tolerate. But I know that I must find a positive way to deal with what could be a difficult situation.

When he drinks, Mr. Cockrell's temper, I am told, sometimes gets out of hand, and he is inclined to want to pick a fight with anyone who crosses him. I have seen his temper flare only once, when his horse was spooked by a horsefly and started acting up while Mr. Cockrell was trying to get the saddle tightened. At that time I heard some of the foul language he had used at our very first meeting when he didn't yet know me. I have made it clear that I will not tolerate swearing in my presence and only this once has he used crude or uncouth language for which he later apologized profusely.

He has told me of things he did before he knew me that give me pause, but I have listened, tried to be sympathetic and understanding. For instance, for a brief period of time he made his living by seeking and returning run-away slaves to their owners. Feeling, as I do, ambivalent, about slavery (I cannot morally accept the idea of anyone owning another human being), the fact that he admits hunting down runaways to return them to a "master" disturbs me. I told him that I probably would have been the one who hid the slave and helped him escape. Mr. Cockrell pointed out that he had to do *something* to make a living and that this was an easy thing for him. I am still uncomfortable with the idea but managed to hold my tongue. There are always things that newlyweds have to work through. This is only one bump on my road to a new life.

The most difficult thing I've learned about Alexander is that he can neither read nor write. You can imagine my reaction when I learned this because I've been so determined that everybody in our family be literate. He is, as I have explained, quite brilliant, quite talented, really well educated, but he does not even write his own name. And he is such a proud man and so full of energy. He can never sit still for longer than a few minutes, so I do not believe he will allow me to teach him. I began to suspect that he had trouble reading when he always tossed letters and newspapers to me when he came into the house and asked me to read them to him. He passed it off as loving the sound of my voice.

When he finally got around to telling me that he could not read, he said he wanted to explain why I had not heard from him during all the time he was serving in the Texas-Mexican War. He repeated how much he had carried me in his thoughts and dreams, how much he would have liked to send word back to me about his longing to see me and have us be together. But he could only hope that I would wait to hear him say the words because he could not communicate them in writing. He was so anxious in revealing this part of his life that I wanted to take him in my arms as I would have a little boy and tell him everything was all right. But it isn't! I want this brilliant person to be able to write words as well as to say them! I want him to enjoy words written onto a page as I do. Perhaps I will never share this joy with my husband, and perhaps I must be content that he is by far the best businessperson I have ever known. He can add a column of figures in his head while I am getting a pencil sharpened! He can draw an outline for a ferry crossing or a lumber mill in ways I cannot imagine. He can debate issues with politicians and clergymen with a lucidity that astonishes me. He can settle disagreements and arbitrate misunderstandings between the Red Man and the white military officers with alacrity—and has. He calls himself a lawyer because he has represented many men in court.

I find it amazing that anyone can be called a lawyer who has the ability to appear in court and honestly represent a client without any official credentials, though I know that my husband is a better lawyer than most men with academic credentials. But I still wish he could read and write and did not have to depend on his oh-so-fertile mind for his court appearances.

Please know that I am not complaining. If I write to you from my heart, I trust you to understand that I must have some kind of outlet for my thoughts and feelings lest they get bottled up and choke me. I cannot, would not, talk to Ma and Pa who, even if they did not say anything, would think "I told you!" There are no friends here in whom I can confide. Mary is so smitten with Mr. Thompson that she is interested only in the romance of life. Our younger sisters are, of course, far too naïve, and our brothers would think I had lost my mind!

Which, in a way, I have. I have lost myself in my marriage. And now I will make it work! I must be gentle with Mr. Cockrell. He must be the leader in this relationship. He will not, could not, tolerate a wife who was in charge!

So, I must be subtle. I know that I must be the silent partner in our marriage that I must support him, must acquiesce to his wishes. And, yet, I know that I must do this in such a way that I am aware of every move that we make. *It must be a partnership marriage.* Because he cannot read and write, I must do this for him. Because he is so brilliant in terms of finances, I know that I must learn from him. I must secure what he accomplishes in ways that will be beneficial to him, to me and to whatever children who are born to us. It is a very large responsibility, but I think not unlike what women have always done. They can be the leaders of their families so long as they do not let the men know that they are in control.

My very first move was to secure a ledger so that I could jot down our records and a container in which to store them. In the ledger, I am keeping a careful file of the assets that Mr. Cockrell accumulates. I have heard that in other parts of the country, there are "banks" which hold the assets of individuals who entrust their money to them. But in our part of the undeveloped country, we do not have such a bank. So, I asked Mr. Cockrell to purchase for us a very small container, a trunk in which I will keep the ledger and all business papers pertaining to our holdings. It seems odd that I should even be thinking in terms of "ours" but my husband insists that this is the way he wants it. Mr. Cockrell bought me a small black trunk on his very next trip to Shreveport. It has a tray and two sets of keys to lock it. One of the keys is on Mr. Cockrell's chain. The other is securely fastened with a small pin inside my chemise where I also have stored a few coins against whatever poverty might be in store and a tiny notepad in which I jot down my most intimate thoughts for whenever I might need them.

I have lingered endlessly on my thoughts, feelings and the conditions of my new life as a married woman and have totally ignored some of the things that are happening in our part of the world and in the larger world.

The Commissioner's Court in Dallas County has ordered a new road from our area in the direction of Dallas and appointed David Cameron as supervisor to oversee its construction. All of us are pleased to have this new promised artery connecting us to the center of downtown and county government. My husband, my father and Mary's future husband, Mr. Thompson have been appointed to a committee to oversee the development of this road.

Yes, you heard me right! Mary is engaged to Mr. Thompson and will soon, also, be a married lady. Can you believe that we are all growing up, getting married and beginning a whole new generation? I find it difficult to think about.

Last month, the Rev. James Anderson Smith, who officiated at our wedding and has been so important in the religious development of

Dallas and of our area, conducted a six-day revival meeting at Webb's Chapel. The revival had an interesting start when the weather turned very cold and the tiny chapel had no heat. The Webbs (Isaac and Mary Hughes Webb), among the first Methodists in the area who had built the chapel, moved all of their furnishings from their house, which was heated and the revival then continued with great success. Ma and Pa and some of our sisters attended every session. But Mr. Cockrell and I only made three of the sermons, which continued morning and night for six days. The Rev. Smith declared the meeting "one of the most glorious . . . it has been my privilege to witness . . . . Preaching was a pleasant task. Mourners came forward weeping and calling for mercy. The Lord was in Zion, her King in our midst. There was balm in Gilead . . . 22 . . . souls were made whole."[2]

Earlier this month, on December 4, Mrs. Bryan Margaret Beeman Bryan gave birth to a baby girl. Her name is Frances Elizabeth, but already they are calling her Lizzie. You remember that her first child died and is buried in the Beeman Cemetery. She has another little boy, John Neely Bryan Jr., who is about two years old. I am so sorry for Mrs. Bryan. She seems so young to be the mother of two children. I am eager to go into the village to see the new baby girl, and Mr. Cockrell says that he will be glad to take me as soon as it is a bit warmer. Mr. Bryan and my husband are good friends. They have a lot in common. Even though Alexander is considerably younger than Mr. Bryan, both left home at an early age and both have been very close to the Native Americans, having lived among them for a long period of time. They seem to be totally in tune with each other when considering the future of our part of the world.

Dear Jane, I feel a part of this community now as I have not felt since coming here with Ma and Pa. Please see what you can do to join us in this new world. It is exciting, and I would welcome you with open arms and so would my husband.

My dearest love,

Sarah

---

[2] *Church at the Crossroads, a History of the First United Methodist Church Dallas*, page 17.

January 1848

Dearest Jane,

Beginning this year I have determined to keep a small journal which I will share with you from time to time when things happen that will interest you. But mostly I plan to keep this journal so that I will have a record of the daily happenings.

Mr. Cockrell is so busy with countless things that inspire him. Beyond listening, encouraging and/or keeping him rooted in reality, I have time on my hands. And now that I am provided with a small trunk in which to keep our most valuable possessions, it occurred to me that with these private jottings I can watch myself grow and change even as I watch my husband help to build the larger community.

This year has dawned with so much promise, and I do not want to miss any of it.

My husband has returned from a trip to Houston. He was gone for 15 days, an unbelievably short time to have made the trip by ox-drawn wagon loaded with lumber on the way there and with supplies for the farm on the way home. It's about 250 miles there, some 500 round trip. A couple of times, he said, he traveled 50 miles in a day and never less than 30 in order to make the trip there and back as quickly as possible. He wanted me to go with him, but realized—and I agreed—that both the weather and the traveling conditions were hazardous. He needed to make the trip as quickly as possible, and I was not conditioned to traveling as he is.

Since my husband's return, I have enjoyed a feast of reading. He brought me several newspapers, a couple from Houston, two from Galveston and one from San Antonio. But my most wonderful treasure is a book called *Wuthering Heights* by Emily Bronte, one of three British sisters who are writers. I have barely been able to put it down. He also brought me a book of poetry including a poem called "Evangeline" by Henry Wadsworth Longfellow. It is so dear to me that my husband, who cannot read this marvelous material, understands that my soul longs for the written word, sometimes even more intensely than my body needs food.

February

On his trip into Dallas yesterday, Mr. Cockrell learned that the Treaty of Guadalupe Hidalgo officially ending the Mexican War has been signed. We have seen nothing in writing yet, but he understands that Mexico has relinquished control of upper California and New Mexico which is roughly one third of the property it claimed before the war. Also, that the Rio

Grande River is the official dividing line between Texas and Mexico. Since Mr. Cockrell served as a courier during the war delivering messages from military posts on our side of the Rio Grande into Monterrey, he is quite familiar with all of the area mentioned as the dividing line between the two countries.

Almost 31,000 men in the regular army, plus almost 74,000 volunteers or mercenaries fought in the Mexican War. Mr. Cockrell was one of the volunteers, which made it possible for him to return home before fighting completely stopped. Almost 5,000 of these men—4,823 according to the latest figures—lost their lives or were injured in battle. I am so glad that my husband came home unscathed, but I have great compassion for all those mothers, wives and sisters who lost their loved ones in war. I hope never to see another war.

Mr. Cockrell also brought word back that gold has been discovered in California and men, by the score, are leaving their homes to go in search of a fortune. It seems that a man named James Marshall, whose home was in New Jersey, had gone to California to help build a sawmill and, while exploring the American River, discovered gold nuggets about 40 miles from Sutter's Fort. I am glad my husband is busy discovering "gold" here and hasn't uttered a sound about wanting to go seeking his fortune in another part of the world although Ma says that some of my brothers are determined to join the gold seekers.

March

I have every reason to believe that we will have a new little member of the family in the fall though Ma says it is too soon to be sure. I have not told Mr. Cockrell and have no idea how he will take the news of a baby. I, who have been with infants and children all of my life, am having mixed emotions. I want children, to be sure, but I find the "little boy" I often discover in my husband quite enough of a child for now. Doubtless, I will be overjoyed when, and if, a baby arrives.

I must tell Mr. Cockrell soon because I will need supplies in order to sew a layette. I must secure soft outings and nainsook to make baby blankets and dresses and diapers. Until then I am completing a couple of tiny quilts using scraps from the dresses Mary, Ma and I have made for ourselves and our sisters.

April

Our part of the world grows, but it seems to me at a snail's pace. James reports that a Mr. and Mrs. John Crockett have moved into Dallas. Mrs. Crockett, whose name is Kate, is the sister of our neighbors, the

William Hords, who we visit occasionally. Mr. Crockett is a lawyer. It makes me wonder how many lawyers one little town needs. Mr. Bryan is a lawyer and my husband claims to be one. I especially wondered about this when James reported that Mr. Crockett had written to friends that "Dallas has 39 residents, half a dozen crude cabins, a dram shop, an open-air tin-pan alley and very little else." Why would anybody want to move to a place with that kind of reputation?

I have confided my condition to Mr. Cockrell, and he is like a little boy in a candy store. So excited! Right away he began grand plans for his son. When I asked what if it was a little girl, he said that would be all right, too. He would be delighted to have a miniature of me in the house. Then he saddled up very early the next morning and went into town for "supplies" for our future child. He came home loaded with soft cotton fabrics and some fine wood, which he immediately set about planing, smoothing and finishing to build a cradle. He hasn't been this excited since the day we were married. And he's almost as nervous as he was then. Every time he comes near the house, he drops in to see if everything is all right. I reminded him that women have been having babies since the beginning of time and that usually everything turns out fine. He said he knew that but he had never had a baby before! As if, he is personally going to do this! I am beginning to feel a bit heavier though I don't think I am showing yet.

Spring has arrived in abundant glory. Wild flowers blossom by the wayside. If I did not feel so lethargic, I would be out digging in the yard. As it is, about all I have wanted to do is sit and read! I have managed to get a garden planted and now must shelter it from the marauding animals, mostly rabbits that want to eat every tender plant as soon as it emerges.

Ma, Mary and our younger sisters came for a visit a week ago Saturday. Pa and our brothers dropped them off on their way into town. Mary and Mr. Thompson have not set a wedding date. Pa and the boys have most of the planting in, but James is more determined every day to join the exodus to California to seek his fortune in gold there. Some of the men from Dallas are already on the trail. I think it is very interesting that the beautiful song, "Oh! Susanna" by Stephen Foster introduced earlier this year in the Christy Minstrels, has become the marching song of men headed for California.

We have had a visitor—Alexander's good friend Charley John[3], who he calls Brother from the days they lived together in Indian Territory. Charley John is Cherokee; he calls my husband Little Older Brother, a name I cannot fathom but which Mr. Cockrell seems to like.

---

[3] John Neely Bryan called his Cherokee Indian friend "My Friend" without naming him. Shirley Seifert in her book, *Destiny in Dallas* gave him the name Charley John, and we have borrowed the name.

Mr. Cockrell was away from home, on another buying trip to Shreveport. I had just completed breakfast and was doing my few dishes when I became aware that I was being watched. I must admit the hackles stood up on my arms. I made myself go to the front door and look out. Charley sat on his black horse some distance from the house. I had seen him several times before, but always when my husband was at home. I cannot describe the stoicism, the serenity, and the stillness that emanated from that stalwart body sitting straight in the saddle and looking toward the east. As soon as he was aware that I had opened the door, he nodded. It took all the courage I had to remember what Alex had taught me— never to appear frightened, to be courteous, to share whatever I could afford and to greet any Indian callers with the few words of Cherokee in my vocabulary. I called to Charley John that he was welcome, asked in my few words and with pantomime if he would like something to eat and, again in pantomime, invited him to dismount and come in. I was vastly relieved when he said, in perfect English, "I wait." I said, "But Mr. Cockrell is not at home at the moment." He said, "I wait," and peering again toward the east, he added, "he come." Since it was a couple of days before I expected my husband, I thought that he might sit out there and wait for a long, long time. But even as these thoughts materialized, I saw the dust at a distance on the path that Alex traveled and breathed a sigh of relief. It was obvious that Charley knew something I didn't. Whether he had seen Mr. Cockrell approaching, or whether he intuitively surmised that the white man he called Brother could not be far off, I have no idea. Nothing would have pleased me more than to have our reunion in private. About halfway through the nine months of carrying this child, I am heavy, bloated and often moved to tears for no reason. Nobody could be happier than I to be expecting a baby, but I cannot seem to control the bouts of depression, the heaviness that pervades both body and soul. Ma says it is a perfectly natural condition for a woman as old as I—approaching my 30th birthday. She says that childbearing, especially for a first child, is for younger women.

So, I closed the door and waited. It seemed an interminable time before Mr. Cockrell stood in the doorway, hat in hand, dust-covered, tired and hungry, but oh, so very welcome. I was in his arms almost before he closed the door.

Who was it that predicted this marriage wouldn't work?

May

Charley asked, and of course was granted, permission for his family and friends to camp in a clearing just this side of a wooded area at the side and back of our house and at a distance near enough that I could observe the activity of the small group. There couldn't have been more than 30 or so Cherokees, mostly women and children. Mr. Cockrell had explained that Charley had several wives and many children. The very idea horrified me, but my husband explained that ideas of morality differ greatly from one group of "God's Children" (that's the argument he used, knowing how strictly I try to practice the Ten Commandments!) to another and that I must not judge the behavior of people from other backgrounds by the same moral standards that are sacrosanct to me. I admit it's hard for me to comprehend such a line of reasoning, but I am trying to be open-minded.

I was almost getting accustomed to looking out the back door and seeing the activity of the little band of Cherokees when this morning I woke up to find them gone! Mr. Cockrell used the occasion to remind me that no harm would come to me from his friend and that he personally was comforted to know that his native American friends were keeping watch over me when he was not at home. I never thought I would see the day when I can almost agree with him, but I do.

Later. We have lost John. Early in the morning, two days ago, I had just awakened and was trying to get energy enough to get out of bed when I heard Mr. Cockrell open the front door and greet someone outside. I strained to hear their low voices while I pulled on my clothes to go investigate. When I stepped out into the front room, my brother, Enoch and Alex turned to greet me, and I knew by their faces that something terrible had happened.

John had died shortly after midnight. I do not have all of the details clear in my mind yet, but this is the story as I remember it. He had come in from plowing the previous afternoon and, instead of getting the bucket and going back to milk the cow, as he always did, he sat down at the kitchen table. His wife, Margaret, interrupted preparing the evening meal to inquire what was wrong, for nobody on earth was more predictable than John. He said that he was just very tired and had a tightening in his chest and thought he would rest awhile before going back to tackle the evening chores.

Margaret continued to set out the food, watching him as she did so. He filled his plate, but took only a few bites before pushing it back, said he was feeling better and left the kitchen to milk the cow. He had been out of the house only a few minutes when, Margaret said, she had the most awful feeling come over her. She ran from the kitchen and out to the shed—and discovered John lying face down, the milk pail still in his hand, the patient cow standing by waiting to be milked. She felt for a pulse and found none.

The funeral was yesterday, the day after John died. The family has rallied around, of course, everybody stunned and not believing that a man in the prime of his life, not yet 40 years old could at one moment be in what seemed the peak of health and the next moment simply not exist.

My mind is in a muddle. Ma and Pa look like they've aged years. Ma was already looking drawn and strained, years older than she is, and now Pa, too, shows signs of being almost senile. John, the oldest, of their 11 children, has always been the strong, steady, silent one of the family. James is the adventurer, Enoch the charmer, Robert the typical baby brother. John has been the steadfast one, so quietly reliant that none of us has ever sufficiently appreciated the role he assumed in the family. He was just always there. And now he isn't.

Most of all I feel for Margaret. She and John had just completed their first home on the 320 acres he acquired before they were married and were looking forward to enlarging both their house and their property. I do not know whether it is good, or not, that they did not yet have children. Good, in one way because Margaret will not have anyone to be responsible to except herself; sad in another because now we have nothing left of our oldest brother.

James has been a brick. I so hope this deters him from wanting to charge off to California to seek his fortune in gold. I know he feels very responsible for the family. It was he who made most of the funeral plans, consulting gently with Margaret all the way. He carved out an acre of his own property, marked it off and designated it as the Horton Cemetery. John is the first person to be buried there. I cringe to think that more graves will follow.

I am too numb to know how I feel. Sad certainly. But mostly just numb. I know that we have been exceedingly blessed never to have had a death before in the immediate family. Not many parents can say that they have lost none of their children in childbirth or young childhood. We have been so fortunate that none of us had ever given a thought that one of us might not be around the next day.

It is not possible, I think, to prepare for the passing of a brother or sister. Somewhere in the back of our minds, we are always aware that one day we will lose our parents, but they are the older generation. When death comes to one of our contemporaries, it is a different matter altogether. It forces us to think of our own vulnerability and mortality.

Doubtless, in the days to come, as the reality of John's death becomes clear, my grief will surface, but right now I am in a state of inertia. I expect any minute to look up and see him ride up to check on me as he has done so many times when he knew Alexander was away on business.

June

The days creep. I am as big as a barrel, have only two tent-like dress-es that I can wear. And still three months to go. Everything I tackle is mechanical, and I am always having to stop to rest between chores. Mr. Cockrell has made arrangement with Ma and Pa for one of my sisters to be here with me because he is away on business so much of the time. I make myself keep our books up to date, but I dread the next two hottest months of summer.

In the *Philadelphia Inquirer* that Mr. Cockrell brought me I learned that Wisconsin has been admitted to the United States, making us now a country of 30 states. Wisconsin is the second state since Texas joined the Union on December 29, 1855 and Iowa was admitted as the 29th on December 28, 1846.

July-August

So little happens that it does not seem right for me to pick up pen and try to make sense of anything. I keep up with the figures on our fam-ily business, manage to prepare a meal now and then. I am grateful for the help of my sisters. Martha is here now. Emma left last weekend. Ma thinks that both Rachel and Lucy should come and stay when the time for my baby's birth draws nigh. I will welcome the help, but it seems such a long way off. The baby is not due, so far as I can calculate, until the last week of September.

I've been reading about the first Women's Rights Conference that met in Seneca Falls, New York, in July (July 19 and 20). I am excited to learn that a few women in this country are now standing up for the rights of women. This need, the female half of the human race, to be acknowl-edged and accepted as equal in our country is long overdue. And I am very pleased that a few exceptional women have begun to do something about it. Now, in the last stages of pregnancy, I am ambivalent. At any other time I would have loved nothing more than to have been a part of that event. But I am eagerly awaiting the time when I am a mother and hold my own special child to my breast! It gives me pause: Must women be a slave to the rhythms of their bodies? Must all women sacrifice the role of wife and mother in order to be full partners in their world? Must we be subservient to our fathers/husbands/brothers? Was it ordained that we have no voice in the rules and laws that govern our lives?

I think not! Every day of my life I am prayerfully grateful that I am wed to a man who values me as a partner, who entrusts me with what he accumulates and who shares with me the largesse of both his worldly goods and his ideas. Sometimes I think the latter is even more important than the former. I even wonder, from time to time, if he could read and write, would he be as trusting of me with our business records?

But this is digressing. It is important to me that such women as Elizabeth Cady Stanton and Lucretia Coffin Mott had the vision, intelligence and creative ability to plan and hold a conference for women. We are years beyond the day when Abigail Adams, the wife of our second president, admonished her husband, "remember the ladies." This has never been done. Perhaps the Women's Rights Convention is a first step. I pray that it will not stop here!

September

I woke at four in the morning. Uneasy. Could not get comfortable. Could not fall asleep again. Awkward. Confused. From my calculations, it was still days ahead of the time for the conclusion of my pregnancy and the arrival of my child.

The day before had been one of the most productive times of my past year. I had awakened early in the morning full of energy and determined to clear and clean the house, do the laundry, be sure that everything was ready for the arrival of a new family member. My sisters, who were staying with me while my husband was on yet another business trip—this time to Coffee's Landing on the Red River—pulled the covers over their heads and begged for another half hour of sleep when I prodded them awake before dawn. I would have none of it. By the time they were up, washed and dressed, I had made corn cakes and was ready to serve them with molasses and fresh-churned butter. They groaned as I outlined the day's procedures. We would wash down the walls, clean the floors, launder the curtains, wash the sheets and remake the beds, sweep everything inside and out, dust and clean all the furniture. And, we would then gather the best of the early fall leaves and decorate the house! They were appalled. This hot house plant, who had barely energy enough to get out of bed for days, was determined to do a week's work in one day!

Nobody had ever told me that a surge of energy often comes just before the delivery of the child. I just knew that I was determined to get the house in readiness for our soon-to-be child.

With Mr. Cockrell gone, we women were alone. While I was mixing the corn cakes, I glanced out to the far field and saw that our friends, the Cherokees, were back in residence. I no longer felt any alarm or misgivings about their presence. In a way, it was comforting to have Charley John and his extended family near.

The house was sparkling clean when my sisters and I retired shortly after dark. Very tired from a long day of house cleaning, I was aware that

Rachel and Lucy were giggling under their covers before I dropped off into a deep sleep.

I came awake with a jolt and lay there quietly trying to get comfortable again so that I could go back to sleep. And then the first tremor came. It was not so much a pain as a disturbance warning me that something momentous might be about to happen. I continued to lie still trying to will my body into a state of rest. Then, about 15 minutes later, a second tiny jolt, a tensing of my body, caused me to remember that Ma had said I should "time" the contractions. I got out of bed, pulled a blanket over my gown, lit a candle and sat down at the kitchen table with a book. Exactly 15 minutes later a third warning signal, the uncontrollable flexing of muscles in my abdomen, caught my attention. From then on, every 15 minutes and then every 13 minutes, I had no control over what was taking place in my body. When the contractions were 12 minutes apart, occurring regularly and each more intense than the previous one, I called Rachel and Lucy. This time they must have caught the tension in my voice because they did not hesitate to get out of bed and were soon dressed, standing anxiously at my side and asking what we should do.

Dawn had come. I remember thinking what a lovely idea—to have a child come into the world with the breaking of another day. It was a Thursday, November 8, 1848. We had several times gone over what each of us should do when the time came. I reminded Rachel that she was to saddle her horse and alert the nearest neighbor woman, or alert a man who would then find a mid-wife and send her to us. I told Lucy that she was to start a fire and get some water heating. I said that one of them should then, as soon as it was light enough, ride over to our home and bring Ma back.

By the time Lucy had the fire underway, Rachel had gone. The contractions were now coming every 11 minutes apart and, with each, there was more squeezing and letting go and the beginning of discomfort. Still no intense pains.

That came later.

I was not at all prepared for the woman Rachel brought into the house, an Indian woman, one of Charley John's several wives, nor was I comfortable with her "take charge" attitude. Between contractions I had been sitting comfortably and reading. My benefactor, with a few words of English but more by demonstrating with her own body, made me stand and walk. When I asked for water, she shook her head. When I became very uncomfortable and wanted to lie down, she shook her head again. As the pains progressed, she propped me up by putting her arm underneath mine—no small feat since I am almost a head taller. And we kept walking. I lost all knowledge of time. I was later told that Lucy arrived with Ma somewhere between noon and early afternoon. I was aware that Ma and the Indian woman were in conference with each other, but Ma did not try to take over. She told me later that she knew immediately I was in good hands and that the labor would go on a long time.

It did. The pains became closer together and much more intense. My body was rebelling every inch of the way. Sweat poured from me. My sisters took turns wiping my face with damp, cool cloths. I was allowed longer periods of rest between the walking, but I was still forced to put one foot in front of the other. We must have made a thousand trips around the room.

Night fell. I remember thinking that I wouldn't have a dawn baby after all. I was aware that other women came and went from the room. They talked in hushed tones. They made coffee and had something to eat. I labored on. In my brief moments of sanity, I prayed. And I cried. Every part of my body was wracked with a pain so intense that there are no words to describe it.

At some point, late into the night, I felt a flood of water gush from my body. Only then was I allowed to lie down. By that time I didn't care. I wanted nothing but to be rid of the pain. The last words I remember hearing were, "Here it comes!" and then I guess I fainted. At some far off place, as if it were a happening to someone else, I became aware of bustling activity. I heard voices, but did not register. I simply let go and fell into a deep coma-like existence.

When I opened my eyes several hours later, the sun was shining brightly. I seemed to be clean and lying on fresh clean sheets. I got a glimpse of Ma putting something on the table and when my eyes focused, my husband was sitting beside my bed. "I am sorry," I said. "I do not remember," and he said, "For what? Why? We are parents of the most beautiful baby. And now you are all right?" It was a question. I felt the tears. I saw the pride. "We have a son," he said, lifting the tiny bundle wrapped in blankets and lying in the crib he had made, and gently placing him into my outstretched arms.

Never has there been a moment of such triumph in my life. Perhaps all mothers feel this way with the birth of their first borns.

Logan Cockrell came into this world shortly after midnight, on September 9, 1848, and with his arrival every dream I had ever had was a shining reality.

In the days since then, as I languished in bed, alternately dozing, nursing my son, reading and listening to the voices of approval of family and friends, I have had lots of time to reflect. Of one thing I am certain: Never again will I be afraid of having the Cherokees encamped near us. Without the help of that Native American woman I am not sure I would have survived. She was both my champion and my tormentor, pulling out of me strength I did not know I had. I learned something else: All women share the blessing of being able to give life. All of us nurture and comfort, love and protect. All of us live in basic harmony with the universe. All of us are sisters under the skin.

For the rest of the year of 1848, I had no time to keep a journal and so there are no entries for the last three months of the year. Logan Cockrell grows and thrives. He is three months old now. He is smiling and beginning to make infant sounds. His father dotes on him. Never in my wildest imagination would I have thought one tiny human being could so captivate my grown, industrious, ever-busy husband. Alexander has been on only one brief buying trip since Logan arrived. He left the first of December to be gone a week and was back in three days and when he returned did not stop until he had lifted his son out of the cradle and held him close.

I keep up with the business ledger, but little else. I wonder often how one tiny infant can command so much time. After I have nursed him, changed him, bathed him, washed what seems like an endless number of diapers, dressed and cuddled him, the day has flown by.

Christmas was a happier and deeper occasion than any of the Yuletides that has gone before because we have this tiny child in our home and our hearts. Because of the cold, Ma, Pa and my brothers and sisters all came here, bringing with them many dishes for our Christmas feast. We acknowledged the empty place in our midst where John used to be and said a prayer of gratitude that his Margaret had gone home to be with the Hopkins, her own family, although we missed her.

Only two small things give me pause. James is still talking of striking out to California, and Robert seems determined to go with him. And, Mr. Cockrell tells me that he must put his mind back on the business of helping to build Dallas. I have so enjoyed having him around, doing odd jobs around the house, looking after the cattle and beginning to add to the herd. When he leaves, I will have again the responsibility of milking the cow and tending the livestock. However on earth will I be able to assume those tasks when Logan requires every bit of my time?

My dearest love until we meet again . . . soon?

Sarah

January 31, 1849

Jane, my beloved sister,

In the midst of being surrounded by well-meaning family members and friends, I sit here isolated to tell you what has happened.

My world has collapsed. We have lost our baby.

Logan Cockrell died six days ago.

He was a roly-poly bundle of joy. At four and a half months of age, he was smiling, recognizing me and his father, gurgling happily, and content to lie in his cradle for longer periods of time allowing me to do a few things other than hold and nurse him and do some of the essential house-keeping chores. He had not had a sick day in his life until the night of January 24. Alexander was home from his travels. He had held the baby after we had completed our evening meal while he regaled me with tales of his latest adventures. I got out the ledger and together we brought our business records up to date. I even lit a second candle in order to complete the records before we retired for the night.

I nursed Logan, wrapped him snugly in his blankets, and he fell asleep in my arms before I put him in his cradle around 8 o'clock. I checked on him before we went to bed around 10 and he was resting peacefully.

I was jolted from a deep sleep in the middle of the night with noises from the cradle and before I could pick up the baby, I knew that he was ill. Even as I scooped him up, he was struggling for breath, a case of the croup. I am sure you know that croup, which results from an obstruction of the larynx and is accompanied by labored breathing and hoarse cough-ing, is one of the dreaded diseases among infants and young children. Ma had told me all about it but had said it sounded much worse than it really was. The trick was to hold the baby upright, soothe his back and help him get his breath. Even as I began to think I must awaken Mr. Cockrell, he was already up and pulling on his clothes. Within minutes he was out the door and within a matter of very few minutes, I heard his horse gallop past.

It was pouring rain. My husband had not even waited to put on a slicker.

Through the night I walked and prayed, alternately rubbing my son's chest with bear grease, juggling him when he struggled so hard for breath that he turned blue in the face, stroking, soothing and willing him to be better.

In my first awareness that the interminable night was ending and dawn not far off, I heard the sound of horse's hoofs. And in the same instant, I also knew that my baby had breathed his last breath and was finally at peace.

The door literally flew open and there was Alexander and the doctor, both drenched and mud-splattered. From somewhere I heard a scream, with no realization that it came from me, but I do remember passing my lifeless son to the arms of his father.

I do not know what happened next. And I have only a vague recall of what happened in the next 24 hours. I must have bathed and dressed my child because everybody has mentioned how beautiful he was. The house was soon filled with people but Alexander was not among them. I learned later that Alex had held his son for several minutes, then laid him gently in the cradle and went out into the rain. He spent the entire day smoothing and finishing the wood for his casket. He would not let anybody assist. When it was as perfect as he could make it, he brought it into the house where Ma and our sisters, who had gone through the scraps of material I'd laid away, lined and cushioned it. Ma knew instinctively that I would want to be the one to lay my baby in his final resting place, so she shook me gently and indicated that the time had come to say good-by.

I am told that Alex chose the burial spot at the highest part of the hill on a bit of level ground just to the south of our house. He did allow our brothers to help him dig the grave.

In the early morning of Friday, January 26, we stood—some 25 of us— in frigid weather around the casket as it was lowered into the ground. Enoch had ridden into town and told the Rev. Smith about the baby's death. I am grateful that the minister took the time to ride out to the farm and conduct the services, but I do not remember anything he said.

My next memory is of Alex saddling his horse. The mourners were still milling about the house. They had made me lie down as if I could ever completely rest peacefully again. Nobody knew how to approach Alex. The minister tried, but my husband did not respond. He did not, in fact, say anything to anybody, not even to me. He left with only the clothes on his back and rode off. I overheard the men—Pa and my brothers, the minister, some of the neighbors—talking. They wanted to go after Alex, force him to return to me and make him face this devastating tragedy. But I begged them to let him be. I know Mr. Cockrell. When he has a problem of any kind that he cannot solve, he goes deeply into silence. I suspect, though I have never been told, that he seeks out Charley John and other Indian friends. I knew that when he had dealt to the best of his ability with his grief, he would return to me. Until then, nothing anybody said or did would help.

For the first time, I understand what kind of "hold" Alex's Native American friends have on him because, without the help of one of Charley's wives—I am embarrassed I do not even know her name—I could have never come through childbirth. But now, all for naught. Or, not quite. I would take nothing for those few months I had. Even in my deepest pain, I would not ever give up those precious moments of sweet communion with my son.

Jane, my dearest, I laid this aside a couple of weeks ago, not able to complete it. I spend too much time sitting, in a stupor. Rational thoughts do not permeate my mind, and the few tears I have been able to shed do not alleviate the pain. I have sent all of our family home, though Ma and our sisters were very reluctant to go. I am all alone. I have not seen or heard anything from my husband. In the late afternoon, I make myself get up and do the evening chores. I have been told that I milk the cow morning and night, insisting that I do this even when the family was here to help. I pull hay out of the loft where Mr. Cockrell stored it and feed the milling livestock. It would help if I could be angry with Alexander for leaving me with this responsibility, but I do not even have the energy to be angry.

Much, much later. March 20, 1849.

My world is still in chaos if not in total collapse. I exist.

It has been six weeks since we buried Logan. I walk every evening to the tiny grave only a short distance from my front door, and then I peer into the countryside knowing that Mr. Cockrell will surely return very soon.

Spring is in the air. We have already had a few balmy days. I have put aside the heaviest quilts and have made myself tend to the housework. Almost every day either Robert or Enoch rides over to see that I am all right.

James has come a couple of times. The last time he came by, I knew that he had something he needed to say to me, but found it hard to begin. After he had checked the livestock and everything around the house, he came in, hat in hand and sat down. Then he began to tell me that the time had come for him to make his long-delayed trip to California. He said that he could not get the vision out of his mind, that almost all of the able-bodied men in the surrounding area had already gone. He was especially concerned not to add to my burdens. He did not mention the baby, but I knew Logan's death had made a deep and lasting impression on him. He did mention that Ma's health was his gravest concern, but he could do nothing personally about her physical condition and that he trusted our sisters and me to see that she was cared for and kept as comfortable as possible. And, he prayed that he would return with a fortune in gold while she was still here to welcome him home. He did mention John. He said that since he was left to oversee not only his own land and the planting of crops, but also had the responsibility of John's farm, he had been torn about leaving. He added that Margaret, John's widow, had enlisted her own family to help with the planting, cultivating and harvesting, and he felt immense relief that he no longer felt total responsibility for Margaret's welfare. He said that he was putting his own future "on hold" until he returned (and he grinned) a very rich man! I knew that he had been courting Jane Phillips and cannot help but wonder how she is taking the news of his departure. He said that Robert is agitating to accompany him to the West Coast and that he will take our younger brother only if Pa is willing and only if Enoch will promise to stay around, help Pa and the rest of us do the heavy work that men usually do.

He then turned his attention to me. I had long known that most of our family is angry at Mr. Cockrell for his sudden departure after we buried our baby. I have not yet heard anything from my husband, but I am still confident that he will soon return, and I told James so. I did not want to hear that Ma and Pa are now convinced more than ever that they were right when they tried to keep me from getting married. I do not condone my husband's behavior. I do not fully comprehend it, but I do understand him better than any other soul. And I am as convinced as ever that I made the right decision. I cannot fathom what life would have been like these last few months without him. And I know I would never have felt the joy of holding a child of my own had Mr. Cockrell not been in my life.

James departed without expressing his anger at Mr. Cockrell and for that I am grateful. I have a pretty good idea what people are saying behind my back, but I cannot let that worry me too much.

For now, I must make myself eat a few bites and do the chores. Maybe then I can read some poetry or, if I can find it, the book I had started before Logan died. I have not touched it recently and have no idea where it is. Our family and friends cleaned and cleared my house in the days following the baby's death and until now I have had no ambition to try to find anything.

Perhaps with the warming of the days, the cold lump in my heart will also begin to warm.

Until later, I am ever

Your loving sister,

Sarah

April 2, 1849

Jane, my beloved sister,

Mr. Cockrell is home.

Two days after I entrusted Enoch to post my last letter to you, my husband came back.

It was late in the afternoon. I had milked the cow, fed the livestock and secured the house for the night when suddenly I heard the pounding of hooves approaching. I knew who it was, didn't even have to look. He rode past the front down to our makeshift barn, which he was planning to replace with a more permanent structure this spring, before I sneaked a glance. He was unsaddling his horse.

It was all I could do not to race out and fling myself in his arms, but I thought better of it. While I waited, I strained the milk and stored it, cleared my supper dishes from the table and set down a clean plate, knife, fork and glass. Then I smoothed my hair, took off my apron and almost held my breath until I heard the door opening behind me. In seconds I was enveloped in loving arms that held me and held me and held. I wanted to shout, sob, spout a million words, but I didn't. I just stood there feeling whole again as if the rest of me was suddenly back in place. I don't know how long we stood in the middle of our kitchen in an embrace that was even more convincing and committing than that of long ago, the night I told Mr. Cockrell I would marry him and the second never-to-be-forgotten night when we first arrived at the White House after our wedding. Only this time the silent pledge was even more complete.

Finally he spoke. "I am sorry," he said. "I will never leave you like that again."

I nodded. In times of greatest feeling, whether of tumultuous joy or of intense sorrow, silence is my only response. Mr. Cockrell, too, was then silent for a long time as he glanced around the house seeming to absorb with his eyes all that was familiar. I recall with such joy the first time he held me so close and how the words gushed out of his mouth. This time I was even more moved by his silence. I do not need words. I can tell by his manner, by his actions, by his presence that he has lived through great sorrow, healing himself in the only way he knows how and that his new commitment to me and to our future is more solid than ever.

I did not ask if he wanted supper. I knew he was hungry, and I set about putting food on the table while he went outside and washed days of grime from his head, hands and body.

For the first time since we buried Logan, I felt at peace. I know my husband did, too.

When he came back inside, he did not immediately sit down, but came around the table, pulled out my chair and indicated that I was to sit with him. There were no words. Only the loving touches. Only the silent promise that we had an impenetrable future.

I did not ask where he had been or how he had spent the two months he had been away. Lacking one day, he had been gone for eight weeks, leaving on Friday, January 26 and returning on Thursday, March 22. I had marked each and every day on the calendar, allowing no visitors to see it so that none of my family had shared the intense loneliness I endured. I will not allow my husband to see it, either, but I will keep it to remind me of the darkest days of my life. And now the resurrection.

The day following Mr. Cockrell's return, he was out of bed and out of the house before I began to stir. I allowed myself the luxury of lingering in bed, reflecting on the days that had gone by and the feeling of a new beginning. When I was up and dressed, Alexander had disappeared. I could see that his horse was still at the barn and that the livestock had been fed and watered. Then I went to the front and looked out. He stood, hat in hand, at Logan's grave which I had visited daily since we buried him there. I gently closed the door and waited for several minutes before I eased out of the house and walked up the slight incline to stand beside my husband. He reached for my hand and we stood there together, heads bowed for several moments before we simultaneously turned to each other and then, hand-in-hand, walked back to the house together. I prepared breakfast while he milked the cow.

At breakfast, Mr. Cockrell began to speak, very quietly and very gently, not about the past but about future plans. He said he had lost two months, that now he had a barn to build, a kitchen room to add to our home and that he had to get into Dallas and find out what had been happening in the town since he left. He was eager to get the ferry he had long ago planned in operation. He needed to get back to Nacogdoches and over to Shreveport and up to the Red River on trading trips. He said he did not know how we would manage it because of the care of the livestock, but he hoped that I would find it possible to go on some of the trips with him.

Then, I told him what had been happening at home, that I had sent the family back to their own place as soon as I felt strong enough to cope alone. I saw him wince. Though he did not speak, it was clear to me that he had thought I would have some of my family with me during the entire time he was away. He later said he could not believe that I had managed by myself, and I could tell that he was again berating himself for allowing it to happen, so I hastened on. I told him that James had gone to California taking Robert with him, that they had left only shortly before his return and that we had not yet had time to hear from them. I told him that, from reports from Pa and Enoch, when he did go into Dallas, he would find that most of the men had also picked up and left for the California Gold Rush. I was vastly reassured when he nodded and added, "Not I."

Two weeks later, April 16. It is early morning, a beautiful day. The sun is shining brightly. I have planted flowers this morning around Logan's grave and other seeds around the front of our cabin. Until Mr. Cockrell gets a fence of some sort built (which he has promised to do) to protect the tender plants, I haven't much hope that they will grow and blossom, but I felt the need this morning to dig in the dirt, to feel renewal in the earth, to be one with the universe.

We have had restoration in solitude together. I have been so grateful that no one has come to disturb our peace. I know that the world will intrude again soon—already has, in fact. But for these past few days of comforting silence, I feel a deep spiritual wholeness again, something I did not believe possible only a few weeks ago. My husband's silent presence has been the balm for my soul. Even today as he hitched the oxen to the wagon for a trip to the village—and possibly on to Nacogdoches, he lingered, seemingly feasting his eyes on the surrounding countryside and coming back to stand near me, occasionally touching me, once in awhile speaking. I knew his reluctance to leave. I knew how badly he wanted me to go with him. But now that James and Robert have both gone to California, there is nobody left to do the chores here. Pa cannot work the long hours that he used to manage so well. Enoch is his only source of help and Enoch is stretched too thin. I could not ask him to assume one more obligation.

Our sisters are willing but have never had the responsibility of taking care of a home and looking after livestock the way you and I have done. Mary and Mr. Thompson, who were quietly married recently, are busy setting up their own home and farm. It is planting time here now and the men are eager to get their crops in the ground. I find myself grateful that my husband is a trader rather than a farmer, for I know I could not manage planting, cultivating and harvesting crops the way some women do. I have managed to get a garden planted in the last few weeks and already have turnip greens and beans thriving. The onions are almost ready to pull and eat. Mr. Cockrell did get a makeshift fence around the garden. It would not deter determined livestock from trampling, so I am constantly watchful during the waking hours to protect the tender vegetables. My most invasive varmints are rabbits. I wish the little critters would eat the tender vegetation all around us and leave the seeds I have cultivated to us. But such is not the case.

Mr. Cockrell did not go to Nacogdoches, as he said he might when he left here day before yesterday. He made a trip into town, found the Trinity almost out of its banks since the recent spring rains and renewed his enthusiasm for opening a ferry and eventually building a bridge across the river. I continue to be awed by the many projects of my husband. So many times, I have learned, people who build mountains of expectations seldom follow through. They are so busy chasing rainbows that they never get around to accomplishing very much. Not so Mr. Cockrell. He is like a bulldog! When he gets an idea, he pursues it constantly and unless he finds good reason to change his mind—it is not right for the community or it is not profitable—he pursues it to fruition. I am glad I keep the family business ledgers. Sometimes I am tempted not to let him know the status of our profits and losses. For where there's extra cash; he is likely to go off on a new tangent of enthusiasm. And, just to think, only a few years ago I worried that I might be an old maid. Now I am concerned that I cannot keep up with a husband who thinks he must single handedly create a whole new world!

Summer has arrived and with it days that are warm to hot. My husband has made three trips to buy, trade and sell, but is home now. Yesterday he took me into Dallas for a visit with Margaret Bryan. I had not seen her in more than a year. Her third child, Edward Tarrant Bryan, was born on June 2 and is a beautiful little boy. You may remember, he is Margaret's fourth baby. She, like I, lost her first-born. Her second son, John Neely Bryan Jr., is now a little more than three years old, and the baby girl, Frances Elizabeth, born December 4, 1847, is 18 months and toddling everywhere. I don't allow myself to envy Mrs. Bryan. But when I held the infant in my arms, I wanted to cry. I so long to fill these empty arms.

I cannot envy Margaret Bryan because she is doing this all alone. Her husband, Dallas' founder, John Neely Bryan, has "absconded" to California in the Gold Rush. He waited until the birth of their son and then, within days, left for California. The Bryan cabin (two rooms) is home for nine people—Margaret and her three children: John Neely, Jr., Frances, the infant Edward, four of her first cousins, the children of her uncle, widower James Beeman, and one young Negro woman Mr. Beeman hired to help with the children before he left with Mr. Bryan for California. The Beeman children range in age from 10 down to 28 months and include Mary Frances, Emily Elvira, Frank and Melissa. Their mother died last year. Mr. Cockrell told me that he was delayed in leaving for Nacogdoches because Mr. Bryan asked him to draw up legal papers for the dispensation of his property and the care of his family in case anything were to happen to him before he and Mr. Beeman returned from California.

When I think of the complaints I had, admittedly mostly silent, for the two months that Mr. Cockrell was recently away from home, and then I think of Margaret Bryan, I cannot but get down on my knees and be grateful for my good fortune. But my arms are still empty.

Later. Early October. I have been so busy sharing personal family vignettes, that I have not mentioned or asked your opinion about many things that are going on in our nation and our world. Mr. Cockrell brought me several newspapers from his last trip, and I am glad that I have finally begun to have a bit of interest in things outside my own selfish world.

I was pleased to learn that our new president, Zachary Taylor, has established a Home Department to the U. S. Government, which I understand has recently been renamed the Department of the Interior and that Thomas Ewing, until recently the Secretary of the Treasury, has been named as its first Secretary. I understand that their charge is to conserve some of our country's beautiful natural resources. I can only hope they do it well.

Mr. Cockrell reports that among the city's newest arrivals are a couple from France, Maxime and Drouard Guillot. They landed in New Orleans on their way to California, but when they came through Dallas he liked it so much that he persuaded his wife to settle here. He plans to open the city's first wagon and buggy factory. The Guillots have a son, Maxime Jr. When I think of this young couple with their small son making the decision to settle in Dallas, my faith in its future and in the "wild" dreams of my husband to be a part of it are renewed. I suppose I am the cautious one! Mr. Cockrell dreams on a much larger scale! I don't want to clip his wings, but I don't want him to go wild, either!

My love of learning and my desire to have had more than a modicum of formal education was renewed recently when I read that a new college has been established in Huntsville, Texas. It's called Austin College, probably named for Stephen F. Austin, one of the founders of the Republic of Texas. The Presbyterian Church founded it. How I long to have been able to advance my education in an institute of higher learning, but alas, Huntsville is miles removed from where we live. And even if it weren't, there is no way a married woman could enroll in a university. When I mentioned this to Mr. Cockrell, he was abashed. "Why?" he asked. "What does being married have to do with learning?" This is from a man who can neither read nor write his own name. And some people wonder why I am so devoted to him?

And, while I am on the subject of women and education, aren't you thrilled that one of US has become a medical doctor? I trust that you are still keeping up with current events as they unfold and know that Elizabeth Blackwell became the first woman in the United States to receive a medical degree when she graduated from Geneva College in Geneva, New York earlier this year. I could never practice medicine. I am almost faint at the sight of blood, but I applaud any woman who is called to a medical profession—or any other profession, for that matter. I wonder how I would survive in competition with all of the men who think they are so great!

Two recent events in our own small world are worthy of attention: In a lovely wedding on September 26, Elizabeth Coats married Edward Browder. You will remember that he is the son of Lucy Jane Monroe Browder, the relative and foster daughter of President James Monroe, who came to this city about five years ago and was its first woman realtor. She sold houses in the Browder Springs area, which her two sons developed. Elizabeth Coats is a direct descendant of Pocahontas, the Indian maiden who saved the life, not once but twice, of Captain John Smith, one of the earliest explorers of this country. The daughter of Indian Chief Powhatan, she laid her head upon his when Captain Smith was about to be beheaded or beaten to death after his capture by her tribe in Virginia. A very young girl at the time, she appealed to her father for mercy and Smith was spared. She saved his life a second time in 1609 when her father, disenchanted with the invasions of the English on American territory, determined to kill him. Learning of the plot, Pocahontas leaked his fate to Smith, who was able to escape. In 1614, after being converted to Christianity, Pocahontas married John Rolfe, an Englishman, and moved with him to England. Elizabeth Pocahontas Cole Browder, is a string of women who have carried the Pocahontas name since our country's founding. She says she will close this chapter of history if she has daughters. I think this is sad because Pocahontas Street in Dallas is named for the family, and the descendants need to know the value of their heritage. Such a romantic story it is!

The settlement of another family in our environs has been of especial note to me as I read about it in our new newspaper, *The Cedar Snag*. (More about our newspaper later!) It is the arrival of Frances Sims Daniel and her family about five miles to the north of downtown Dallas. Mrs.

Daniel is the widow of a Methodist minister, the Rev. John M. Daniel. She came from Alabama in a covered wagon with six of her eight children and her sister, Nancy Sims Harlan. Seeking the land grant she was promised, she veered north of the village and camped on a gentle hillside.[4] The next day, seeking a more auspicious place to establish her home on the 320 acres she had acquired as a widowed, single person, she moved a few feet north where water was more available, and settled with her family. I would love to meet this Alabama widow. She sounds like my kind of person. Having lost her husband and with no idea where her future lay, she left her village in an impoverished part of the country and struck out for a new Promised Land.

The most auspicious occurrence that convinces me we are headed for a new era in Dallas is the arrival of our own newspaper! James Wellington Latimer (known as Weck) and his wife, Lucy Jordan Latimer, arrived in town several weeks ago from Paris, a town in Northeast Texas, where he published a newspaper. I don't know who convinced him that Dallas was a better place for a newspaper, but I am so glad that the Latimers are now among us. He simply packed up and headed southwest. He and Mrs. Latimer arrived in Dallas in a covered wagon with all of their possessions including his printing press and her piano. As soon as they were spotted, the word went out and men, including my husband, poured out to greet them. When they saw the piano, the men immediately began to beg Mrs. Latimer to play. She tried to postpone her performance, explaining that she was weary following the long journey and in addition, the piano should be tuned before it was played, but the men persisted and finally she sat down, on the wagon, in the middle of Main Street, and played a piano solo, to which her audience responded with loud applause and calls for an encore. Mr. Cockrell enthralled me with his report on the incident and made me long to have been present for the very first musical performance in the city.

Mr. Latimer has rented a small building on the west side of Houston Street at the southwest corner of Commerce and has already turned out his first newspaper. Mr. Cockrell brought me a copy! Now called *The Cedar Snag*, the paper's name will soon be changed to the more appropriate name, *The Dallas Herald*. Mrs. Latimer hopes to teach music lessons. I don't know how this is going to work out because there are no other pianos in the area and, thus, no way for children to practice.

The year has ended on a happy note. Our neighbor, Mrs. Hord, told me about it. During the recent holidays, ten couples got together for dancing on Christmas Eve at William Beeman's Dallas Tavern and had such a good time that they repeated the festivities on New Year's Eve.

---

[4] Frances Daniel and her family camped on their first night in the area on the very spot where SMU's Dallas Hall would later be built.

Mrs. Hord said most of the town's leading citizens, including Nat M. Burford and his wife participated. They danced to the music of a fiddle, but she didn't say who played the fiddle.

Now that 1850 has dawned, I wonder what life has in store for us in the coming year. I continue to miss you terribly.

All my love,

Sarah

P.S. I was not going to tell anybody yet, but can't keep a secret from you. Mr. Cockrell and I will become parents again in the spring. Only Mr. Cockrell knows and he's being so good to me. I have not told any of our family, so mum's the word when you are writing to us.—*SHC.*

1850

My dearest sister Jane,

Throughout the year I have penned notes and letters to you, most of which have been written in my heart and never put on paper and none of which has been mailed. I hear from you through our sisters, as I know you hear from me.

This has been an eventful year and now at Christmas-time as the end of this year approaches, I am compelled to put a few thoughts on paper. So much that has happened in this year of 1850 is anti-climatic because we have finally begun to legalize what we were already doing. For instance, Pa's deeds to three parcels of land he has been farming almost since we arrived were officially granted on November 15, including Patent No. 386 for 442.8 acres, Patent No. 1447 for 37.2 acres and patent No. 1437 for 160 acres. Three days later, Alexander's certificate No. 449 issued by Peters' Colony became legal—640 acres on Patent No. 51 and 320 acres on Patent No. 52. Because I keep the books on all our transactions and continue to be involved in the business of our parents, which I began to do the moment we arrived in Texas six years ago, I had been gravely concerned about the lack of legal papers to prove our claims. Now I feel a great deal more comfortable. There is still much to do, but at least we now have legal claim to our property. The promises of Peters' Colony agents that lured so many of us to settle here have not, in many instances, proved valid. We have yet to see the outcome of it all.

This country is new. Its inhabitants have arrived from many states to settle here bringing with them laws from all parts of the country. Not yet have we established binding laws of our own. I think now we are beginning to do so.

At least we are now legally a county with Dallas as county seat. Last January the state legislature passed an act declaring that an election be held in August to establish a permanent county seat. Since several attempts had previously been made to effect this legislation, I held my breath until it actually happened, which came about on August 15 with a run-off on August 31. Three towns in the county were in hot competition to be named the government center—Dallas, Cedar Springs and our Hord's Ridge. Mr. Cockrell and I had divided loyalties—both in our business life and in our personal lives! Mr. Cockrell favored Dallas from the start. He already had a number of businesses started in the small central village and was loathe to move. I favored Hord's Ridge because of its proximity to where we live and because we already know so many people here. I still think it would have made the ideal county seat. I wonder if we would not have won had we established a makeshift seat of government and given ourselves a new name. Somehow, Hord's Ridge does not sound to me like a seat of government. Cedar Springs to the north of Dallas has a growing population of very prominent people. So we had no idea what the outcome of the vote would be.

On August 15, 470 votes were cast. Dallas edged the other two with 191 votes to Hord's Ridge's 178 and Cedar Springs 101. This meant there had to be a run-off, and the campaigning for the next two weeks was fierce. On August 31, 460 votes were cast—244 for Dallas and 216 for Hord's Ridge. So, we lost, but I haven't grieved about it. At the end, I was just glad to have something done! It helped that Dallas already had been doing business as the temporary seat of government. Since Mr. Bryan and my husband are friends, and since I like Margaret Bryan so much, I think it would have hampered our relationship if we had won and they had lost.

I am amazed that so many votes were cast because the entire county population is only 2,743—the number of us counted in the first federal census ever taken here, which came shortly after the August vote. When you consider that at least half of that number are women who do not have the vote (whenever are we going to change that?), that many of the remainder are children and that the 207 slaves do not have a vote, it is amazing that more than 450 ballots were cast.

As soon as Dallas was designated as county seat, "we" began construction on a courthouse. It's only 16 by 32 feet and was completed by the men of the area in about a week. I am so glad we have this central location to house the court files that have been transferred from Nacogdoches, our former county seat to the east. Mr. Cockrell says we had to pay Nacogdoches $100 for the transcription and delivery of the records. I think that is exorbitant! And, I am not sure whether the files from Old Franklin in Robertson County (our part of the county seat west of the Trinity) have arrived here yet. The new courthouse is not big enough to accommodate all of the legal proceedings, so courtrooms continue to be rented in various parts of the county. I was appalled to learn that Adolphus F. Goughnant's barroom was rented for $7.50 recently to hold court. Imagine a seat of legal justice in a bar!

Mr. Cockrell continues to envision a modern utopian city in this wilderness, and I continue to try to harness his multiple enthusiasms. I think he is reckless with runaway dreams, and I know I tend to be too cautious. I often lie awake nights wondering how we would survive if I did not occasionally put a damper on his exuberance. On the other hand, his investments usually turn out well. The ink was hardly dry on the law designating Dallas as the county seat when he asked me to write a petition requesting permission to build a highway from Dallas through Johnson Station and on toward Fort Worth. When the petition was ready, Alex got the signatures of almost every man in this part of the county and presented it to the court in October. The court took the petition into consideration and designated Mr. Cockrell, A. G. Harris, J. J. Metcalf, Samuel Stacks and S. B. Hopkins as a committee of five to review the possibilities for such a road and report back to the next session of court.

I think it highly entertaining that Mr. Cockrell is on the committee of five to determine the advisability of such an undertaking. Were I opposed to it, I would strongly object to having one of the petitioners chairing the committee to investigate, but since nobody has voiced an objection, I keep my thoughts entirely to myself!

Alex is so certain of its approval that he has already begun laying the roadway! It will, of course, lead from the city of Dallas across Cockrell Bridge on Mountain Creek and onto the western boundary of the county toward Fort Worth. In the meantime, he is working with leaders in Fort Worth to start from their downtown eastward toward Dallas County.

I feel sure there are times that Mr. Cockrell wishes he had not said at the time of our marriage that I should always be a full partner in "our" business endeavors, for I can see the look on his face when I often douse cold water on his wildest dreams. When he brought the trunk home and said that I should keep all of the family records, he gave me carte blanche to become the full partner he promised. I keep very careful records. I do not ever want to clip his wings or curtail his enthusiasm. But when he comes up with one wild scheme after another, I watch with both fascination and fright. I sometimes think he would gamble the last dollar we have on ventures that, in my limited view, haven't the slightest chance of succeeding. The truth is that most do succeed! Sometimes, I admit, I stash back a few dollars that he doesn't know we have—because I do not ever want us to go hungry.

There is no doubt that Mr. Cockrell has become the town's business leader. He not only has instigated the opening of new business enterprises, but everywhere he goes, he talks about the future of this place and lures new people to settle here. Mr. Bryan, who was such a visionary in originally building the town, has very little interest in it now. He recently returned home after seeking his fortune—which did not happen—in the California Gold Rush. We are very good friends of the Bryans. As soon as Mr. Bryan arrived back in town, Alex went to see him, convinced that the two should become partners in the town's future, but Mr. Bryan expressed little interest. Mr. Cockrell says he seems to have lost all passion for progress. I overheard the men talking about how he has taken to drink and often seems morbid and depressed. I feel so sorry for Mrs. Bryan. She is so young and lovely. I, too, am married to a man who enjoys his liquor, but Mr. Cockrell never drinks to the point that he does not know what he is doing.

It's not only the new road that has made Dallas a popular place to trade, but the expansion of a stage coach line that links us to cities beyond our borders. At 7 a.m. every Monday, Wednesday and Friday, the Dallas Houston Railroad Express Stage Coach leaves from the courthouse through streets that are little more than mud bogs to make its way to Houston on our south and to Jefferson on our east.

Our growth is phenomenal. From a population of 39 within the "city limits" a little more than a year ago, we now have 2,743 in the county, 2,536 whites and 207 blacks. What's more, we have a large number of new businesses. The first federal census, only recently completed, shows that the city of Dallas has 430 people living within its town limits (and that does not include those of us who are very important but live in the countryside surrounding the town!)

I think any city in the country would be glad to claim the caliber of people who make up the foundation of our town. I am amazed that we have so many professional men. The professionals include nine lawyers—Nat M. Burford, John Neely Bryan, John M. Crockett, Felix Eakins, John N. Elkins, Smith Elkins, J. W. Latimer (who is also the newspaper publisher), John C. McCoy and Samuel G. Newton; five physicians—Samuel T. Bledsoe, Perry Dakans, S. B. Pryor and A. D. Rice—and one dentist,

James B. Bryan. These professional leaders are enhanced by three merchants—Madison M. Miller, James M. Patterson and John W. Smith. There are also three wagon makers—B. F. Barrow, Edward Mills and Gide Pemberton, and then there's Charles Newton, a carriage-maker. Our hotel proprietor is Thomas Crutchfield, and our chair-maker, John Shurlock. The others of the in-city population include Adam Haught, a ferryman (everybody knows he made his money as the keeper of the city's first saloon), B. O. C. Pound, a saddle-maker, William M. Wallis, a printer; Aaron McDaniel, a gunsmith; A. M. Keen, a surveyor, and four blacksmiths—J. W. Lyttle, A. J. Marvin, E. T. Myers and Robert Ray. William Briton and John A. Jackson listed themselves on the census as traders; Worley Carter as a hunter and William McDermitt as a coffeesmith (whatever that means!). So, you can see what a wide variety of careers are included in this first census. I asked my husband why he was not listed as a lawyer among the professionals in the city, explaining that Mr. Madison Miller who lived a long way south of the city was on the list, but he had no answer!

Mr. Cockrell has laid out plans for a grand new hotel that he hopes to open within the next few years which will be, he says, the most elaborate lodging site in the country. He is also talking about building a bridge across the Trinity River.

The splurge of city growth, marvelous as it is for the county, has brought with it a shifting population, thrill seekers and charlatans, the negative side of prosperity. For the first time, there is an increase of lawlessness in our area. I suppose it is always so—those seeking a "fast buck," a short cut opportunity to "get rich quick" seek out the areas of rapid growth, make their mark and move on. So, we have had a rash of brawls, fights and, occasionally, a murder. Those of us who expected the growth of our area to produce and enforce laws to protect all the citizens have learned instead that we are often at the mercy of a vastly exploding, quickly changing populace. It seems to me that at this time last year we knew just about everybody in the area or at least we knew friends who did. Now, there are days I feel that I do not know anybody any more. As new businesses open up, the demand for unskilled labor grows. Lone men wander in without ties to anybody, work until they have enough money to move on to seek their fortunes elsewhere and leave their jobs—often having picked the pockets of anyone with whom they came in contact. I have warned Mr. Cockrell repeatedly about the need to check the background of those who apply for work, but I have to agree with him that this is not easy. When a business is desperate for workers to fill the orders coming in and when communication is so slow and unreliable, it is almost impossible to know—and sometimes even to care—who is filling the orders as long as the business gets done.

As a woman of faith, I am especially horrified at the number of gambling halls, saloons and brothels. A woman of "refinement" is not supposed to know about the "ladies of leisure" that always seem to follow prosperity, but, of course, we know!

Where I once was horrified that an open barrel of whiskey with a dipper attached for drinking was available in almost every business in the town, I now long for the day when I could be certain that my long-overdue husband was safe and drinking with his friends in a known establishment. Even though I trust him, there are times I sit up late at night darning socks in the flickering glow of candlelight and have misgivings.

The year 1850 will always be marked for me by two dramatic personal changes, one sad—the death of my mother—and the other joyous—the birth of our daughter.

Ma, as you know, had been ailing for a number of years. I sometimes think that leaving her home and her own family in Virginia was the beginning of her letting go. Even though we know that death is inevitable, it is never easy to say good-by to those we love. In Texas, Ma was never the serene and comforting presence you knew. Even on the trek from Virginia here, while she was doing her best to put a good face on all of the hardships we endured, she could not hide from me her misgivings about all the people and surroundings she left to begin this new life. She said all the right things, but her heart was never in it. Caught unaware, she often had the far-off gaze of someone who is misplaced, of someone who does not exist in the present.

From time to time she rallied, as she did when I announced that I was going to marry Mr. Cockrell. And also to give support or voice disquietude at the choices each of our younger sisters and brothers made for their lives.

Most of all, she continued to support Pa. It was so clear that they loved each other! Even as they faded, her eyes would light up and her voice seemed stronger at the appearance of Pa in her bedroom.

On April 7, she died very quietly, just as she had lived, surrounded by those of us who loved her best. Absent only were you, our brother John, who pre-deceased her two years ago, and our brothers, James, and Robert who have not yet returned from the California Gold Rush. Pa seems to have given up since she went away. We laid her to rest in Cockrell Cemetery near our brother, John. Hers is the cemetery's second grave.

I am very lonely.

But, whether it is a parent or a child that leaves us, the future lies beyond our grasp. And it is the future that brings me to the triumphant end of my tale of 1850. I am again a mother!

On May 25 Aurelia Effie Cockrell was born. I cannot begin to tell you what a joy she is.

I had no idea how Mr. Cockrell would react to having a daughter. Even as I carried this child, I worried that my husband would be disappointed if I gave birth to a girl.

I could not have been more mistaken!

Aurelia is a magic child!

She is the image of her father, even more than Logan was. She has his coloring, his complexion, his eyes, and, heaven help us, his determination! Sometimes I think they conspire against me! They are bonded in a way that I cannot intrude, even if I wanted to do so. I only rejoice in their attachment to each other.

And so, as this year ends, I rejoice in the rest that our Mother has found in her heavenly glory. And in the coming of my daughter. But most of all in a future that I still think will also include my beloved sister and her family. When are you coming?

My abiding love,

Sarah

1851-1852

My beloved sister Jane,

This is likely the last letter I will address to you in Virginia, and I couldn't be more thrilled. Only yesterday your short letter with such wonderful news arrived! At last you are moving to Texas! I never gave up hope, but as the years have gone by and so many things have happened in your life and in mine and in the lives of our family, I often wondered if we would ever be together again.

Now it is happening! I am busy preparing the house for your arrival. You will stay with us, of course, until you and Mr. Bradshaw find your own property and can build your home. Mr. Cockrell joins me in welcoming you—all of you! I could sense a concern in your letter that you would need to separate your children into the homes of various relatives when you wrote that you did not expect any of us to have sufficient room to house all 10 of you. But I know you will be anxious enough making adjustments to new surroundings without having the added concern of worrying about the welfare of your children. Sure, we will be crowded, but we have been crowded before, and there is always a way to accommodate beloved family members.

As soon as you have selected property, Alex, James and Enoch are ready to help you build a house—and, I am sure, neighbors will pitch in to help. Everybody is so generous to assist each other in any time of crisis or need. It is one of the great joys of living here.

I cannot believe that your John is 16, almost a man! And that your three oldest daughters are now into their teens. Henry was a baby, just beginning to walk when we left Virginia and now he is 10 years old! You also have added another daughter and two sons to the family since we parted. What a reunion this is going to be!

You may not have time to receive this letter before you set out on your journey. But since you said you have not been receiving my letters, I will add a few things that have gone on here in the past two years to try to prepare you for this place to which you are coming.

I did send you a line when Pa died, and I know that one or more of our sisters have been in touch with you. After Ma died, we could see Pa fading before our eyes every day. He just could not seem to rally. As far as I could tell, there was nothing really wrong with him, but he just gave up. Nothing interested him. He would sit for hours gazing out the window or occasionally walk alone out onto the farm land. He would disappear and I'd find him standing at Ma's grave, often talking softly—whether to himself or to her, I could not be sure.

We were planning a surprise birthday party on Saturday, March 22 (1851) for his 76th birthday hoping that we could persuade him to show some interest in living again. The birthday cake was baked and decorated and all of us were cooking his favorite foods. He went to bed before dark on Friday, which was not unusual. When he did not come for breakfast on Saturday morning, Lucy went to see about him and found him. The doctor said he died sometime before midnight. Enoch rode over immediately to tell me what had happened. Together my sisters and I prepared his body for burial while the men made the casket. Instead of the festive birthday supper we had planned, we gathered around the table in the kitchen where Lucy and her family had lived with him since she married and exchanged bittersweet stories about our lives together.

It was comforting to have James home when Pa died, even though he brought more sad news, that Robert had died in California. He said he had written to tell us about it some weeks back, but the letter did not arrive— and still hasn't. James got here two weeks before Pa's death. He had far more luck in California than most of the returning men, who have deemed the California Gold Rush a Gold Bust! James said he was sorely tempted to stay out west and would have except for two things—his property and his wife-to-be back home. The day after he rode in, he was over at his farm laying out the area. He and Jane Phillips were to be married the day after Pa died, but postponed it for another couple of weeks, during which time they got the house nearly completed so that they could move into it.

You will be glad to know that you are not coming to the frontier town we found when we arrived eight years ago. Every time Mr. Cockrell goes into Dallas, he brings back newspapers and usually a book or two. I am getting quite a library! And I treasure every book that comes into my hands. We are especially delighted to have a newspaper of our own. The Latimers are doing quite well with the *Dallas Herald*. Mr. Cockrell advertises in every issue.

When Mr. Latimer was elected chief justice shortly after Dallas County was organized, Lucy, his wife, took over the major role in publishing the paper. It was highly amusing to me to overhear the men talking. Most were absolutely certain that a mere woman could not handle a newspaper and most strongly opposed her trying. If the truth be known, I think the paper improved a great deal under her guidance, but then as it matured it was bound to get better.

Mrs. Latimer was really overwhelmed. Not only was she getting out a weekly newspaper, but would not give up her piano students.

About a year after Mr. Latimer was named chief justice, John W. Swindells came to Dallas from New York and purchased an interest in the paper and became Mr. Latimer's partner. He is said to be courting Minerva Crutchfield, the daughter of Tom Crutchfield, our town's hotel owner. Mr. Swindells' contributions to the paper have vastly relieved Mrs. Latimer, who continues for now as the chief publisher.

While I am on the subject of reading, I wonder if you have read *Uncle Tom's Cabin*? Written by a woman, Harriet Beecher Stowe, it was first published in a series of articles in the *National Era*, an anti-slavery tract in Washington, D. C. last year. It was widely circulated and, I am told, became a topic of conversation and debate at elite gatherings across the country. Even in our own small part of the nation, it has been much discussed. When it came out in book form earlier this year, Mr. Cockrell ordered a copy for me and I couldn't put it down. It's one of the most conclusive writings against slavery that it has been my experience to read. And it has divided the country even more completely between those who are for slavery and those who oppose it. It has further convinced me—an opinion I had already arrived at—that ownership of one human being over another is in opposition to the very freedoms on which our country was founded. I find that those who most vehemently oppose the book haven't even read it. I defy any thinking individual to read it through and come away without serious questions about slavery.

It seems that every time I write, I am juxtaposing sad family news alongside the good. I recall that I told you about Ma's death in the same letter that I reported the birth of our daughter. She was two in May and continues to be the apple of her father's eye.

Now, as I outline details of Pa's death, I celebrate the arrival of another child to our family. Robert Benjamin Cockrell was born on January 16, 1852. This time my health was excellent throughout the waiting period, and his birth was much easier and faster than that of the other two children. He's such a dear little one and looks not at all like the other children. He's roly poly, already an armful. He has my coloring—the gray eyes, the olive complexion, darker hair than mine but not as dark as that of Alexander and Aurelia. Maybe experience has taught me the art of mothering because I have not fretted nearly as much over this child. I do not worry every time I put him to bed that he might stop breathing, as I did with Aurelia after we lost Logan. I am far more relaxed, too, with my housework. If there is dust on the table or the floor is not swept and mopped, I don't panic any more. I thoroughly enjoy nursing my baby, and I love reading and playing with both Aurelia and Robert. She is learning to sing lullabies along with me. Mr. Cockrell declares that she carries on conversations with him when he takes her for a stroll or lifts her up into the saddle with him. I doubt that anyone other than her father could understand what she is saying, but I go along with his version.

We are a happy family, as I am sure you can tell. My only concern, still, is that my husband is impatient to turn this country into the biggest and most illustrious city in the Southwest and feels very keenly his role in making it come about.

The area continues to attract settlers from many different parts of the country—and also from foreign lands (and thereby hangs quite a tale, which I will get around to relating a bit later). We have acquired our first photographic studio. It was recently opened by Adolphe F. Goughnant and is located on the courthouse square. It's called Goughnant's Art Saloon. I am not at all surprised that it is a "saloon" because, as you may recall, he made the money to establish it by operating a saloon where hard liquor held sway. Even so, he has the only establishment in town that can reproduce the likeness of people in a system called the daguerreotype. I was thinking of having pictures made of both Aurelia and baby Robert, but now that you are coming, there are few people back in Virginia who would be interested in looking on the likeness of my children. I am certain that Mr. Cockrell's remaining relatives in Missouri wouldn't want a picture.

We also have a new town in our county. Called Lancaster, it's to the south of us in another fast developing section of the county. Mr. Cockrell prophesies that before we are finished, there will be small towns dotted all around Dallas.

Mr. Cockrell recently brought me a copy of the *New York Daily Times*, which purports to be the best newspaper in the country. I have only one copy, which I read and cherish. I save every scrap of written material and intersperse reading newspapers and books with daily reading of the Bible. Sometimes, when he is at home, I persuade my husband to sit and listen to me read. Energetic as he is, he usually does this reluctantly. One of my most cherished memories is of us sitting by candlelight, him holding Aurelia and me with baby Robert at my breast, while I read the 23rd Chapter of Psalms.

I was devastated to read that a fire in the Library of Congress destroyed 35,000 volumes of books and materials, which the story said was two-thirds of the Library's collection, including many donated by Thomas Jefferson.

Except for the birth of our son, I have again saved the most pertinent part of this story until the last.

You, my dear sister, are arriving in a land that my husband and I now mostly own. If anybody had told me eight years ago that I would be a part of the history of this place, I would have considered them insane. When I married Alexander Cockrell, I could never have envisioned what was ahead. Now, that I am a partner with a visionary/dreamer/entrepreneur, the future seems unlimited. I admit, as I have written to you in the past, there have been many times when I have tried to hold my husband's enthusiasm in check. It never worked! This is my latest tale:

On the morning of August 2 (1852), Mr. Cockrell rose early, tended the livestock and after a hearty breakfast, said that he would ride into town to take care of some business. When I questioned him, he seemed a bit secretive. In any event, I nodded, watched him as he rode away and busied myself with the cleaning of breakfast dishes, bathing and feeding Aurelia, changing Robert's diaper, dusting the front room and putting some deer meat and potatoes on to boil for our meal.

It was, as I recall, a very hot summer day—August 2, 1852—and all had gone exceedingly well. I had completed my chores and was sitting down with a book of poetry. I was feeling at peace with my world, celebrating my good fortune, a healthy seven-month-old son at my breast, a beautiful two-and-a-half-year-old daughter busily pulling my books off the shelf and scattering toys as two-year-olds do. I was experiencing a moment of complete satisfaction. WHEN, it seems to be in retrospect, I was suddenly jarred into the reality of a new day!

I heard, rather than saw, Mr. Cockrell approaching, riding hard on his favorite pony. Still holding my baby to my breast, still aware of everything Aurelia was doing, I opened the door to a husband/father who looked like a mad man! Having ridden hard, (as evidenced by the sweat on his faithful steed), he approached our house waving a paper over his head. "Mrs. Cockrell," he shouted, still waving the paper as he pulled his horse to a halt and dismounted at our front gate, "Mrs. Cockrell," he shouted repeatedly. "Mrs. Cockrell! Come look! I bought you a town!"

Never in my life have I been filled with such mixed emotions.

I had no idea what he meant. I dreaded to find out! But soon enough the truth was out. He bounded into our front room, scooped me up in his arms, Robert and all, then reached and embraced Aurelia with us. And announced again:

"I bought us a town!"

When he had calmed down enough to make sense, I got the story—and what a story. He had been to visit the Bryans and found Mr. Bryan more melancholy that usual, talking of leaving town again, struggling with debts and determined to rid himself of all responsibility for the town he had founded. He offered to sell the rest of the township to my husband, who tried his best to talk some sense into his friend. When he was finally convinced that Mr. Bryan was determined to sell all of the remaining parts of the town to somebody, Alex agreed to purchase it.

Apparently the deed is binding. We have acquired all of the property that remains in Mr. Bryan's name in Dallas, which amounts to at least one-third of the townsite and some surrounding acreage. Mr. Bryan had sold some of the lots and given away dozens to new arrivals as wedding presents. The deal also included transfer of the ferry to Mr. Cockrell.

For the "package" my husband paid Mr. Bryan $7,000. Mr. Cockrell admits that he does not know exactly what he purchased and won't know until all of the legal work is completed. So ownership will not come into our name until all of this is completed early next year. The agreement signed by both Mr. Bryan and Alex reads that we should take possession by the latter part of March 1853.

When, at last, Mr. Cockrell calmed down, he went off to the barn to unsaddle his horse and take care of the livestock. I got Robert down for a nap, gave Aurelia lunch and read her a story, put our lunch on the table to await Mr. Cockrell's reappearance from the barn. I just sat in my rocker by the window and gazed out over our property. My emotions were—and are—so confused that I do not know which way to turn. I know that Mr. Cockrell has liquidated most of our assets to take on this indebtedness. He talks of moving into town where he can keep a close eye on the developments he plans. He talks of the buildings he will erect, the business he will lure into town, of building a better bridge across the river to replace or augment the ferry, of a grand hotel he envisions. In all of his plans, he simply assumes that I will be a full partner—and I will be—but at what cost? We have been so happy here in the White House on Mountain Creek. My husband talks of a whole new way of life. I don't know how we will pay for everything—I am, after all, the keeper of financial records—and I don't know at what cost to our future happiness.

There is an additional concern. I so hope Mr. Bryan will not be sorry he made this deal. I worry about Margaret and their children. I hope she does not think that Alexander took advantage of her husband during one of his low and lonely periods. I cannot bear to think that any business deal could jeopardize our friendship.

And, so I wait and ponder! Whoever would have thought that I, a country girl from Virginia, not all that smart and late wed, would assume responsibility for an entire town in a faraway state?

In the meantime, I await your arrival! Through everything, this has been the shining goal of my life. Come soon!

With all my love,
Your sister,

Sarah

1853

My dear sister Jane,

It is so wonderful having you here. Even though the miles between where we are in "downtown" Dallas and where you are at Mountain Creek make it impossible for us to see each other often. But I know you are there, and we can be together from time to time. I cannot begin to tell you how wonderful it was to talk to each other face to face after nine long years. I don't think we could ever catch up with our sisterly chats.

It must seem strange to you that I continue to write, but my letters to you since we arrived in this unsettled part of the world in 1844, have afforded me the opportunity to pour out my innermost thoughts. And often, in so doing, I work through some difficult times and make decisions I might otherwise have found impossible. Because I am a private person who mostly keeps her own counsel, I find that I must have an outlet. And so I write.

I could just keep a journal, but I find that directing my thoughts to you are by far the best way to communicate with myself!

And so I will continue to write to you, my wonderful sister. You may never receive any of the letters. I shall keep them together with our financial records, deeds and most cherished mementos in the small black trunk Alexander bought shortly after we were wed to serve as a bank. I really do not intend for you or anyone else to read these missives. I intend to destroy my words before I reach the end of my life—but, perchance, they should survive me, please know that these are my impressions alone. If someone else were "keeping score," keeping the records, the results would be entirely different. I want you to know, also, that many of the things I share here, I will—to the limit of my ability—have shared with my husband. But he is male. And men look on life from a perspective entirely different from the female point of view. That is why I have to speak to you from my heart. And, if someday you should perchance read these words, you will know that the message is not only from sister to sister, but from woman to woman.

What a year this has been!

In March of this year, 1853—March 21 to be exact—Alexander Cockrell became the sole owner of Dallas.

There is no mention in the deed of transfer that I, Sarah Horton Cockrell, am any part of this arrangement. And, for that matter, there is no mention of Alexander's heirs. Our children and their children may some day inherit the "fruits" of our labors, both the benefits and the problems that such a heritage entails, but for now the town belongs entirely to Alexander Cockrell. I say "ours" because I have a very large role in this. Had I not kept account of our finances and persuaded my husband, from time to time, to be more cautious with his spending, we would not have had the money to make the purchase. But since women are legally nobodies in this new State of Texas, I am a silent partner and have no idea how our daughter, Aurelia, who is the apple of her father's eye, will be treated. Will she one day be able to inherit? Or will the property we acquire be given over entirely to her brother? When I try to talk to my husband about these things, he either walks away or teases me that women were meant to be protected. And he intends to do just that, so I am not to worry. How can I not worry when he continues to build so many castles in the air?

My husband's enthusiasm knows no boundaries. In August he assumed full ownership of Dallas. The legal transfers were accomplished by the two men—John Neely Bryan, the seller, and Alexander Cockrell, the purchaser—a simple straightforward business deal. But the transaction affects the heart and soul of two women—Margaret Beeman Bryan, wife of John Neely, and me, not only the wife of Alexander Cockrell and the mother of his children, but also his secretary, record keeper and business manager.

Among the many points of agreement between the two men was that we would exchange houses! The Bryans would move into our home at Mountain Creek, and we would become residents in the Bryan home on the banks of the Trinity River in downtown Dallas. Neither Mr. Bryan nor Mr. Cockrell asked Margaret and me if we were agreeable.

I was shocked, at first incredulous and then horrified when I first heard about the plan. Mr. Cockrell explained that he could not manage the improvements he had in mind for the downtown if he had to ride in every day from where we lived in the country. He would waste half a day every day just riding back and forth. I could understand the logic of this, but it did not help the way I felt. It was a sad day, indeed, as I began packing for our move. I went as a bride to the Mountain Creek home. There I gave birth to three children, Logan, Aurelia and Robert. Almost every day I walk out to the top of the little mound at the side of my home and stand at Logan's grave and bow in silent prayer. It was all I could do to keep from crying as I packed.

I knew I was putting an end to a phase of my life. I tried to be happy about it. I think I did manage to be cheerful, both for the sake of my husband and our little children. Even so, moving day was awful. As the loaded wagon pulled away from the White House, I dared not look back lest the tears that filled my heart erupt into my eyes and destroy my good intentions. The plans were that we would meet the Bryans approximately halfway, they on their way with their furnishings to Mountain Creek and us on our way to their cottage on the banks of the Trinity. As it happened, we were almost all the way into Dallas before we met them, so eager was Mr. Cockrell to be on his way. We stopped only long enough to greet each other. And I could tell by Margaret's face and the few words we exchanged that the move was as painful for her as it was for me. All I could manage was to wish her well in a house that had held both the greatest happiness and the greatest sorrow of my life.

The two houses are approximately the same size, ours two rooms downstairs with another two rooms in the loft. Theirs, in which I am now making a home, is a double cabin, actually the third house which served as a Bryan home. Even though the weather is dry now—we are experiencing quite a drought—I am well aware that another flood could take everything we have.

Our furnishings fit quite nicely, but it will take some time for me to feel at home here on Commerce Street right in the middle of downtown Dallas where the view outside is not of trees and flowers and the changing of the seasons, but of mud streets, a few buildings including the courthouse—and the river. It is a world apart from anything I have ever known in my life. Caring for my two children, babies really, has also required a different approach. In the country I had to be alert for Indians, for snakes and other predators when Aurelia was outside toddling about the farm. Here I have to be aware of city dangers—wagons in front of our house, possible run-away teams or horses, and the need to protect her from the riffraff of unsavory characters. Robert, still in arms, will grow up in this environment and will never know the difference. But I wonder what kind of impact her earliest experiences on the farm will have on my daughter. I do not want my children growing up in this kind of environment where taking the Lord's name in vain is an every-day occurrence.

Mr. Cockrell helped me set up a makeshift office in one corner of our bedroom. There I have my trunk with all our official papers, a small desk and chair that he built for my writing materials and me. Mr. Cockrell's successes are a source of pride. I was very concerned when he spent almost all of the cash we had to purchase the town. Seven thousand dollars is a fortune, but then I remember that almost everything he touches proves to be a success. I am the cautious one!

Alexander is busy making improvements to his town. He has put some of his best men in charge of the sluggish, slow-moving ferry and has considerably shortened the time it takes to cross the Trinity. The sawmill, just as he predicted, has been a real boon to the community as building progresses, but he is planning to move it soon to a better location, right to the edge of his land where the timber is more plentiful. His most ambitious project thus far are plans to construct a bridge across the river, not to replace, but to augment the ferry. He says there will be a continuing use for the ferry to transport heavy loads, but a bridge is imperative for foot traffic, horseback riders and smaller wagons and teams. Almost every day he comes in to tell me that he has bought another piece of property, or that he has his eye on land that will be very valuable in the future. He is, in fact, so busy with projects in town that he hasn't had time to go to Shreveport or down to the Gulf Coast on buying trips, but says he must do so soon. He did make a speedy trip up to the Red River and was gone less than a week. It is good to have him home, but he's barely here when he is here. The growth of Dallas keeps him occupied day and night.

Our country increasingly agonizes over the subject of slavery. It is such a complicated subject and I predict before the issue is resolved that there will be great conflict, perhaps even a war. Presumably there is a clear delineation between the north and the south over slavery.

I have personally always been opposed to any human being owning another human being. But, as a child of Virginia, a stronghold of slavery, I have been indoctrinated with the conditioning of my rearing and have simply avoided the issue. As we quilt together and share our thoughts, I learn that most women oppose slavery, but then my circle of friends does not include wealthy women who rely on servants to do their housework, cook their meals and take care of their children. For the most part, when these conversations take place, I get the feeling that most women are mouthing the opinions of their husbands, fathers or brothers, but not in this instance. At first there is a tentative "feeling out" of each other with mild, almost questioning observations to elicit response. On the issue of slavery, many women take a different view from that of their husbands. My husband does not have strong feelings either way, though we do not own slaves. And when he employs slaves owned by his friends, he insists that a portion of what he pays be given to those doing the work. Two incidents in the recent past have focused my attention on slavery and left me in what I am certain will be permanent opposition.

The first is my reading of *Uncle Tom's Cabin*, the book by Harriet Beecher Stowe that I mentioned to you earlier. It has created shock waves across the nation. Even if, as southerners claim, slavery as depicted in the book is exaggerated, the point remains that many of the incidents have the ring of truth. More than 10,000 copies of the book sold within a week after it was published last year, and it continues to sell in great numbers across the country and in England. It made me consider all of the ramifications of slavery and led me in my first overt opposition.

The second "incident" is closer to home and far more personal. On May 27 an ugly chapter in Dallas County culminated in its first legal hanging when a slave woman was executed for killing a white man. Her name was Jane Elkins. Owned by a prominent Dallas family, she was sold to a Mr. Wisdom whose wife had died and who needed a woman to care for his three small children. Nobody knows what happened in the Wisdom house until the morning that he was found in bed, covered in blood and dead. There was no doubt that a nearby ax, also covered with blood, was the lethal weapon. And there was little doubt that Jane Elkins wielded the ax—though I do not think the court case proved her guilt beyond reasonable doubt. In any case, the entire trial was a farce. As a slave, she was a non-person who was not allowed to speak in her behalf. She had no lawyer. The woman who was her former owner declined to comment and was not subpoenaed. The children were not questioned and were, in any case, too young to testify. The entire process sickened me. From what I overheard and read in the *Herald*, I am convinced that there is far more to the story than was brought out in court or that we will ever know because Jane went to her death without anyone ever uttering a word in her behalf. We women wonder what could have provoked a slave with no apparent past meanness to have committed such a heinous crime?

In the last presidential campaign, hot heads on both sides of the slavery issue almost came to blows. When Franklin Pierce, a northerner who supported slavery, became president, the south said his victory made it clear that the constitution guaranteed their right to slave ownership. But, President Pierce was a compromise. When the Democrats could not agree on a candidate, they put him on the ballot. Though he carried 27 of the 31 states in the Union, most of the stories I read and many of the people I hear talking think his victory was more because of his personal charm than because he was the most qualified person to become the country's leader. His promise to gain new U. S. territories peacefully was very popular even when the issue of slavery was creating headlines in every major publication. And, everybody is gravely concerned over what might happen if he died or became too ill to function because he has no vice president. Poor Mr. William R. King, who took the oath of office as vice president in Cuba as a political bow to President Pierce who wants to annex Cuba, died in April less than a month after taking office. For now, the President retains sufficient popularity to function largely because he has been focusing on transportation.

When the men get together, the talk about extending rail service dominates the conversation. In March Congress in session appropriated $150,000 for a survey to find the most practical transcontinental rail lines. In its first published finding, the commission chose a route through the Gadsden Purchase south of the Gila River as the best route to link Texas to California. Naturally, the men including my husband, are ecstatic. He is doing everything he possibly can to get the rail line in operation.

I continue to be very interested in what women are doing and to hope that it will not be long until we have the right to vote. Earlier this year a petition to permit woman suffrage was presented to the Massachusetts Constitution Convention. It was the work of Mrs. Amos B. Alcott, whose husband, an educator/writer and social reformist, encouraged it. I hope you and I live to see the day when we will be allowed voting privileges.

It has been extremely dry this year. The drought, in fact, has parched the Southwest destroying many crops before they were ready to harvest. Mr. Cockrell says the unpredictability of the weather proves that he must continue to expand his businesses. One simply cannot rely on farming for a livelihood. The White House ranch has suffered, not because we had crops growing, but because the water for our livestock has been so low.

I face the New Year with determination to make our "new" home in downtown Dallas a place of comfort and joy. I have my work cut out for me!

With abiding love,

Sarah Horton Cockrell

1854

Dearest sister Jane,

I have been far too busy to put pen to paper and record the growth of this city and county and my personal thoughts and feelings about what is happening.

All of my written records are recorded in our business journals because my husband continues to enlarge our holdings, purchase and develop our land, construct new buildings, improve those he already owns and dream about an unlimited future. I cannot begin to keep up with him, but I do record all of our business dealings and am his confidante. I don't think he ever really listens to me, but somehow my ideas get across and most of the decisions he makes have my blessing as well as his! It is a good feeling to be in partnership with a man whose vision of the future is so unlimited. I have also taken to reading something to him almost every night when he is at home. I have learned that when I choose news stories in which he has a vital interest, he is far more inclined to sit still and listen, though he is still too excitable to tarry for long. I still wish he would learn to read and write.

When I have completed the family ledgers and have done my house-work—the cooking, cleaning and sewing—and have cared for the children, I am exhausted. There has been almost no time for anything other than pressing responsibilities of each moment. I can't imagine I ever had the time to brood!

I am fortunate to have you, my dear sister, and our other sisters near enough for an occasional visit. Aurelia loves to come spend time with you and her cousins. I hope it will keep her connected with her birthplace on Mountain Creek. Being with family and attending worship services are my only diversions.

Much has transpired since I last put pen to paper with personal thoughts. In this I will only hit the highlights.

You will never know how much it meant to me that you were here for the birth of our son in August. The hours we spent together, catching up on family and friends on the night of August 28 made me feel so very warm and loved. I knew I was terribly uncomfortable as I prepared for bed, but attributed it to the awful heat. I was quite surprised when I woke before dawn with contractions. It was so comforting to have you here! You sent for the doctor, who came promptly and together you delivered Francis Marion Cockrell before noon on August 29. Even though he is an early child, he has been so good from the very beginning.

Mr. Cockrell was so surprised when he got back from his trip to Shreveport to find that he had become a father again. He, too, is taking this baby much more casually.

Frankie is so different from Aurelia and Robert. He is a placid baby, content to lie in his cradle. Even at the age of only a few months, he observes the world with a look of wisdom. Robert has always been restless and mischievous. You have but to look at him to know he is planning something that will not meet with my approval. From the time of Robert's birth, Aurelia has been his protector and, sometimes, his nemesis! Because she reports everything he does! Most of all, I am happy that my children seem healthy and all are so bright. Aurelia started teaching herself to read a few months ago and now can sound out most words, needing my help only occasionally. Mr. Cockrell says she is just like her mother! Leave either of us alone for a few minutes, and we can always be found with a book in hand. I know that secretly he is pleased that we both are readers because he almost never comes home from any outing without new books for us. If I have any concern at all about Aurelia, it's that she assumes too much responsibility and could miss some of the fun of her childhood. I worry sometimes that I expect too much from her. Before long I plan to enroll her in school.

I still miss very much being out in the country on Mountain Creek. In October Margaret Bryan gave birth to a son, Alexander Luther Bryan, in "my" White House. I know she wishes, as I do, that our roles were reversed—she with her new son in her home here on the banks of the Trinity and I with our new son in the country. Perhaps one of these days that can happen for her. Alexander is talking about building a larger house for us, and we do need more room.

In February of this year his application to form the Dallas Bridge and Causeway Company was approved by the State Legislature, and he is now spending most of his time working toward the bridge he plans to build across the Trinity River. He has enlisted the services of W. C. Brown, a civil engineer from Houston, who has already provided tentative plans for the construction of the bridge early next year. I am excited about the building of this bridge because I think it will go a long way to alleviate the animosity that still exists among settlers west of the Trinity River who are still upset that they lost the election to have the county seat located on their side of the river. As original West-siders, both Alexander and I understand their chagrin. It pleases me that my husband is going all out in his efforts to connect the two sides peacefully. As we wait for early spring and warmer weather to begin actual construction, Alex has been busy relocating our sawmill nearer the site where the bridge will be constructed. This will result in a lot of time saved that would have been wasted in hauling the material.

Our county's growth is about to be greatly increased if a new endeavor by European entrepreneurs comes to pass. A Frenchman, Victor Considerant arrived in the area recently to purchase property for the founding of a "utopian" community in our midst. Among our citizenry there is consternation—both the promise of a great many new people to add to our population and concern over what they believe will be the founding of a socialist movement that is, as one put it, "the work of the devil in our midst." Most of all, there is great curiosity. My husband—who, as you know, believes that the "work of the devil" knows no religious boundaries—inclines toward the positive in this new development. He thinks that anything is good that brings new settlers with skills to enhance Dallas. I am in a "wait and see" attitude. From a Christian perspective, I am not eager to embrace any purely socialist movement. On the other hand, I have seen much good come from individuals who are deemed "savage " and "outcast" from the established norm. In looking back, I don't know whether I would have survived if an Indian woman had not been with me when Logan was born. Also, my life has been greatly enriched all along the way by people from other walks of life who have moved into my orbit.

But, a bit of the background: Two years ago, Considerant, whose "radical" ideas had exiled him to Belgium, made a trip to America seeking the ideal place to create a utopia based on the teachings of Charles Fourier, a social philosopher. Fourier founded a movement based on the idea that it was possible to create a community in which everybody cooperated rather than competed. I have no idea what caused Considerant to make a trip to Texas, but he came. During his visit here, the temperature was ideal. Flowers were in bloom everywhere (I can just see the bluebonnets spread like a blanket over hill and meadow!) The community was new, but growing. Everybody was excited about what was happening here and, no doubt, imbued him with the belief that everything good was possible, that what he saw during an ideal time was the norm all the time. The result was that he returned to Belgium and wrote a book entitled *Au Texas* in which he extolled the virtues of Texas, selling our area as the new "promised land" much in the same way that John Neely Bryan had extolled it in his earlier days. *Au Texas* was received with great enthusiasm by Europeans determined to leave the countries in which they felt bounded for the promised freedom of a new lease on life. They signed up in great numbers even as Considerant was forming a Colonial Association. He capitalized it for a million dollars and shortly it reached $300,000 with stock that bore a five per cent interest.

With this as capital, Considerant and Francoise Cantagrel, an agent for the company, came to buy land. Together they purchased 2,000 acres about three miles west of Dallas on a plateau and in a fertile valley. They called it La Reunion.

Mr. Cockrell says they could have done better in choosing a site for their "ideal" community. Unaware both of the condition of the soil and of weather vagaries, they chose unwisely, he said. The land, though pretty with its captivating hillsides rolling into lush-looking valleys, is a sight to behold in good times, but the soil is limey, my husband said, not arable, not given to the agricultural endeavors the future residents will find profitable. I do not know. I only know that we are all awaiting the arrival of our first La Reunion residents, which we hope to welcome in the spring of next year. I know that their coming will not be universally welcomed, but I intend to hold out the olive branch. I know how important it is to my husband that the growth of this, his new city, be inclusive, but also that I would never fail to hold out welcoming arms to anyone who joined our community in good faith that they would have a better life.

In the meantime, I am captivated by a couple of recently published new books. I can barely wait for your next visit to share with you *The Charge of the Light Brigade* by Alfred Lord Tennyson and *Walden, A Life in the Woods* by Henry David Thoreau. Mr. Cockrell brought both to me from his last buying journey to New Orleans. Some days, when I allow myself solitude and meditation, I am overcome with the educational and cultural advantages that are apparent in parts of the world removed from ours. When my husband returns from these soirees, I always probe to find out what is going on in the rest of the world, but we always wind up with him convincing me (or, trying to at least) that we are on the cutting edge of a world that is just awakening to its leadership possibilities. Why do women always acquiesce to the men in their lives who are so convincing that economic leadership is superior to everything else? I would not, for one moment, discount the advantages of money, but I am equally convinced that moral and spiritual leadership is just as important!

And, with every newspaper that comes into my life, I follow the world beyond my own limitations. The advances of transportation in our country amaze me. When we made our trip across country from Virginia here only ten years ago, our route was mostly through rough terrain where, oftentimes, nobody had gone before. We had to make our own way, often along trails that were rough-hewn if at all. Now, railroads are stretching for miles in every direction and with limitless miles yet to come. I am amazed that a rail now extends to the east from the Mississippi River and picks up again across the Mississippi westward. It has not reached us yet, but I am assured that it will and very soon.

Texas has suffered one of the worst drought seasons in its history. Within the past year, lacking rail transportation, ranchers from this area drove their cattle overland long distances with the first Texas longhorns reaching New York City. The papers tell us that Easterners were appalled at the tough and stringy meat from our famous longhorns. But, what could one expect after miles and miles of being herded on hoof from our part of the world with limited forage on the long trek cross country?

I am especially intrigued by the new electric light invention. Can you imagine flicking a switch and having a whole room light up?

On the political front, I read about the establishment of a new party, organized earlier this year (in February) in Ripon, Wisconsin, that combines the former Whigs and some disappointed Democrats, both of whom oppose the spread of slavery. It's called the Republican Party. I wonder what will be the outcome of this? And, I'm also glad to know that our government has approved a new agreement called the Elgin Treaty that establishes reciprocity including many trade agreements between ourselves and Canada, our neighbor to the north. Wouldn't it be wonderful if our dealings with other nations could be so amiable? I think of you and all those I hold dear. More later.

Your loving sister,

Sarah

1855

Dear beloved sister Jane,

Since I spent so much time in my last letter telling about the bridge that my husband planned to build across the Trinity River and, then about a settlement called La Reunion about to open up in our county, I begin this letter with an update on those two significant things.

The bridge is open! Since February 8, 1854, when the State Legislature sanctioned the building of the bridge by an almost unanimous vote, Mr. Cockrell has not let a day pass without making his dream come true. We have been fortunate for this project that the drought left the river bottom accessible to the construction of the bridge. It is located at the foot of Commerce Street across the river bottom. The circular saw mill, which my husband had earlier established further south along the banks of the river, was moved to the south side of Commerce Street so that lumber was readily accessible for the building. Red cedar trees were cut in the adjacent forests and hauled by ox teams to the mill where they were planed into lumber, making boards 10 by 16 feet. The boards were then notched, pinned together and filled with limestone rock. At either end of the bridge, piers were sunk into the ground to a depth where they rested on a slate foundation so that the bridge had a rock base. Abutments at both ends of the bridge were massed in such a way to give the greatest stability possible to the construction. The two-spanned arched bridge is further fortified in its very center by beams that reach far into the earth, also resting on a rock foundation. Our on-site engineer and superintendent, Andy Burtis, a local architect, was there every day during the construction to supervise everything. But, wouldn't you know? Not even the expertise of this professional kept Mr. Cockrell from being there almost every moment for the entire time it took to build the bridge.

Don't you know that the professionals he hired wish that Alexander would fade into oblivion and let them supervise the work they were hired to do? But, I learned a long time ago that he is a "hands on" person, and I am doing my best to learn his management skills in case I were ever to need them. I am especially pleased that he looked after the men he hired to construct the bridge. Since many of them were from other parts of the county and the state, he erected a two-story building near the site to house his employees.

In the waning days of last year (December 18, 1854, to be exact) the County Commissioners appointed a committee composed of J. W. Latimer, Ed C. Browder and Adam C. Haught to inspect the bridge. Their hasty approval was our Christmas present and the bridge opened to traffic.

The official opening was announced in an advertisement in the February 24, 1855, edition of *The Dallas Herald*: "The undersigned has completed and has now in complete repair the largest and most commodious bridge across the Trinity River opposite the town of Dallas ever constructed in the State of Texas. The bridge is entirely new, 520 feet long, weather boarded and covered with a substantial roof. The whole bridge was constructed of good substantial material and in a workman-like manner. It is on the main thoroughfare of travel from all the western and southern states and from Eastern Texas to the western and southern portions of Texas. This is by far the best and cheapest crossing on the Trinity River and immigrants and travelers will find it both more convenient and pleasant to cross at this point that any other. The charges are regulated by a charter from the State Legislature and are very moderate." It was signed Alexander Cockrell, Proprietor.

Now that the bridge is complete, the sawmill turns out lumber for the entire county, which is on a building boom. The sawmill, the first steam-circular mill in the county, is strategically located because a primeval forest of cedar, oak, ash and other timber native to this part of the country lies just to the east. The mill turns out all basic lumber needed for building. Finishing lumber is hauled in from the pine forests of East Texas.

News of the bridge has spread afar. From all over the western part of the county, men have brought their families to view and to marvel at it. Women and children, who almost never ventured into town from the outer edges now make the trip with their husbands and fathers. This has greatly enhanced business. Lucrative new businesses have sprung up and older ones have had to increase their supplies and add a greater variety in order to keep pace. More important, as the news has spread beyond our own boundaries, we've had a flow of people from other parts of the country moving here. The building boom requires architects, contractors, mechanics, carpenters, brick masons and investors. Factories and other businesses have followed. Hunters and trappers who have always gone to the Red River to sell and swap their wares are now coming to Dallas. A contract has been let to construct a new two-story brick courthouse on the Village Square, the tiny one now in existence long since having proved to be too small.

The view from where we live is both enhanced and diminished. A grove of beautiful trees still exists in the square. Wooden sidewalks have been constructed on each side of the street, all to the town's improvement, but the splurge of building is an eyesore. Almost everywhere you look, something is going up. The noise level is sometimes horrible with the sound of hammers and saws from early morning until dark. The building boom has also added to the lawlessness. The opening of new gambling halls and saloons lures a shiftless class of people. We've had brawls and fights right on Main Street.

Mr. Cockrell continues to talk about a much larger new home for us, but I've just about given up thinking it may happen because he is so busy building the town that he seems often to forget our personal needs. Naturally, I'd like to move back to the country, but I can't see any hope of ever doing that.

In my last letter, I mentioned that a group of Europeans had purchased 2,000 acres about three miles southwest of the village of Dallas to establish a utopian community. A Belgian, Victor Considerant came to Dallas three years ago and on his visit found ideal weather and went home and published a book, *Au Texas* extolling the virtues of our tiny community. He claimed that he had discovered a land where the climate was mild, the weather sunny and bright, and the terrain, similar to that in the grape-growing regions of France, ideal for growing fruits and vegetables. Tomatoes, he wrote, grew as large as watermelons in Texas.

Considerant had an immediate response from hundreds of Frenchmen and a few German, Swiss and Belgians. In April of this year the first few arrived. They were mostly the construction crew to prepare living accommodations for a much larger contingent that would come during the summer. The workmen laid out a philanstery, a series of buildings around a U-shaped park. The development is called La Reunion.

On paper, the idea sounded wonderful. Everybody would live in their own separate houses, share everything—the chores and the benefits, eat together in a central dining hall, buy their supplies from a central store, worship together, pray together and play together. When I heard about it, I told Mr. Cockrell it sounded like something I would like to try. He laughed. He said it would never work! He was right, but I don't want to get ahead of my story.

I shall never forget June 16, 1855. That's the day 200 bedraggled, road-weary settlers struggled into our downtown on their way to their utopia. Rumors that they were on their way from the Gulf Coast to Dallas preceded them, but we could not in a hundred years have imagined the sight that greeted us about noon on that early summer day.

Most were walking, many alongside ox-drawn carts loaded with household goods and implements. A few rode horses. Some of the smaller children and a few of the women rode in the carts. Their clothes were very strange, some ragged from their long walk and exposure to the elements. Many wore wooden shoes and the clatter along our board sidewalks could be heard, it seemed, for miles.

For all this, they seemed a cheerful bunch with bright and smiling countenances. Mr. Cockrell was one of the first to extend a handshake, but it turned out that nobody could understand a word they said and they certainly could not understand us. I am ashamed to admit that many, including me, stood in our doorways or along the city streets and stared. I am also ashamed that the greetings were not unanimously positive. A few men, most of whom were tipsy, lurched in open saloon doorways and jeered. Fortunately, the newcomers could not understand the words hurled at them— "furriner, socialist, communist" among the milder of the epithets, but they could understand the body language, and some of us did our best to shield them.

Shortly Maxime Guillot, the saloonkeeper and more recently owner of the first wagon-manufacturing yard, arrived and took over. He spoke their language and became the self-appointed interpreter. It was a joy to see him meet and converse with them, to speak his native language and introduce them to the rest of us.

Only a few women live in downtown Dallas, but it didn't take long for those of us here to rally and do everything possible to welcome the newcomers. Even while the greetings were going on, I asked some of the women to bring their children into the cottage where, through sign language, I offered them water and rest. Other women who lived near and around the city square did the same thing. We quickly put together the best we had of food and within two hours had spread a picnic on the city square in front of the courthouse. They seemed so grateful. It does not take words to convey hospitality and together that day we bonded.

Mostly, I am proud of us. And, I am certainly pleased about our new citizens who seem so gracious and appreciative. Mr. Cockrell says they are fine folks, but he wonders how they will survive because they are not used to the kind of lives we live here on the frontier. They are all from a more settled part of Europe, some aristocrats in the Old Countries. They are artists and craftsmen, writers, musicians and poets, jewelers, wine-makers and chefs. Some owned their own businesses back in France and Belgium. Among them is a botanist, a stonemason, a lithographer, a milliner and a tailor. How will they make their living in this land that is so undeveloped, that has no need of couturiers and hat makers and land-scape painters?

Before sundown, the rag-tag group that by that time felt like old friends to many of us, made it known that they must be on their way to their new home. Mr. Cockrell offered them free passage by ferry across the river. I was so proud of him! I am told that in the purple glow of the western sunset that June day, they claimed their dream. And I am glad for this beginning of their utopia that already is unraveling.

As they made their way through the forests, they looked to the south over a carpet of greenery and flowers—the last of the fading bluebonnets and the daisies toward the bluffs overlooking the fertile valley that would be their new home. Cattle grazed on the hillsides. They were a bit too late for the wild game—the buffalo, deer and antelope that only recently had bounded through the forests—for now, behind them was the start of a city of industry. But, for them, they envisioned the promise that had been projected in *Au Texas*. One among them put it this way: "Watch worn and weary, our cares flew away, and visions of happiness danced o'er our minds, and we reached the Utopia of our dreams."

What an ending this must have been for the 200 or so who made their weary way through our streets that June day. I was to learn later about a few of the hardships that they had endured to reach us. Promised that they would sail from their native countries to Galveston, they would find river transportation to take them up the Trinity River to Dallas. They arrived in the coast town to find that the Trinity was not navigable and they would have to find alternative ways to reach their destination. Already worn from a long sea voyage, they made their way, mostly by foot to Houston taking along supplies, some of which were unbelievable. One woman had brought 13 trunks loaded with finery! Where on earth would she wear her satins and laces in our frontier village? An elderly man had slipped on shipboard and broken a leg. Both he and the trunks were loaded on carts and shipped, as cargo, for three cents per pound from Galveston to Houston.

In Houston, unscrupulous tradesmen took advantage of them and sold them decrepit carts and oxen to haul their supplies to Dallas. Undaunted, the immigrants loaded whatever conveyances they could find with their supplies and headed north. It took them 26 days to travel overland, mostly by foot from Houston to Dallas. How they could arrive with their dreams still intact amazes me. As 1855 comes to a close, settlers for La Reunion continue to arrive, even while some of those who first came have moved out. Mr. Cockrell says that socialistic living cannot work. This country is new, raw, based mostly on survival of the fittest, and the European emigrants are people of culture, education and giftedness. But I predict that the talents they have brought to us will continue to enrich everybody here in the future.

I end this report of 1855 on a sadder note. Early in the year while we were having breakfast, a courier arrived to tell Mr. Cockrell that Mr. Bryan wanted to see him across the river. Alexander left immediately, one of the first people to cross the new bridge before it was opened to the public to meet his old friend on the west bank. For a long time Mr. Bryan had not been himself. As I mentioned earlier, my husband had done everything possible to awaken his friend to a new enthusiasm for the city he had founded, but to no avail. On that morning in February, Mr. Bryan told Alexander that in downtown Dallas he had shot and wounded a man who probably would not live. Mr. Bryan was certain that he would be arrested and said he could not bear to be locked up or endure a long trial. He gave my husband power of attorney, asked him to look after Margaret and the children, mounted his faithful Neshoba and rode west. We have not seen or heard from him since. It has been ten months. I feel so sorry for Margaret. She and her little ones are still in our house on Mountain Creek. Mr. Cockrell is doing his best to look after them and their interests. I can provide only care at this long distance, but I've asked my family who live nearby to drop in and keep an eye out for their welfare. As soon as possible, I want Margaret to have her house here in town back. She needs it!

So much has happened this year. I wonder what the next will bring and if I am able to withstand whatever prevails! Life moves on.

Your loving sister,

Sarah

February 1856

My dearest sister,

This year I am taking a new look at the purpose for these "records" for I realize I am writing more to myself than to you. I don't suppose it will make a lot of difference in the future, but I've always been a private person and hope that my words, written to give me perspective, will not be foisted off on others!

I begin on this cold February day with personal reflections.

I have just become aware that I am to be a mother again, a secret I am keeping in my heart until I sort through my own emotions. It is impossible to relate in words what my children mean to me. Maybe, because I had given up the thought of ever marrying until Mr. Cockrell came along, I think I value my children more than most women, who seem to take it for granted that they will be wives and mothers. Each one of mine has been such a precious gift. Losing our first-born was, as I have written in the past, almost more than I could bear. Then Aurelia came along and the world turned right side up again. How I love this little girl! She is now almost seven years old and is the delight of my life. Her father sees me in her, a reflection I cherish even as I point out that in so many ways she is her father's child. She has the same streak of creative genius that marks his existence even while she often exhibits the caution that compels me. I love watching her expand her world through reading and, quite often, through reflection. I come upon her in moments when she is sitting with an open book looking off into space as if she sees a world unfolding out there.

Robert is my happy child! He's never known a moment of solitude and is still only when he's asleep—and sometimes not even then as he flounces about in his bed. I think, perhaps, he had the most mothering of any of my children. When Robert came, we were still living at the White House on Mountain Creek. Even though he was a restless baby, he was an easy one, fitting into our lives effortlessly. I was not so stressed with housework and with managing the family books. Life was simpler. I could hold and nurse and sing lullabies in a way I had never done with the first two. Robert loved it. He has been a deeply affectionate child from the moment of his birth, simply absorbing my attention as if he is entitled. His father says I spoil him, which is probably true.

Frank is my wise child. Even in the cradle when he was only months old, he had the appearance of being all-knowing. He is not as outwardly affectionate as his older brother, but I see in him a depth of caring and, even at age two, a sensitivity to others that is lacking in his older brother. Frank is an original; he looks like nobody else in the family, as least as far as I can tell. There are so many unknowns in Alexander's past that I am not sure which of those ancestors may have passed on genes to my children. Perhaps there is something in his name, Francis Marion, that harks back to his father's family because Alexander named this little boy for males in his own family. Frank will, I am certain, grow up to be dependable and responsible, characteristics I treasure even as I hope he will not miss some of the joys that only childhood offers. His father says I must call him Frank so that he grows up to know his name, and stop referring to him as Frankie, which Alexander says is feminine!

As for the child I now carry in my womb, I do not know how I feel. There are moments when I am glad we are adding another child to the family, but there are also times when I think I cannot take on another. The care of three children and all the housework plus the increasingly full-time job of managing the business leaves me so tired that I often feel overwhelmed. Mr. Cockrell is gone much of the time and though he leaves good instructions to his foremen and workers when he goes away, I am left with the responsibility of making decisions when unforeseen problems arise. I still miss the country. Our house is too small and there's no escape. Where I once could take a book and seek solitude away from the hub-bub of a big family in a small house, this is now impossible. Beyond my front door is a world of clamor I abhor and, in any event, I cannot leave my children unsupervised. I often feel that the walls are closing in on me, and I need somewhere to escape. But where?

Later. Having read this over, I have a strong inclination to tear it up! But, I would be defeating my purpose, so I continue. . . .

My husband is the linchpin of my life. Even while I try to rein in his impetuosity, I know that he has brought me a wonderful world of excitement and adventure beyond anything I ever imagined possible. We are very good together. He is the wild schemer and dreamer, and I am the anchor. There are things I would like to change about him. I worry about his drinking. Until I met Alexander, I had lived such a sheltered life. Only through reading did I know about liquor and its possible consequence. It's not that Alexander drinks beyond his ability to know what he is doing, it's just that I've never been around anyone who imbibes in hard spirits. And, morally as well as intellectually, I oppose anything that diminishes our ability to think and act in a responsible way. To be honest, I think drinking is sinful. Recently he had a letter from Mr. Bryan, who is wandering somewhere out West, and I could not keep from reminding him that liquor has been the undoing of that visionary man. I suppose, in a way, I am scared because I see what is happening to Margaret Bryan, and it makes me angry that her husband has left her with so much responsibility. My husband got a far-away look in his eyes and clammed up, so I shut up. I know that if I push him too far he will stop confiding in me and might even find solace elsewhere. Even though he has responded well to my care and has come to depend on me both in his personal life and in the business, there is a core of him that is still private and untouchable. Most of all, he is an excellent provider and a wonderful father. I think he is as baffled at the joys of being a parent as I am.

I worry, too, about my husband's temper. I see little of it, but I hear things. His outbursts sometimes create problems that I am left to resolve. Just before he left the last time on a buying trip, he had such strong words with the supervisor of the office building being constructed on Commerce and Jefferson that the man was devastated. Although Alexander cooled down immediately, he left town without apologizing or saying anything to the supervisor about continuing the project. The poor man came to me later and asked if he was still on the payroll. My husband had not even mentioned to me that he and his employee had words, so I was totally in the dark. When he explained what had happened, I reassured the man as best I could, asked him to continue on the job and promised to speak to my husband when he returned. This I did, only to find out that Alexander did not think there had been any problem at all. He said he was just under pressure and blowing off steam. This is only the latest example relayed to me about Alexander's temper outbursts. I can't get through to him about his behavior because I don't want him to think I don't trust his judgment. He is very sensitive when he thinks I am criticizing and once said that I don't trust him and simply treat him like one of the kids. I bit my tongue to keep from responding that when he acts like a small child, my response is to treat him like one.

Now, having blown off steam of my own about my private life, I move on briefly to some of the things that are going on in the wider world.

Earlier this year, even as I was writing the words above, our town was legally incorporated. For a long time the leading citizens of the town have been talking about the need to incorporate and elect leaders, especially a mayor and policemen. Everything was just talk until early this winter when the son of one of our most prominent citizens was found cheating at cards. His victim, a shady character new in town, pulled out a pistol and shot the man. The man's watch deflected the shot and he suffered only minor injuries. But the incident, with all of it humorous aspects, served as the impetus to draw up the papers and quickly get them approved by the legislature to make Dallas a "city." Some city! We are still a little more than a frontier wilderness. But we are on our way!

March

John Beeman, Margaret Bryan's father died yesterday (March 12, 1856). Margaret's husband, John Neely Bryan, is still "missing" somewhere out West. Alexander has had another letter from him, but Margaret tells me she has heard nothing. The Beemans, among the area's first settlers, lived east of town where they proved to be very successful at farming. I hope that when his will is probated, Mr. Beeman will have left sufficient property and holdings to Mrs. Bryan that she can comfortably rear her children. She is still living at our White House but has been staying with her mother for the past several weeks during her father's illness and death.

As a way of keeping correct notes for posterity, I include here a copy of the letter Alexander received from Mr. Bryan:

Creek Nation
February 25th, 1856

Mr. A. Cockrell

Sir, I received your letter of December the 4th a few days since and I was very glad to get it. I have received from my wife only 2. I am living with Jesse Chisholm in the Creek Nation about 40 miles north of Fort Arbuckle. Chisholm is a half Breed Cherokee and an old friend of mine. I have done nothing yet to make a living. I have been out on the Plains 3 times to look for the gold mines but did not find them and I think I shall start again soon but will return hear (sic) again. I some times think it would be best for me to go into the western part of Texas and make me a new home for I want to see my Family and shall not be satisfied untill (sic) I am again with them. I wish you to write to me and advise me in regard to this course and let me know if it would be safe for me to do so or not. I was in a storm some time since and a tree blowed down on my horse Neshoba and broke him down in the legs since which time I have had to borrow.

I am surprised at Col. Stone and other attorneys of Dallas for turning against me and I shall meet them yet when they may least expect it and then I will know the reason why they do so. If I have any friends among the People of Dallas I want you to write who they are.

Give my love to my Wife and Children and say I will be with them as soon as I can. I shall depend upon you to act for me as well as you can and I hope to live to thank and pay you for it.

Give my Respects to your Lady.

I remain your friend always

JN Bryan

Write soon and direct to Fort Arbuckle Chickasaw Nation.

After I read the letter to Alexander, I could not help but have a few strong words to say about Mr. Bryan. Why is he writing to my husband instead of to his wife? The two or three times I have seen her since he left more than a year ago, she seemed so sad. I did not want to pry. But I finally asked her if she had received any good news from her husband, and she said she had not heard directly from him at all. He indicates that he has written to her. And there's always a possibility that the mail has not come through, but I doubt it. I don't know what kind of demons are disturbing him, but the clarity with which he communicates to Alexander indicates that he could most certainly write to his own wife and children. I wonder how he thinks they are being supported? He trusts Alexander to do what he can for them and doubtless he knows that her family will look after them. She continues to stay with her mother now that her father is gone.

Summer

It's the middle of June and already seeringly hot. I wonder how I am going to endure it when the really intensive heat arrives. Our living accommodations are so meager . . . the house so tiny. The dust and dirt are almost unbearable. The clatter of hooves and the rumble of wagons on the street in front of our cottage make it impossible for me to keep anything clean. It does not help that the child I am carrying is restless, as if he or she (I hope it is a she so that Aurelia will not be the only girl) is in a hurry to be born. S(he) could not want it more than I do!

Mr. Cockrell keeps talking about building us a bigger home, but he is also eager to build the hotel of his dreams, and I know which will take priority. He has just completed a two-story brick building at Commerce and Jefferson as office space for the new businesses that are moving into the area, and he is like a small boy with a new toy.

Since he is so seldom at home, he cannot imagine why I think these two rooms are too small. Very puzzled, he said to me "But, my dear Wife, you tell me that you have trouble keeping this place in order. What would you do if the space you desire were doubled or tripled?" I am so amazed at this kind of male thinking that I had no reply. Then, I thought about it and decided that the only way I am ever going to get a bigger home is to appeal to his masculine pride, so last night just before we fell asleep I pointed out that a man of his stature in the community needs to have a home and a family that is worthy of him. I also pointed out that it would be so good if we could move out of this house and let Margaret Bryan and her children have it back. I hope that these arguments sway him.

July

The long, hot summer continues. The children are almost as lethargic as I am. Mr. Cockrell is away from home almost all of the time. When he returns, he usually brings me a new book, probably thinking that will keep me from complaining! And, I admit, it often does. The only problem is that these books with their forward-thinking ideas give me ammunition for thinking beyond the boundaries of our frontier community. Then, I have to take the ideas up with him later. And he always is amazed that I, the homebound person in our union, should have opinions different from his when he is "out in the world" all of the time.

Privately, I think that Lucy Stone, the women's rights activist, had the right idea. When she married Henry Blackwell last year, she insisted on keeping her birth name and he agreed. I wonder if there is a woman in the world who ever really sees herself as Mrs. Married Name. I know I don't. Oh, for a time in the first flush of romance after the wedding, especially if you come to that state as I did after giving up all thoughts of ever being a wife, you see your new status as an affirmation of a new person . . . but then?

October

I am a mother again. Our fifth child, fourth son, was born on September 6. I cannot imagine that I had ever thought I wanted a girl. From the moment I held him in my arms, I knew he was exactly what I wanted. Mr. Cockrell was out of town at the time of this child's birth, so I took advantage of his absence to name his son for him. He is Alexander—no other name, no embellishments. I suppose when he is older for purposes to distinguish father from son we will need to call him Alexander II. When the other boys were born, my husband would not let me give any of them his name. He said one Alexander Cockrell was quite enough. There are times I think he is exactly right! But now we have two. May it be God's will that this child inherit only the best of Alexander I!

This baby fits into my heart and into our lives as if he has been a part of the family always. He is a good child, even though I forget every time how difficult it is to "launch" a new baby. I am bone weary tired. One of my sisters has been with me at one time and another and without them I could not have made it. Nursing the baby every three hours for the first month took most of my time. It seemed that I would just complete a feeding when it was time to stop and nurse him again. Now that he has decided he has come to stay, he is beginning to go for a bit longer periods of time between feedings. And I can do some of the essential chores that have either been done by my sisters or have been left undone. I read that I am supposed to just let everything go and rest when the baby rests. The "experts" who write this nonsense obviously have no children. You can't just let everything go. Other children have to be fed. Aurelia at 6, Robert at 4, and Frank at 2 still require more time than I have, and I feel guilty at having to neglect them.

In addition to the cooking, the laundry is a constant time drain. The baby runs through eight to a dozen diapers a day and since I have only two dozen, I have to do laundry almost constantly. I try to rinse the diapers as they are used, but sometimes this is impossible. Other chores often demand immediate attention and during the night I do not have the energy to do any washing. There is one bright spot. Mr. Cockrell provided a cistern at the back of the house shortly before Alexander's birth, the first time I've had water on hand. Always before I've had to wait for someone to haul it from the river and then boil it to remove the impurities before we could use it for drinking and cooking. Having water handy is a great luxury.

If I thought we were crowded in these two rooms with the three children, the addition of an infant has pushed me to the limit of my patience. I've told my husband that we must treat ourselves to the house he has long promised. He said he would get onto it right away. I will not let up this time until I have my house.

As much as I love this baby and as much as I now know we could never have done without him, I do not plan to have any more children. It is beyond me how I will accomplish this. But I know the limit of my endurance, and I've reached it. I am doing three full-time jobs now. I need a secretary, a housekeeper and a nanny. I've looked around the neighborhood for a young girl I can hire, but no one comes to mind. I have thought of asking one of my sisters to let one of their daughters move into town and help me, but there is no room for an extra person in the house. And, in a way, I would be taking on the responsibility for yet another child. I do think it would be wonderful to have a young niece here and provide her with a chance of schooling, which the girls do not have at Mountain Creek.

Having the daughters of some of the La Reunion families in our midst has added greatly to the educational possibilities of our community. And it's that which has made me think more and more that it is time for me to get more help with the housework and the children so that I can focus a bit more on schooling for Aurelia and our sons. I am happy to say that Mr. Cockrell is just as eager for our children—he says "our sons"—to be educated as I am. He has made me promise that if anything were to happen to him, I should enlist the help of the men in his own family back in Missouri and the assistance of Dallas leaders to see that the children get an education.

Your loving sister,

Sarah

Spring 1857

My beloved sister Jane,

With the greening of the earth, my energy has renewed and my spirits have soared. But oh how I miss the country where I would now have a garden well along its way and flowers blooming. Here in the noise and dust, I can but hope that before another year goes by, I will have a bigger house and the space for a garden.

The children are thriving. Baby Alexander, at seven months, is a roly-poly armful. Robert was five in January and so far shows no interest in learning to read or in simple mathematics. Frank at two and a half, may turn out to be the best "scholar" among our children. He will sit in my lap quietly for as long as I will hold him and listen to stories, and he tries to copy what Aurelia does when she sits at the table with her pencil and paper. I am so grateful for little things. The writing material—paper, pencils, pens and ink I so longed to own when I was a girl growing up—I now have in abundance. Mr. Cockrell provides stationery, books, ledgers and writing implements every time he comes home from a trip. Only those who have done without these simple tools can understand how special they are to me. Our children, of course, take them for granted.

I have written previously a little of the story of La Reunion. Now this update: At first their behavior, their clothing and their different languages made them suspect, and we were both intrigued and sometimes dismayed by them. As a colony, the experiment in socialistic living is a failure. Even as the legislature was approving their articles of incorporation last September, the group was falling apart. When the little band walked into Dallas two years ago, they were in high spirits despite setbacks at every step of their journey. Most determined to make a go of living here. At first, remember, we welcomed their arrival with a picnic on the city square. They loved it, but declined our invitations to tarry. Our initial hospitality diminished into hostility in some quarters when we learned that they were desecrating the Sabbath by throwing lavish parties with music and even dancing on Sunday nights!

Then, a few of the more daring Dallasites started venturing out to these parties and were warmly welcomed. Before long the gossip that they were sinful faded to tolerance and slowly to acceptance of their ways as "different." It was not long until a few of the most outgoing young swains were romancing the daughters of these "weird" colonists.

Victor Considerant was a disaster as a leader and manager. Upon arrival, the colonists found an office building for Considerant—a building for the making of soap and candles, a laundry, a forge, a chicken house, a cottage for the executive agent, a kitchen and a communal dining room and two dormitories of eight apartments each. The first rumblings of discontent came because Considerant had built for himself both an office and a home and had left the 200 others to share space in the two dormitories until they could build their homes, which some immediately set about doing. They were each allotted 66 by 132-foot lots. Mr. Cockrell says that Considerant quibbled over details leaving the overall management slighted. He disapproved of the trees they cut to build their homes, declaring them too small to make good lumber.

The communal dining hall sounded like a great idea, but it didn't work. On the assumption that men ate more than women and that women ate more than children, plans were drawn up, menus planned and food cooked to serve a set number of individuals. Food was apportioned to each table and passed around with people serving themselves. The first served took larger portions than the allotted amounts, leaving less for those as the platters were passed, sometimes resulting in no food at all left for those at the end of the line.

Hungry people are not happy people. Considerant advised them to work out the problem. They didn't.

Vague and lacking in experience for handling large groups of people, Considerant first pled, then threatened and then gave up. He was the first to leave the living experiment, declaring it a failure. He took his aristocratic mother-in-law, Madame Vigoureaux, a conversationalist who had espoused socialism to all who would hear, a brilliant pianist and a published poet to San Antonio and thence back to France.

Disgruntled, the colonists deserted the village. Some went back to their homelands. Many moved into Dallas, but even as they deserted their failing village, others arrived from Europe and moved in. Because of the lag in communication between our village of Dallas and the Old Country, new arrivals had no way of knowing what had happened until they arrived. In all 350 people, maybe more, made their home in La Reunion before its final demise.

Just as I predicted, the gifts and talents that the La Reunion residents have brought to Dallas are beyond measuring. Both in our homes and in our businesses, most of us have hired French teachers, or more correctly, we have exchanged talents. They teach us French and we teach them English. Our two existing schools have hired French teachers. Even Mr. Cockrell is learning French, as indeed he must! His expanding businesses make it imperative that he hire carpenters and wood finishers from La Reunion because they are by far the finest craftsmen in our midst. While they are making us aware of some of the finer things of life, I like to think that we are sharing with them our survival skills.

Mr. Cockrell hired a lovely French girl to help Aurelia with her language and to teach her music. When he brought a piano home from New Orleans I almost fainted. He said it was only temporary—that as soon as he completed the hotel, the piano would be moved into it. What to do in the meantime? As much as I wanted Aurelia to have it for her lessons and for practice, I could not see that we could possibly find a place for it in our two tiny rooms, but find it we did. With his practiced eye and making the impossible happen, Mr. Cockrell simply moved the beds together and had the piano placed along the wall where the bed used to be. Now we not only all sleep in what appears to be a communal bed, but we have only inches between the bed and the piano, barely space to crowd the stool in for Aurelia's lessons. I have to move the stool out every time I turn the covers down or make the bed in the mornings.

The boys are not eager to learn music. Bob (Mr. Cockrell says we must begin to call Robert "Bob" just as he taught me to say Frank instead of Frankie) would be outdoors all of the time if I would let him. When his father is not away from home, he follows every step he takes. I am not happy about this. The crude behavior of many of the builders and the swearing that Bob overhears leaves me trembling. Mr. Cockrell says to let him alone, it will toughen up the boy.

Frank is not much into music either, but he loves to draw and has asked his father to buy him some paints.

Baby Alexander just looks wide-eyed at all the activity around him. Mr. Cockrell says I must stop calling our youngest Baby Alexander. Since I insisted on giving him his father's name, how are we to distinguish the two? I tell him that since most everybody calls him either Mr. Cockrell or Alick, the baby can be Alexander.

Late Summer—July/August

Such a busy year this has been!

The men view the new two-story brick courthouse right in the middle of the square as a building of priceless beauty and efficiency. It is, no doubt, efficient for conducting county business because we outgrow one building after another. But to me it is an eyesore because it cuts off my view of the distant horizons, which were already sadly limited, and now there is another monstrosity. Within the past few months a double log jail has been built alongside the courthouse. If I were not already nervous about having my children so close to the lawlessness of this community, I can now point right outside my front door and see where the criminals are locked up. I suppose that is better than having them roam the streets although they also roam the streets. The Commissioner's Court in February passed a resolution requiring vagrants who are locked up there to be released daily to work on building roads.

Just as he predicted, the new business building Alex opened last year on Commerce at Jefferson is attracting a lot of new businesses to town.

A new general merchandise store, Hirsch & Shirek, was the first to move in. The business took up the entire main floor of the two-story building. Hirsch & Shirek moved here from Hopkins County. Since Weck and Lucy Latimer moved here eight years ago from Red River County and started publishing *The Dallas Herald,* a number of businesses from that northeast corner of Texas have moved to Dallas.

John C. McCoy rented office space on the second floor of the building. Mr. McCoy came here as the attorney for Peters' Colony, but when it ran into trouble, he opted to remain. Mr. Cockrell hired him a couple of years ago to manage our legal business, and he's been indispensable. Alexander will listen to him much better than he listens to any other person or me. I like Mr. McCoy, who seems to understand me and my contribution to our business. When Mr. Cockrell is out of town, Mr. McCoy has several times consulted me about what is going on.

We do need legal counsel! Mr. Cockrell has begun construction on the hotel he has long dreamed of building. I have never seen such plans! It is a brick building, three stories tall—our city's first skyscraper, a new word in my vocabulary meaning "reaching far into the sky!" He hopes to have it open next year.

When he told me that he was drawing up final plans and beginning to hire the construction crew to build the hotel, I convinced him that we had waited as long as we could for the house he has long promised. So we are into that at the same time the hotel is going up. It took some persuading, but at last the foundation is laid. Though it's not on my ideal location, the southwest corner of Commerce at Broadway, I am so grateful to be getting a house after all this time that I was willing to compromise. Mr. Cockrell insists that he needs to remain right in the thick of things downtown to oversee everything. I didn't respond to that "reasoning," but I wanted to point out that he is not the one in the "thick of things." I am. And our children are. He is away so often on business and for long, long stretches of time that he has no idea of how claustrophobic I am all penned in here and surrounded by increasingly tall buildings.

Last week the *Herald* printed a story requesting books and/or money to establish our first public library. I am delighted. I tucked a few small bills into one of my much-loved books and took it right over. Volunteers will run the library. I wish I had time to help. It would be such fun. I imagine that some of the beautifully educated French girls and women will help to open and run the library.

The expansion of public education and the establishment of a Lyceum are two very important additions to our town and prove that we not only are growing in numbers but are making an effort to become an intellectual and a cultural center as well. The state gave us $3,710.42 in taxes this year toward public education, and we were able to hire two new teachers. Although our school terms are very short, and our teachers are required to handle too many subjects, this is a beginning that I applaud.

The Lyceum is another matter. Created by Mrs. Latimer and two other ladies, it holds public speeches and debates, recitals and musicals, and even had one poetry reading. It meets in the women's homes, and once Mr. Cockrell gave them a room on the second floor of the business building for a program. I would dearly love to attend these programs, but so far have been able to make it only once when Aurelia was asked to play and sing with a group of children.

Only a few men attend the Lyceum programs, but the women, starved for intellectual stimulus, crowd in. The one time I went I saw almost all of the women who live near downtown Dallas, some I knew from church, several I knew slightly and others I had only read about. I would like so much to know several of these women better. I've known Mrs. Latimer better than most of the others because she is Aurelia's music teacher and publisher of the *Herald*. We've chatted several times when I go by the paper to drop off the ads for Alexander and I find her delightful. She has become a principal leader in creating educational and cultural programs here.

I met Mrs. Alexander Harwood and her beautiful sister, Miss Juliette Peak at the Lyceum. They are the daughters of Mr. and Mrs. Jefferson Peak who live east of Dallas. Instead of farming, Mr. Peak is developing his property into a residential area. He's laying out streets and naming them for his several children—Carroll, Worth, Junius, Wallace, Sarah Ann, Flora—and others. Several families have bought property from Mr. Peak and are building homes in the area. It's a part of the building boom that is so profitable for us. Mrs. Harwood is young, married to Alexander Harwood, one of our county officers. She has a year-old son. Miss Peak is the town beauty.

Mrs. William Cochran is another woman I would like to know better, but I'm sure she's even busier than I am. She moved here with her family the year before we did and lives north of town where she's started Cochran Chapel Methodist Church. She named it for her husband, one of the first men elected to the state legislature from Dallas County, who died four years ago, leaving her with six children. The oldest is now 18 and beginning his studies to become a doctor.

I'd like to be a part of the Lyceum, but I'm just too overwhelmingly busy to give much time to "cultural enrichment," a term that made Mr. Cockrell laugh when he overheard me using it. He said "We are as rich as anybody in town and going to be more so. Why would you need further enrichment?"

I do wish that Mr. Cockrell would be more careful of his retorts of this sort. I know he is so excited about all his projects, and like a kid with a new toy, holds nothing back. But I am aware that he is making himself unpopular in some circles. I hear things. It is no secret that he intends to be the richest man in town, if he isn't already. His excitement in sharing his ideas often comes off to others as bragging and that coupled with his abrasive way of handling employees makes him seem to be unfeeling and even mean to those who do not know him well. Bob reported an incident recently that gives me cold chills. Against my better judgment I sent Bob down the street to a local saloon to deliver an important message to his father and tell him that dinner was on the table. Mr. Cockrell was drinking with his buddies and didn't notice his son hovering in the doorway. He and another man were in a terrible argument that would have likely wound up in a fight if Alexander had not spotted Bob and immediately calmed down.

The children and I see the softer side of my husband, but others don't. He won't allow it. Like most men, and especially those who have had to raise themselves to survive for most of their lives, Mr. Cockrell honestly thinks that being kind and gracious is a sign of weakness. He can be generous to a fault, but often he appears cold and unyielding to others. Once, I even overheard him described as "cruel" when I walked into Hirsch & Shirek to pick up a new pinafore for Aurelia and overheard a couple of women shoppers. I pretended not to have heard, but I could tell by their flustered behavior that they were not convinced. I've given a lot of thought to how to approach my husband and convince him that he is making enemies. I've thought of talking it over with Mr. McCoy, but can't bring myself to "air our dirty family linen in public."

People can't seem to tolerate the good fortune of others, no matter how hard they work to achieve it, and the very people you most help are often the first to turn on you. I suppose that's because nobody likes to be beholden. It seems to me that the closer the connection, the more likely we are to have people turn on us. Maybe it is human nature to dwell on the bad rather than the good in others. There's no doubt that prosperity in others creates contempt in the recipients. And I am beginning to believe it. The writer, Edmund Burke, said it most succinctly: "... they will turn and bite the hand that feeds them."

Even our beloved friend, Mrs. Bryan, held herself at a distance when I went out to Mountain Creek Lake recently to see her. My reason for the visit was two-fold: I wanted to tell her that as soon as our home is complete, she and the children must move back into their downtown cottage. I know she wants this. Mr. Bryan is still "missing." He's been gone now for more than two years. If he corresponds directly with Mrs. Bryan she never mentions it, but he writes to Alexander now and then. The last letter was but a note inquiring about his "business," but in her husband's handwriting, and I thought she would want to have it. I'm sorry I did not keep a copy. Margaret even seemed reluctant to invite me in—and this to my beloved White House home!—but warmed considerably later. Even so, I had to carry the conversation. Her burdens seemed too heavy to participate. She thanked me for the offer of returning to Dallas to live in her cabin. I think she misses it as much as I miss the White House. But she seemed ill at ease and when I gave her the letter, she put it in her apron pocket and said she would read it later.

I have finally ventured out to take a major role in the establishment of a new business, albeit with the sanction of my husband and with my brother as a partner. Earlier this year my brother, James Horton, and I entered into partnership to open a gristmill at Eagle Ford. James is the partner in control and the day-to-day manager. I am the "silent" partner. With Mr. Cockrell's blessings (he said it was time I decided to "go out on my own") I provided most of the capital. I decided since I am the business manager for everything we own that I should learn how to manage something of my own.

Heaven only knows where this will lead. I pray not astray!

Yours for now,

Sarah

1858

Dear Relatives and Friends,

My world has collapsed.

I am writing this in the winter of my life. Just as this is the winter season, the last week of December 1858, I must detail some of what has happened. I have kept notes, both personal and financial all year and now two days after Christmas and before a new year dawns, I recall the way my year has unfolded.

We moved into our new home in late January. It was a clear, sunny day, unseasonably warm, reminiscent of that day in November 14 years ago when I first arrived here. Even though we were moving only a very short distance from the cabin we occupied for the past five years, it took us most of the day to load and unload our possessions. I had limited the furnishings in the cabin to the bare essentials, simply because the living space was so crowded that I would have had no room at all for the family of six if I had indulged myself in the beds and dressers and armoire of my dreams. But, when I started to pack, it seemed everything multiplied! I could not imagine that so many things had been crammed into so small a space. It took me a full week to pack everything, and it took three wagonloads to move us. Mr. Cockrell was at the cabin supervising the loading, and I was at the new house directing furniture placement. The children were so excited!

Even though I had watched the construction of this house from the first moment the foundation was laid, I could not have dreamed how much I would enjoy it and appreciate it. When I mulled over its history, I was astonished. It is located on the exact spot where Dallas Founder John Neely Bryan built his first log cabin, the one that was home to Margaret Bryan when she was a bride. Located on the southwest corner of Commerce Street at Broadway, the house is Greek Revival style. It is two stories and constructed of the finest lumber. When Mr. Cockrell was convinced that it was time to build our home, I think he personally chose each board. Downstairs a small covered porch gives way to a wide entry hall and to one side the living room, sitting room and, at the end of the hallway opening onto a large enclosed and covered back porch. To the right as you enter the front door is the bedroom which I have claimed as mine and Mr. Cockrell's, with a separate small room adjoining it which is our office. There I can keep an orderly file of both our business and our family papers. When I looked at the house plans, I insisted on this addition. Beyond the office is the dining room and back of it the kitchen, again opening onto the back porch which stretches the full length along the back of the house. Having the kitchen within the house deviates from popular norm in this region. For reasons of safety and temperature (the summers are sweltering here) kitchens have always been located in a separate room at the back of the main structure.

From the central hall inside the entryway at the front, a stairway ascends to the second floor, which has a small balcony above the downstairs porch. Aurelia claimed the upstairs room on the right facing

Broadway. Across the hall to the left is the room I have designated as "guest room" because it will be the easiest for me to reach and clean when we have visitors. Back of it is the bedroom that will be shared by Bob and Frank. They complained, each claiming that there were enough rooms for each to have his own and adding that they would be glad to move in together when we had company. I prevailed because I must have one room that I can keep clean and ready for a guest at any time. I couldn't do that if I had to move a boy out each time someone came and spend a whole day getting the room ready for the guest. Boys create an amazing amount of clutter, and I thought it best if I put the two clutterers together. I do have misgivings because Bob and Frank have such different personalities and interests.

Back of Aurelia's room is the nursery. I thought I would have liked it at the front of the house (where Aurelia's room is) so that I could reach it handily, but as it turns out, the location is ideal. When I reach the top of the stairway, I turn right and the doorway to the nursery is right there! Alexander is our only child still in the nursery, and he won't be for long. At age two, he is showing his independence far faster than any of the other children. He quit nursing before he was a year old and tossed out a bottle before he was two. He eats with us at the table— sometimes so messy that I wish I were still feeding him—consuming foods far beyond what his older sister and brothers ate at his age. When his father is at home, Alex sanctions the appetite and consumption of food of his youngest son and namesake. But, I don't. I just want him to be a wonderful little boy who grows up to fit into this family.

After we moved, Mr. Cockrell left almost immediately on a buying trip to Shreveport, thence to New Orleans, then to Galveston and back to Dallas. He said he would be gone for no longer than six weeks, but he was away for two months, from January 20 through March 21. By the time he returned, I had everything in the house in place. Mr. Cockrell's trip was primarily to buy furnishings for the hotel, but he told me to add what we needed for our new home and I did. It was good to have new bedding, storage chests and even a small desk for myself. I will keep the trunk, which has been my repository for all our business and personal files, but it is getting crammed.

Even while we were in the process of moving, Margaret Bryan was packing to leave the White House on Mountain Creek and return to her beloved cabin which we were vacating. The day after we left, she and her children arrived back home with their household furnishings. Even though I was still overwhelmed with getting things in place and seeing my husband off on his trip, I took the time to drop by to see her and take a pound cake as a welcome back present. She seemed far more cordial than at our last meeting. I know how difficult life must be for her, especially since she lost her father who was her stalwart supporter after Mr. Bryan went away. I understand that Mr. Beeman's will is soon to be probated and hope that he has left something for his daughter.

When another letter arrived for Mr. Cockrell from Mr. Bryan a week before my husband's return, I was tempted to take it at once to Mrs. Bryan, but decided I must not because I had no idea of the contents. I have since shared it with her. He wrote:

Jamestown Cal.
January 2, 1858

To Mr. Alex Cockrell

Sir, I received a letter from you which was written in June last and I answered it at the time of reception, but I have not heard from you since. I received one from my wife at the same time and have not received any since. What can be the cause is a mistery (sic) to me. But I continue to write to my ...by every mail. I hope you will write to me and let me know the cause if any. I do not write to anyone at Dallas except you for I cannot place confidence in any (of) the rest.

I am not able to come home yet but as soon as I can I shall start home on the mail route from hear to El Paso. I have worked harder than I ever did in my life but it take all I can make to pay my expenses and every one hear (sic) that I am acquainted with is in the same situation. I sometimes get out of heart and conclude I will not be able to see my wife and children again.

The gold mine is worked out so much that men can make but little now and still a man's expenses is the same (as) they were before the mines failed. I am mining now but the watter (sic) freeses (sic) up and I can make nothing. You could not believe that this was in this country and hundreds of them that were almost on the starve, but such is the case. And there is but few but what eates (sic) up at night what he makes in the day. It is the hardest country I think on earth.

I shall be on the way as soon as I can make the money. I shall not remain hear (sic) one day longer than I can help for I want to see my wife and children. When I mention that is the cause for my coming home you know I am in ernest (sic). I want you to see my wife. Tell her what I have written and say to her that it is not my fault I do not come home.

Give my love to my wife and children. My respects to Mrs. Cockrell and any others that you know to be my friends if I have any about.

I remain your friend

John N. Bryan

P.S. If you write direct your letter thus:

Col. John N. Bryan,
Jamestown, California.

If letters come hear (sic) after I leave I have friends hear that will send them too me wherever I go. I do not want any more sent to Stocton (sic) for their is to many their that know me. J.B. Bryan[5] was their (sic) not long ago.

JNB

When I gave the letter to Mrs. Bryan, she said she had been writing to her husband, but had received no letters in reply. She asked if she might keep the letter. I told her Mr. Cockrell had asked me to bring it back because he wanted Mr. McCoy, our lawyer to see it. I promised to return it to her soon. I suppose she is comforted by seeing her husband's handwriting, but I cannot understand how any woman can continue to be so loyal and faithful to a man who has been gone for more than three years.

Only a few days before Mr. Cockrell arrived home, the town elected A. M. Moore as its new Marshall. I had a bad reaction when I heard about it because Mr. Moore owed us money that Mr. Cockrell had not been able to collect, and I knew my husband intended to have it out with him when he returned home. Having it out with a private citizen is one thing; locking horns with a lawman is entirely different.

After being away for two months, Alex spent a full week following his return in finding out what had been happening in our business. First, we sat down together, and I showed him all of the records I had kept and gave him an update on our financial status, which are considerably less than before he left Dallas on this trip. He spent lavishly for furnishings for the hotel, far beyond what I would have thought proper. He had purchased a lavish crystal chandelier to hang in the hotel entryway and a grand piano among other furnishings. He was like a kid when he told me

---

[5] J. B. Bryan was a brother of John Neely Bryan; he was a dentist.

about the piano, saying he thought the one he had previously purchased for the hotel was too small and, besides, since we had our new house Aurelia should keep it to practice her music lessons. When I tried to find out exactly what he had bought, he waved his hand in dismissal, said there would be five wagonloads coming soon. I could stand alongside as the merchandise was unloaded and make careful records of everything. His wagon boss, Rudy Horst, was in charge of getting the five wagonloads home safely. I knew that was exactly what I must do. To be so good at business, Mr. Cockrell was a disaster as a businessman!

After hearing my report and successfully evading my probing for answers, Mr. Cockrell set off to see for himself how our various businesses were faring. He checked in with the foreman at the lumberyard and, to hear him tell it, was convinced we'd soon make a fortune. He wasn't as optimistic about the brickyard, said we were only breaking even there, though my books clearly showed we were beginning to make a profit which would increase as soon as people learned that brick, though costing more, would be much more substantial in the long run. He checked in with the office building and was delighted that since he left, I'd rented space on the second floor to Mr. Gougenant for his photography studio. He stopped by and visited with Berry Derrit who he'd left in charge of the toll bridge and the ferry. But he spent most of his time with the foreman of the hotel, which was his grandest dream. He was convinced that the hotel would enhance the image of Dallas and bring travelers and traders here for both business and pleasure.

He was in fine humor. Things had gone so well in his absence that at dinner that night he told Aurelia and the boys that he planned to go away more often and for longer periods of time because I ran the business better than he did. When Aurelia burst into tears, both Bob and Frank looked at him with wide-eyed disbelief and baby Alexander followed his sister in sobs. Their father hastily retracted, assuring them that he was only kidding.

April came. In all of the rest of my life, I will replay that morning. We had an especially close connection the night before. After the almost-fiasco at dinner on Friday night, Alex had played with the children until they were tired and then left for a conference with Mr. McCoy. I begged him not to end the evening at a saloon, but of course, he did. He came home totally sober and said that on the morrow he would complete the rest of the unfinished business so that he could go on to greater things. When I asked what that meant, he said he would confront Mr. Moore and demand that the debt owed us be paid. Since Mr. Moore was a public servant, he not only had the money to pay, but he owed it to the citizenry to be free of past obligations in order to uphold the law.

I listened quietly and then, very gently, I thought, admonished him to be careful. Mr. Moore was young, a newly named law-enforcement officer, determined to prove his mettle. I told him a bit about the gossip I had heard in his absence—that the man was "trigger happy," in a hurry to take over Dallas and not interested in the common good but only in what profits he could make. He responded that my concerns were not valid, that he would meet Mr. Moore, have a friendly talk with him and be done with it. He said Mr. McCoy had told him how to handle the situation, and I was not to worry. He even promised me that when he went out the next morning, he would leave all firearms behind. We had a very special evening with each other.

Saturday morning dawned bright and beautiful. The children were all abed, and I allowed them a rare opportunity to sleep in. I got up before dawn, lighted a candle and checked, one more time, over our business obligations. Then, I went to the kitchen, fired up the stove and waited while reading a book of poetry by Henry Wadsworth Longfellow that Mr. Cockrell had brought to me from his recent journey. I didn't know why, but I was almost moved to tears by two of the lines from the poem "Santa Filomena" which read: "Lo! In this house of misery A Lady with a lamp I see." It was written to honor Florence Nightingale, that beautiful nurse who undertook the most horrendous circumstances to nurse the war wounded. But it spoke to me.

By the time Mr. Cockrell came down to breakfast, I had made spoon bread and set it on the table with butter and molasses. He paused to inhale the fragrance of the cooking sausage and to give me a hug—rare, but so very special because of its rarity. My disposition soared even as I fried eggs and set the whole in front of him. He asked, "Now, what am I going to do for an excuse when I meet Mr. McCoy and Nicholas Darnell for breakfast?" and I responded, "Anything except stop by the local bar for a quick one!" He laughed.

I was so surprised, and so pleased later when I went into our bedroom to set it in order, that his ammunition belt and firearms were lying there. I straightened and made the bed, cleaned and cleared the bedroom and laid the firearm belt neatly across our new dresser. By that time the children were beginning to stir, and I went downstairs to see that they were fed and dressed and ready for the day. I don't know why, but I scrubbed each one and had them put on their "Sunday clothes." And, all the while, I struggled with a feeling of doom that would not leave me.

During the morning, I completed my household chores and cleaned the kitchen. I loved keeping the new home sparkling. Not since living in the White House had I enjoyed so much space. At noon when Mr.

Cockrell had not come home for lunch, I fed the children, sat down with my darning and worked for a couple of hours, then decided to take the children with me and go up to Hirsch & Shirek for groceries. When I returned somewhere before four and five that afternoon, I went into the bedroom to put away my bonnet and reticule and my heart sank. The ammunition belt was gone. So was the shotgun that my husband kept stored above the door.

I tried to keep busy, folded a few pieces of clothing I'd laundered earlier and put dinner on. There was a knock at my door and even before I could get there, Mr. McCoy was opening it. It took one glance. His friends had brought my husband home on a makeshift stretcher. That was my first thought, even though the "stretcher" was one of the boards from our lumberyard. I could not take in then, and I haven't been able to remember since, who was there or what they said. All I remember is that Mr. McCoy said Dr. McDermitt had been alerted and would be along soon. I lent over my husband. He was conscious, but barely. He looked up at me and said:

"Educate our children."

Nobody can know what those three dying words spoke to me. "Educate," he said, he who had scoffed at "classroom learning" even while he hired the best tutors and musicians he could find to give our children lessons. "Educate," he said, even when he laughed at me for my reading and book learning and said he was so smart that he did not need an education to be "schooled" in the most basic of life's lessons. "Educate," he said, "*our* children, not mine, not yours, but *ours*." That, I shall carry in my heart forever. He had promised me from the beginning of our marriage that we were partners, but because of his rearing and conditioning where he'd always had to be a lone survivor, responsible for himself, he usually spoke about what "I" have done, what "I" own.

My husband died.

We had been married 10 and a half years, 3,869 days. He left me with the greatest treasure any woman could want: Four beautiful children—Aurelia, 8; Robert, 6; Frank, 4; Alexander, his namesake (oh, how glad I am, I named this child for his father!), 2, and our first-born, Logan, buried at White House Ranch, dead as an infant, that I will never overlook.

I still have to sort out what happened. I know that the morning started with Mr. McCoy, Mr. Nicholas Darnell and Mr. Cockrell meeting to talk business. Alexander wanted to engage Mr. Darnell to manage the new hotel.

At some point during the morning my husband found Mr. Moore and they had words, but parted without my husband collecting the debt.

Nobody knows what happened after that. It depends on which person you believe or what stories you listen to. I think I have heard them all.

Dr. McDermitt looked at his watch, shook his head, looked at me and said, "I am so sorry." It was the end of a wild but wonderful time that had taken me from a quiet, often boring maiden through a tempestuous wife and mother, the end of an era. I could not know that it was the beginning of a new one.

Mr. Cockrell was dead.

My life, as I had envisioned it, was over.

What now?

It depended again on which voices I listened to, but I knew, even in my state of numbness and inertia that only I could answer the questions threatening to overcome me. I had our children. I had the businesses that he and I had started together. And I had my husband's trust that I would carry on. There was nobody but me. I had no time to grieve. I had to take charge.

I thanked the friends who had brought Alexander home. I had them lay him out on our dining room table, the only space long enough. I dismissed them. Said I wanted to be alone. Held his hand and prayed. Cleansed his body. Dressed him in his best suit. Asked two of the Negroes who worked for us to help me move him to the living room sofa. Called our children to come and say good-by. Sent for Mr. Gougenant and had his picture made. Dismissed everybody. And stood alone in our new home in my grief. At some point soon after these basic needs were completed, Reverend Smith arrived. I was grateful. I knew I must plan a funeral. People began arriving, bringing food and faltering words. Nobody knew what to say and that was all right. I wouldn't have known how to respond. My sisters came and took over greeting friends, employees and relatives. My sister-in-law brought the dress and the bonnet she had worn when her husband died, I was vaguely aware to be grateful for the bonnet that would shield my face from curious on-lookers.

My immediate reaction was to take my husband back to the White House ranch and bury him beside Logan, but Reverend Smith pointed out that the distance would make it difficult for many people to attend, so I agreed to bury him in Pioneer Park Cemetery near downtown Dallas, within walking distance of our new home. Alexander was one of five men, including the Rev. Smith, who had only the year before on March 21, 1857, deeded three acres of their property for the cemetery.

Later that evening when all of the people had departed and the children were in bed, I lit the new kerosene lamp that Mr. Cockrell had brought home from New Orleans only a few days before, opened my trunk and laid everything out on my new desk. I spent the rest of the night going over our finances. I stopped only once to refill the lamp with kerosene and relight it. A new day was dawning when I finished. I knew almost to the final penny what we owned, what we owed, what bills I must immediately pay, what debts I might collect and which might have to be written off. Whatever else I did, I knew I must collect the debt from Mr. Moore because I had learned by then from Mr. McCoy and others that he had fired the shots that killed my husband.

I knew I had to reassure our employees that the businesses would go on, not the way Mr. Cockrell would have managed them, but that they would continue to have jobs and that I would be able to meet our payroll. I sent messages to the manager of the lumberyard and the brick yard and the foreman of construction of the hotel to see me the day following the funeral. I assured Berry Derrit that he was still in charge of the toll bridge and of the ferry and that anyone coming to the funeral from west of the Trinity should be passed free of charge.

Many people have commented about my composure all during that horrendous time. I am told that I took my little children by the hand and walked out of the funeral services and took over the business, but that is melodramatic. The truth is I was in a trance, doing what had to be done.

When the weekly *Herald* was published the next Saturday, April 11, it carried a tiny item in the middle of page 3.

FATALE RECONTRE

On Saturday evening last, a distressing and fatal recontre occurred in this place between A. M. Moore and Alexander Cockrell, two leading citizens of town, resulting in the death of the latter. Both parties were armed with a double barreled shot gun and revolver, and Moore at the time was attempting to arrest the deceased, under a writ for violating a corporation ordinance. Eight shots from Moore's gun took effect on deceased, most of them in the lower portion of the abdomen. He survived about an hour and a half. As the whole affair will undergo judicial investigation we forbear making any comment or from stating the circumstances in detail, as we do not wish to prejudge or to prejudice the case one way or the other in advance of the trial. Moore was admitted to bail in the sum of $5,000. We will only add that this unfortunate occurrence has thrown a gloom over this community. It is a distressing affair that cannot be too much deplored.

Immediately after the funeral, I hired Mr. McCoy to prosecute Mr. Moore. The story Mr. Moore told was that my husband was drunk and rowdy and that he was only doing his duty in trying to arrest him. Others say the two men had almost come to blows in their earlier encounter, and Mr. Moore had challenged Mr. Cockrell to a duel. Whatever the circumstances, there was no excuse for what happened.

I wrote to Mr. Cockrell's family in Missouri as soon as I could get my wits together after the funeral. His brother (half brother), Francis Marion Cockrell, for whom our Frank was named *had* read law and was practicing in Johnson County Missouri. I desperately needed him to come and assist Mr. McCoy in the prosecution. This is a portion of the letter I received in response:

Warrensburg, Johnson County, Missouri
May 9, 1858

Mrs. Sarah Cockrell
Dear Sister,

Your letters of April 10th and 11th were received two days ago. I was deeply pained to receive the bad news of Brother's death. So untimely and so foully caused. I truly sympathize with you and your children in the sad bereavement and loss of a kind husband and father. And, may God help you to bear this heavy loss with Christian fortitude. And God will be the God of the widow and father of the fatherless and will never forsake you...

I have no doubt from the statements in your letter that Moore killed him willfully and premeditatively without any cause . . . but from the fact that Brother had been arrested and fined and had a gun in his possession and Moore was ordered by the Mayor to take him, and in pursuance of that order shot him, it would be very difficult according to our laws to convict him of murder in the first degree, which would be hanging. I should advise you to do everything you can to have Moore punished with the very heaviest punishment that can be inflicted upon him under the laws of Texas.

Upon his trial, show Moore's former hatred and ill will towards Brother, his threats and vows that he would kill him and that he sought this opportunity and means to execute his threats . . . and in fact did kill him willfully . . . though the shooting was done under the color of authority. . . .

> *Employ able lawyers to prosecute or assist in prosecuting him ...See that his murderer reaps no benefit from his death.... I would be very glad to come and see you and attend the trial if possible, but I do not now think I can come. The health of my wife is very bad at this time. We have two children, both boys, the oldest named John Joseph is three tomorrow, the other William five months old the third of the month.*
>
> *We are now living in Warrensburg. I am practicing law in partnership with a Mr. Charles O. Sullivan.*
>
> *Write as soon as you get this letter—write fully and all about the business, when Moore's trial comes off, what will probably be done with him, how you are getting along, whether you have friends and relatives who will protect you and your rights and see that Moore is punished.... Write about your children. I am always glad to hear from you....*
>
> *May God bless you and your children and help you to bear the loss. Trust in Him for He is a friend that will never leave you or forsake you.*
>
> I remain your affectionate Brother,
Francis M. Cockrell

For a few days after the funeral, business in Dallas almost came to a standstill while everybody speculated what would happen now that the man who employed almost half of the town's population was gone. This is not my opinion alone. John H. Cochran, our town's most outstanding chronicler told me, "Alexander was the most energetic and enterprising man living in the town of Dallas. His unfortunate and untimely death has caused all much needed work to cease."

Nobody understood that I would not let the work cease. They did not think that a mere woman could carry on—and when they began to understand that was exactly what I planned to do, many were appalled. Some of the town's leaders—all male, of course—advised me to sell out and get out. Even those who claimed they had my best interests at heart, including a few in my own family, told me that it was unseemly for a woman to dirty her hands with business. I doubt that I could have found half a dozen people in the entire town who supported my decision to follow through on as many of my husband's visions as I possibly could. Because I had been so deeply enmeshed in the business end of his enterprises, I knew that good intentions would not get the job done. I prayed for the physical strength, the mental tenacity and the moral fortitude to guide me through.

The trial was a farce. Even after it was brought into evidence that Mr. Cockrell fell on the south side of Commerce Street between Houston and Broadway in broad daylight and that he was not aiming a gun at Mr. Moore, the jury found Moore innocent. I did not testify. I wish Mr. McCoy had allowed me to do so. The question that still rankles more than any other is how eight shots could have been pumped into my husband by a man innocent of any crime. Even though Alexander had been drinking—there is no doubt in my mind that he had—and even though there had been a major disagreement between the two men, how is it possible that the perpetrator can go completely unpunished? I think Mr. McCoy did as good a job as anybody could under the circumstances, and I intend to continue to hire him as my attorney.

The most galling incident came at the close of the trial when the "not guilty" verdict was read and the entire courtroom burst into applause. I had long since accepted the fact that we were not popular in Dallas, but I had no idea how deep the rancor went. The only time I have wanted to fold up and walk away was at that moment. I wanted to walk out of that courtroom and just keep walking.

I don't know how much longer I can listen graciously to the countless words of "good advice" I hear constantly. I desperately needed some of Mr. Cockrell's Missouri family with me in preparation for and during the trial, but all I got was that one letter from his brother. I did not hasten to write to him about the verdict because there was absolutely nothing he could do at that stage. In October I wrote to R. B. (Reuben Bradley) Fulkerson, Mr. Cockrell's brother-in-law and asked that he relate the outcome to any of the family who was interested. The response to that letter arrived only yesterday and came from Francis M. Cockrell who wrote, in part:

Warrensburg, Johnson County, Missouri
Dec. 1, 1858

Mrs. Sarah Cockrell
Dear Sister—

Your letter of Oct. 16th was . . . the first news we got about Moore being acquitted. I was prepared to receive the news from what you had written and I had heard . . . his acquittal does not render him less guilty in the sight of God. We tried to make arrangements so we could come . . . but failed. Nothing would please us better than to come and see you and your children. . . .

I do not know Brother's age, but if I can find out his age, I will write you immediately. I was glad to hear that Brother left a will for I was very fearful that his estate would be involved in law and a great deal spent and wasted. The way he left his property will no doubt be for the better.

I am glad to hear you have the children in school. Send them all to school as much as you can and give them a good education. Tell them I say learn fast, study their books well and learn to write so that they can write to me. . . . I would like to get a letter from them.

We hardly know what to say about coming to see you. . . . In the fall and spring, I am more busy in my law business. Our courts come on in April and in October and before courts for a month or two we are busy in bringing suits. . . . I would be glad that you . . . come and see us. . . . I would like to know how you get along with your business and if you . . . will get it settled up without much trouble.

Amid all your trials, troubles, afflictions and bereavements, put your entire trust and confidence in God and God may in all his mysterious providence make them all work for you and your children. Train up your children in the nurture and the admonition of the Lord and tell them, I say, be good children and mind your mother . . . ."

It is a profound mystery to me that everybody feels compelled to remind me to trust in God. If I didn't have a foundation of faith, I could never be doing what I am doing. What I need is their help to accomplish God's will! Now I am being profane!

On a personal level, I knew I had to have some help. Whatever else I did, if I failed with our children, my life would be worthless. I explored every option I could think of. I prayed diligently. I took long walks around Dallas, observing the building of the hotel, which I had implored the foreman to continue. I visited the lumberyard and reassured the employees there. I turned the running of the ferry and the bridge completely over to Berry Derrit, and then I went to visit my sister Mary at Mountain Creek. Even though nothing had been said, I knew that Mary (almost everybody calls her Polly for some reason) and her husband, Marlin, were experiencing some rough financial times. I needed someone to be a stabilizer for our family while I put our Cockrell business into order and more than anybody else in the world I trusted her to do this. I also told them I needed Mr. Thompson's expertise and guidance. I would find them a house near mine and see that they both were gainfully employed. I wanted to be sure that it was a business proposition as well as a family commitment, for I had seen problems develop among too many families when someone felt under-appreciated. I probably felt more keenly about this than most women, for by the grace of God and the arrival of Alexander Cockrell, I could easily have been the old maid daughter and the maiden aunt who would have been the caretaker of my parents in their declining years and then forever dependent on my sisters and brothers.

I was incredibly grateful when the Thompsons took me up on my offer. My children were skeptical. Bob wanted to know why he must still share a room with Frank when the extra bedroom I had withheld for guests would now be designated as his aunt's so that she would have a space of her own when she stayed overnight? Aurelia was concerned that her aunt and cousins might now take the place of the mother in her life. Frank looked wide-eyed and skeptical about the plans as I explained everything to my children. Alexander was too young to care. All he wanted was to be one of the big kids!

The Thompsons moved into Dallas in the middle of June. They have a house two doors from ours. Mary is here all of the time in this transition period while Mr. Thompson goes back and forth to complete this year's harvesting on Mountain Creek. I cannot begin to explain what a relief it is to have someone totally capable of running our home, someone I love and who shares the values present in our lives. It is working well. When the nightmares come, when I awaken in the wee hours of the morning with all of the world's problems on my heart, when I am so lonely that I cannot stop the tears, I am comforted by knowing that Mary is with me in the upstairs bedroom and that she is committed to helping me see it through.

The summer was sweltering. June melted into July with unrelenting heat. Even as I tried to grasp the enormity of our business responsibilities, to reassure the workers, to see that the hotel was on schedule for completion, to have what seemed to be countless meetings with Mr. McCoy to resolve our legal problems, to complete negotiations with Mr. Darnell about running the hotel, to accept and pay for materials and accessories that my husband had purchased on his last buying trip, to keep an open door and an open mind to the countless problems of our many employees, I moved through the days automatically. I tried to keep my wits about me, but, oh, how hard it all has been. My work is complicated, too, by Will Toomy's illness. He has been the administrator in charge of our affairs during the countless times Mr. Cockrell traveled. He was always Alex's right hand man, and I have come to depend on him more and more. Alex's death seems to weigh heavily on Mr. Toomy's already declining health, and I do not know what I will do when I no longer have him to depend upon.

Most of all, I knew I must keep in touch with my children. Not only keep them safe but also guide and direct them. And, as Mr. Cockrell said, *educate* them. I will never forget that challenge.

When I had just begun to get my head above water, or thought I had, the real water came down! The rains started. Unbelievably and unseasonably, the rains started in mid-August. And continued. And continued! We were all grateful for the respite from the heat. We all reveled in the rains. My children insisted on going out and playing, lifting their faces to the downpour, shouting and running about in the puddles that formed in the streets in front of our house. Even I felt my spirits lifting.

And then came the day. I was at my desk, checking over the latest income/outgo figures when Mary interrupted to say that Berry Derrit was at the door. He wasted no words. One arch of the west span of Mr. Cockrell's bridge had given way and fallen into the river. Even as he gave me the bad news, I heard the remainder of the west section falling. Again I was on automatic response. This meant, I told him, that the bridge should be closed immediately on both banks and that the ferry should be made available to provide transport across the river until we could repair the bridge. I had no idea what this would entail. I only knew that we must continue to provide passage for people from the west of Dallas County to reach the center of county government and trade. I later learned that Col. M. T. Johnson was the last to cross the bridge before it collapsed, and I am eternally grateful that neither he nor anyone else lost their lives in this fiasco.

Most assuredly, other things have been going on in our world even as I am preoccupied with my own personal corner of it. This was the year that Minnesota joined the Union, our 32nd state; President James Buchanan was inaugurated last year as our 15th president and urged Congress in his State of the Union address to purchase Cuba, so far to no avail; the year, I read, that a religious revival is sweeping the country. I must admit, I don't see much of it. Closer to home, the year that Margaret Bryan inherited 40 acres of property when her father's will was probated. I am so glad for Mrs. Bryan. Her husband has still not come home. This makes two missing Dallas men—Mr. Bryan, its founder, and Mr. Cockrell, its inheritor. How will we survive? Only this I know: We Must!

Yours in good times and bad,

Sarah Horton Cockrell

June 1859

Notes to all who care about Dallas:

The world goes on, even when there are many days I don't want to go on with it.

I move automatically through each day trying to accomplish what needs to be done, both for the good of my children and for this area. My husband was the visionary; I was the cautious executor of his dreams. Now it is up to me to be both the dreamer and the builder.

Having Mary here to supervise the running of our home, to help me see that my children's needs are properly met, to supervise the planning and cooking of meals and the general housekeeping has been my salvation. Without her clear direction and steady hand I could not have survived. Through all of the many dark days I have had since Alex left us, it has been Mary who has kept me on course. I know that I could accomplish miracles in the community, but if I did it at the expense of my children, my life would come to naught. Mary reminds me of this often. While she does many of the things that are required in the care and nurturing of the children, it is I who must be in touch with each of them daily.

Aurelia was 9 in May. She is a serious, studious little girl doing well both at school and with her music lessons. I am so glad that her father insisted we move the piano into our crowded two-room cabin. It now is the centerpiece of the parlor in this house and where Aurelia goes every day without prodding to practice. She misses her father, I think, more than any of the boys. From her birth she had a special niche in his heart. I sometimes scolded him for his open favoritism to his daughter, and he always responded that a girl needed protection whereas boys had to grow up to be tough and take care of themselves. I did not believe this and I still don't, but I understand what Alex meant. Having his mother die when he was a wee boy and his father so busy with his remarriage and the rearing of several other children, Alex left home at 14 and survived on his own until he found me! I tried to give him the attention and love he did not have while growing up, but I wonder if it is ever possible to fill in those vacant spots which apparently leave holes in the heart of a growing child.

Robert continues to be my happy-go-lucky child. He is seven, almost eight, still not very interested in academic pursuits but begs me to take him with me to the mill and to the construction site of the hotel. Last week he did not answer when his aunt Mary called him to supper, and we were all growing concerned when he showed up just before dark acting surprised that we thought him lost. He said he had asked me if he could go down and watch the construction crew at the hotel, and I had nodded. I don't remember that, and I am not sure that Robert isn't faking just a bit, but I must be more aware of what I give the children permission to do. I know that when my mind is on so many things at once I am inclined not to tune in to the nuances of their needs. The point is that I would never have given him permission to go alone to the hotel if I had been aware of it. Not only is there danger that he could be injured, but I do not want the boys subjected to unsavory characters on the streets, especially in the late afternoon and early evening when men are staggering from the saloons. I went up to Robert's room after we ate and had a mother to son talk with him, and he promised he would do better.

Frank is just five, but is already learning to read. He and Aurelia had a small fracas recently when she missed two of her books. Mary found them under the covers of Frank's bed. He is a sober little boy who pointed out to me that he would not have borrowed his sister's books if I had given him some of his own. This is a clear challenge to me that I must be aware of his needs, and I wasted no time in ordering some "boy" books for him. He is ready for school now, but the public school, which is becoming quite good, will not take him until he is six. Most children do not begin their formal education until age seven or eight. When I walked into the dining room yesterday, I found Frankie lying flat on his stomach with a pointed stick meticulously tracing letters from the *Herald*. I must get him paper and a pencil.

Barely three, Alexander is still my baby. He is a happy little boy, constantly in motion during every waking moment and running off a lot of his baby fat. I am concerned that he will not remember his father at all, but all I can do is keep his memory alive in all of our children as much as possible. At every meal, when I say the blessing, I ask God to let the best of their father live on in their lives. One of my most difficult tasks is not to coddle Alexander too closely to fill the vacuum in my aching heart. His father would find that intolerable.

My challenge is to fill the lives of my children with abundant love coupled with firm discipline while being alert to their individual needs. How do I know that Aurelia misses her father the most? How can I be both mother and father to Bob, Frank and Alexander?

My life outside the four walls of this house is every bit as challenging as my role of mother/protector.

I pray to let bygones be bygones, not to be vindictive, not to dwell on the injustices that seem clear to me to have been perpetrated on the Cockrell family, but I have to admit that having Andy Moore pay his debt was very satisfying. It was such a trifling amount for which Alex lost his life. Immediately after the funeral I gave Mr. McCoy the IOU that Mr. Moore had signed and told him that his first priority was to collect that debt, which he did. I felt like framing the $50, but Alex would not want me to do that. It was also a source of satisfaction to me that Mr. Moore was voted out of office in an election held shortly after my husband died. Perhaps there is not so much rancor against us as the court trial would have me believe.

I have so enjoyed getting acquainted with George W. Guess, the young lawyer who moved to Dallas to join with Mr. McCoy's law firm. Alex had told me about him. When Alex was shot and placed on a stretcher to be brought home, for some reason still not clear to me, he removed his watch and handed it to Mr. Guess asking him to give it to me. In the confusion following Alex's death, the young man left the house with the watch still in his hand, but returned a short time later and gave it to me. He was a witness to the entire fracas and, at my insistence, gave me all of the details. When I had started to bathe and dress my husband following his death, the watch was missing. I noticed because he always wore it, and I wondered what had happened. The watch is the one thing of Alex's that I will keep and treasure always because he was so proud of it, and all the years of our marriage it ticked faithfully over his heart. It will be my link to our past.

Mr. Guess is very bright. He has helped Mr. McCoy with every detail as we have settled the estate, and I respect his ability as my legal counsel every bit as much as I trust Mr. McCoy. I don't know what series of events transpired to have Mr. McCoy invite Mr. Guess to Dallas, but I find their personal lives ironically similar. Mr. McCoy came to Dallas only a month after the Horton family arrived in 1844 with Peters' Colony as its agent and surveyor. Upon its disintegration, he fell heir to the Colony, severed his connection with the original owners and set about helping Dallas citizens who were caught up in the debacle to resolve their legal entanglements. In so doing, he opened his law offices. Alexander admired him very much, as did everybody else in the community, and hired him as our attorney. At the time of his arrival, he was a handsome bachelor, who, it is said, broke many hearts when he chose the much younger Cora McDermott as his bride in 1851. He bought the corner lot on Commerce at Lamar five blocks up the street from us and built a lovely home there which became the entertainment center for leading citizens in downtown Dallas. He still lives there with assorted family members. Mrs. McCoy died in July of 1857 in childbirth not long after they moved in. She was only 25.

Mr. Guess came to Dallas with his wife, Molly, a very ill child-wife—only 17. They had been married for two years. She is suffering from tuberculosis, and Mr. Guess said he brought her here to a warmer climate for her to recover her health. But it is not working, and he fears there is no hope for her. This doubtless accounts for the prevailing look of sadness that permeates Mr. Guess's face. He is only 10 years younger than I, but I treat him like one of my sons.

In April 6 only three days after the first anniversary of Mr. Cockrell's death, we lost another leading citizen of the community when Mr. Latimer died following a freak accident. He, along with his wife Lucy, and later a partner, John W. Swindells, had published the *Herald* weekly since the Latimers arrived here in 1849. Not only was his newspaper a great addition to our area, but he personally was one of our best-educated citizens. On the evening of April 5, while carrying an armful of firewood into his home, he tripped and fell fracturing his skull. He died the next day.

I have decided to dispose of the sawmill. It has been a difficult decision because it was one of Mr. Cockrell's most prized creations, but it is simply no longer profitable. Almost all of the desirable wood in the area has been cut and harvested. To transport logs from distances away to be cut into lumber would be almost prohibitively expensive, and I know that if my husband, had he lived, would already have sold. I have no idea whether anyone will assume ownership. If not, I will simply shut the operation down and go on with other parts of Alex's business.

The most pressing of this "other" business is the completion of the hotel. It is almost finished. I have concluded negotiations that my husband began with Nicholas N. Darnell to manage it. He is perfect for the job, not only in ability and experience but also with the necessary polish and urbanity that such an enterprise demands. He was a captain in the Indian Wars of 1839 distinguishing himself in battle. He is a devotee of the Masonic Order, which is a must in this community for any successful businessperson. He was speaker of the House of Representatives of the Texas Congress in 1842 and elected lieutenant governor of Texas in the first elections in 1846. He was a candidate for governor in 1847 and came very close to being elected. He attained great popularity throughout the state with connections far and wide throughout the country. Convincing him to take the position was not easy. I learned from Mr. McCoy that he was very near to signing a contract with my husband when he died, but like so many people, he did not think that a "mere" woman could own and manage business. When he and I met in Mr. McCoy's office with Mr. Guess in attendance for me to try to persuade him to take the position, I had (as my husband used to say) "an ace up my sleeve!" I told him if he became manager, the hotel would be named for him.

And so it will be—the St. Nicholas Hotel. This was a hard decision for me to make because I had intended for it to be named for my husband, whose dream it was. I could just see the wheels turning in Mr. Darnell's mind before he reached for the pen and signed the contract. When Mr. Guess escorted me out, he was grinning from ear to ear and congratulated me on "pulling a rabbit out of the hat"—whatever that means!

Mr. Darnell was immediately put on the payroll after the contract was signed, and we have been daily in negotiations concerning the opening. I was strongly resistant to having an elaborate ball to open the hotel. I am still in "widow's weeds," and think it inappropriate to appear in public at any social event. It has been only a little more than a year since Alex died, and I still hurt every time I think about his death. But, I have allowed Mr. McCoy, Mr. Guess and Mr. Darnell to convince me that a grand hotel of the stature of the St. Nicholas deserves a lavish send-off, so we have scheduled a gala ball in July. They have assured me that I will not be required to do anything except be present. Mr. Darnell seems to have no reluctance to stand in the spotlight, and Mr. McCoy has agreed to lead the grand march at the opening. The men said we would "evade" my period of mourning by announcing that the grand ball was being sponsored by the "leading citizens of the town." All I have to do is wear black and fade into the woodwork. I wonder what my husband would have to say about this?

Sometimes I think I have lost my mind because I have agreed to spare no expense to make this event the most important in the history of Dallas. Invitations are being engraved. Special couriers will personally deliver them to invited guests throughout this area. Invitations are being mailed to leading citizens in the state and the nation. We have signed the band and secured the services of a caterer and barmen (how I hate to serve liquor, but my male advisors insist it is imperative!)

I have also spared no expense to furnish the hotel and provide it with the very latest conveniences, because I know that is what Mr. Cockrell had planned. The building is grand in scale and in furnishings. It is our town's first skyscraper, a three-story brick building on the northeast corner of Commerce at Broadway. The painting, finishing touches and furnishings are now being put in place. I did not dare look when the crystal chandelier was being installed in the main entry. Mr. Cockrell had bought it on his last trip to New Orleans, and it was on its way to Dallas when he was murdered. Nor, could I bring myself to be present when the grand piano was being installed and tuned, the one that replaced Mr. Cockrell's first musical purchase for the hotel, which had been installed in our home and replaced by this much grander one

We have been most concerned about the hotel lighting because all of us are so aware of the potential for starting a fire. The chandeliers Mr. Cockrell bought are all illuminated by kerosene, which is much safer than candles, but still presents a fire hazard unless handled with extreme caution. So I have directed that one man be hired to light, watch over and extinguish the flames. We have installed wall brackets, also with kerosene as the fuel, between the windows in the main ballroom and have furnished each table with an oil lamp. The guestrooms are also furnished with oil lamps and our special "fireman" will light the lamps every evening when a guest is in the room. We will trust them to blow out the flame when they are ready to retire!

The very thought of everything "I" am doing—that is, I am paying to have done—makes me tired. My advisors assure me that everything will come together. We shall see. In the meantime, I must go check on my children.

December 1859

I cannot believe that the last entry I made in this journal was almost half a year ago just before the opening of the hotel.

The grand ball that officially opened the St. Nicholas in July was splendid beyond my wildest imagination. It lived up to every expectation I had been promised by Mr. Darnell and "the citizens of Dallas" in whose names the invitations were extended. We had turned the dining room into a ballroom, hung the walls with tapestries lent to us by our oldest and most influential families which they had brought from their ancestral homes. Windows were garlanded with wild flowers interlaced on boughs of cedar and other evergreens. We turned the lighting of the chandeliers and the wall brackets low so that a mellow glow was cast over ceiling and walls. The half circle balcony with balustrade was draped in flags of the United States and Texas and had chairs for honored guests behind it overlooking the ballroom below.

I caught my breath when I arrived early in the evening and saw Mr. Cockrell's dream come true. The space that only days before had been swarming with carpenters, painters and other workmen was transformed into a work of art. I wore my best black alpaca dress. My only decoration was a broach my husband had brought me shortly before he died. In further deference to the occasion, I left off the mourning bonnet and veil, which has been a part of my uniform almost constantly every time I went out since his death. I was seated at the front at a side table away from the entry so that I could observe everybody and everything without being conspicuous. I even allowed my children to stay up for the first part of the evening and sit on the stairway where they could see, but would not be obvious to the guests.

The livery stable had been sold out for a week before the actual ball, and we had a hard time finding accommodations for the number of horses and carriages that had to be stored awaiting the close of the event and the emergence of their owners again. Just before dark the first guests arrived. They came in surreys and stylish carriages drawn by highly groomed horses decked out with garlands of flowers and ribbons.

And, my, the guests! They came from throughout the state and some even from other surrounding states. Many of the ladies had ordered their ball gowns from St. Louis, Boston or Philadelphia. Others had opened long-sealed trunks to resurrect satin and lace and taffeta and ribbons and have garments restructured into the latest fashion. Most had tightly fitted bodices with high necklines over full flowing skirts, their fullness enhanced with hoops. Some had flowing trains. Many had leg-o-mutton sleeves. They had brought out heirloom jewelry—diamonds, pearls, rubies, and even emeralds—cleaned and polished to a high sheen and worn for the first time on Texas soil. The men were equally splendid, gleaming white shirts with jeweled studs and cuff links; black suits fashioned with frock tailcoats. Both women and men wore white gloves, the ladies' to their elbows and beyond. Almost all of the ladies carried flowers and many had flowers woven into their elaborate coiffures.

As the guests arrived, Frank Leonard, who would later lead the band, presented a symphony of melodies on the violin that brought tears to my eyes. I have always loved the violin. When the music stopped, there was a hush, and then from a distant room a bugle call, at the conclusion of which Mr. Leonard lifted his baton and the orchestra on a raised dais began the haunting strains for the grand march. From the farthest doorway, Mr. McCoy, with a lovely young lady in a white gown looking every bit like a princess leaning on his arm, emerged and led the grand march. The couple was followed by an almost endless row of elegantly dressed ladies, married and single, escorted by equally debonair escorts, husbands and sweethearts and the town's leading young bachelors.

When the grand march ended, the orchestra swung into a waltz. As hundreds of gas lights flickered on the chandelier, the scene was a fairyland. And it took me back to what seemed like an eternity ago when a handsome young prince in his army uniform whisked me from the kitchen out under an oak tree, declared his everlasting love, asked me to be his wife and rushed me back into the living room of the Wesley Cockrell home to announce our plans. He then held me as if I would break and led me in a waltz where, I feel certain, my feet never touched the floor. I closed my eyes at this fabulous beginning of Alexander Cockrell's beautiful hotel and was transported back those many years to the beginning of our dream.

The night went on forever, it seemed. Nobody tired. Nobody left. They danced the schottische, the mazurka, the polka, the lancers, the Virginia reel and the graceful, dignified minuet and again and again the waltz. I think Mr. Leonard surprised the younger guests by knowing and playing most of the popular songs of the day, "The Yellow Rose of Texas," introduced only last year, and "Dixie," introduced just recently. When he played "Dixie" the dancing halted, and all stood around in almost awe joining in the rousing words of the song. He played many of Stephen Foster's "hits," including "Jeanie with the Light Brown Hair" and "Come Where My Love Lies Dreaming." And he played the oh-so-popular "Listen to the Mockingbird."

Some of the young ladies who have been east to school were astonished that our little Dallas was so advanced!

To be honest, I was surprised myself. I have been so busy for the past few years learning and then running the Cockrell business that I had not kept up with the finer things of life. I try to keep up with books and literature, but I confess ignorance with music and art, to which I seldom have access. I was amazed the morning after the big event when I heard Aurelia picking out the notes of "Listen to the Mockingbird" on the piano. I must remember to get the music for her.

At midnight the music ceased. Mr. Darnell stood in the spotlight and announced that dinner was served. Then, from every entryway, it seemed to me, white-coated waiters bearing trays of food prepared in the kitchen adjacent to what would tomorrow again be the dining hall, whisked through the ballroom laden with a feast. It did not take long for the dancers, who at first grumbled at having the music stop, to take to their tables. The feast was shortly consumed. The waiters bore the plates away, cleared the tables and the music started again. Still, nobody left! Mary had long since taken my children away to their respective bedrooms and to happy dreams.

The revelers simply would not let the party end, and Mr. Darnell seemed determined that it go on as long as Mr. Leonard and the orchestra would play and as long as the dancers were on the floor. It was not until the purple hues and the orange glows of a reflected rising sun heralded the dawn of a new day that the last guests seemed ready to go home. I had sat at my table through the entire night, amazed as the culmination of Mr. Cockrell's dream unfolded before my eyes. Oh, how I hope in some distant paradise, he sees and knows what happened on this night!

Finally—finally, the orchestra played the goodnight waltz, which was sung by Mr. Leonard and some of his musicians:

> *We will hang up the fiddle and the bow ...*
> *We will hang up the fiddle and the bow ...*
> *You've danced all night till broad daylight.*
> *We will hang up the fiddle and the bow!*

As dawn broke over Dallas, I walked alone the few blocks back to my home on lower Commerce. Mr. Guess, Mr. McCoy and even Mr. Nicholas were appalled that I insisted on making the few blocks alone. But I needed that time. Time to reflect on what had happened here this night. Time to be grateful to God for giving me the strength, the fortitude, the courage and the wherewithal to make my husband's dream come true. Even as I entered the front door of the house, I was not sleepy. Much had happened on this night.

I have been so busy running my own home and businesses that I have all but ignored what is going on in the world beyond the boundaries of Dallas. So only the briefest of mentions:

The rumors of war are everywhere—in our local newspapers, in all national publications I have seen, in the conversations of most of the men I overhear (heaven forbid that a woman voice an opinion, so I listen, learn and keep my mouth shut!) The latest event to rally the troops and divide our nation into pro-and-anti slavery camps occurred just a few weeks ago when John Brown was hanged in Charlestown, West Virginia, on December 2 for inciting rebellion against his country. Mr. Brown had been our country's most outspoken opponent of slavery. In 1855 he moved his family including his five sons and their families to Kansas with the purpose of seeing that Kansas entered the Union as a free state. Since that time he has constantly fomented rebellion. Earlier this year, with 21 men, he seized the town of Harper's Ferry, Virginia, and held it until a local militia led by Robert E. Lee defeated the holed-up group. Ten of them were killed. Brown was captured, tried for treason and hanged. Out of this has come a new song, popular with the young folks and with all who are opposed to slavery, "John Brown's Body Lies A-mouldering in the Grave."

I know that a recent act by the Georgia legislature has left the hard-liners in both the pro-slavery and the anti-slavery camps at dagger's points with each other. Georgia has legally prohibited the post-mortem freeing of slaves by an owner's last will and testament and, further, the same statute permits free blacks to be sold into slavery if they are indicted as vagrants. I still do not know where my loyalties lie—first, to this town that my husband "gave" me when he purchased the unsold lots of John Neely Bryan's Dallas, then to my country.

My abiding prayer is that conflict can be avoided.

In Dallas, the break-up of La Reunion and the continued arrival of immigrants who were to become a part of that settlement has increased our population and enhanced our educational and cultural advantages. It has also expanded our city's residential areas. To our east, a new town is growing. Henry Boll is completing a brick home on White Rock Road about two miles from downtown. I haven't seen it, but have been told that it is a narrow one-room-deep two-story dwelling fashioned after his ancestral home in Aargau, Switzerland. As soon as I can get away from the responsibilities that keep me busy every day, I want to take a trip around Dallas and see for myself what is happening. Mr. Boll's house is located on the northeast corner of White Rock and Germania. Mr. Boll has recently been joined by his brother, Jacob Boll, a pharmacist, who I am told intends to open an apothecary here. He is a naturalist, they say, whose chief interest is investigating the mineral resources and studying the natural history of Texas. I am amazed at how far and how fast Mr. Cockrell's dream for a vibrant Dallas is expanding.

Our religious community is growing, too. Maxime Guillot recently brought a circuit-riding priest to his home to say Mass and is determined to establish a Catholic church here. I know there are people of the Catholic persuasion among the La Reunion settlers who have felt alienated because there has been no place for them to worship. I think Mr. Guillot will be successful and I hope he is. I would be bereft if I had no place and no community of my own faith in which to worship, for on Sunday morning in church the cares of the world are lifted from my shoulders.

The Reverend Smith, who has been so important to our family, is a wonderful preacher. When listening to his sermons, I always feel the presence of God. But I also feel supported and cared for by my fellow citizens. I need that! Even though I still miss the country, I am so grateful to be in Dallas where, on Sundays, I can attend worship services. This was impossible when, most Sundays, I had the care of the children while Mr. Cockrell was away on business trips and had nobody to help me hitch up the wagons so that I could go to worship services. And most of the time those meetings were so far away that it would have taken all day just to get there and back. I am strongly considering donating a city lot downtown for the founding of a new Methodist sanctuary. Every time I think of this, I smile, because my husband always teased me about being a "Methody woman" and reminded me that our very first meeting almost denied him a second chance to prove his mettle!

Our post office has moved. It is now located in the Crutchfield House. I thought seriously of bidding for it to be located in the St. Nicholas, but was discouraged in doing so by Mr. Darnell and now I am glad. Even if I had been successful in relocating it to our hotel, somebody would have had to sort the mail, look after the customers and be responsible for everything. And it would doubtless have turned out to be me. I simply could not take on this responsibility.

Though I have had so little time to read—and how I regret that—I know that this has been a great year for the publication of new books, both fiction and poetry and lovely new hymns.

I am eager to read *A Tale of Two Cities* by Charles Dickens, but it is just out, and I know it will be some time before it is available here. Three other books, *Adam Bede* by George Eliot, *The Idylls of the King* by Alfred Lord Tennyson and *The Rubaiyat of the Omar Khayyam of Naishapur* published into an English rhymed version have been recently published. I must find a copy of the poem, "The Children's Hour" by Henry Wadsworth Longfellow. I think it perfect for my young Frank. Or, is he yet too young for:

> *Between the dark and the daylight*
> *When the night is beginning to lower*
> *Comes a pause in the day's occupation*
> *That is known as the children's hour.*

I think not. Poetry is a gift for all ages, and children brought up hearing beautiful words must surely have an educational advantage. Or, at least, I like to think so and wish I had more time to read to my children and to expose them to books that have so enriched my life.

Last Sunday Mrs. Latimer, still in her widow's all black, introduced our church to the new hymn, "Ave Maria." I am told that the music is based on Johann Sebastian Bach's "The Well-Tempered Clarichord." I don't care from whence it came; I could sit and listen to it all day long. I heard another new hymn, "Nearer My God to Thee" at a recent funeral. The lyrics were written by a woman, Sarah Adams, in the early 40s, but only recently have been set to music by Lowell Mason of Boston. Both the music and the words moved me to tears as I recalled my late husband.

I have taken the plunge and asked the State Legislature to renew the application it granted to my husband to build the bridge across the Trinity River. The ferry, which I reactivated as soon as Alexander's bridge fell last year, is simply not adequate to take care of the traffic. Businesses to the west of the Trinity, especially around Lancaster and, to a lesser degree, around Mountain Creek and Hord's Ridge are growing by leaps and bounds. Merchants, promoters, traders and other businessmen cannot wait for the ferry to transport them across and return for the next load. I want to erect an iron bridge. I know it will be costly, but for once in my life I have followed the vision of my husband, thrown caution to the winds and am ready to do whatever it takes to see that a new and more substantial bridge spans the river.

In October, through my lawyers, I filed an official application with the Legislature for the renewal of the charter to build the bridge naming as directors nine of the town's most prominent citizens—W. J. Clark, A. J. Gouffe, John W. Haynes, Sam S. Jones, T. C. Jordan, Ben Long, A. B. Norton, W. H. Prather and James E. Scott.

I was totally unprepared for the broadside of resentment that followed. On November 25, a petition directed to the Speaker of the House of Representatives of the Legislature of the State of Texas, signed by 56 outstanding business men asked that the lawmakers deny the renewal of my charter. My lawyers obtained a copy of the petition, and I was horrified to see the signatures of many men I thought had become my supporters. Almost all of the downtown businessmen, some elected officials and professional men signed the petition. J. W. Smith and J. M. Patterson, our town's first merchants, were among the signers as was Alexander Harwood, county clerk; John F. Crockett; the druggist, W. W. Peak; William J. Crozier, John F. Stemmons, and my good church friend and sometimes hotel competitor Thomas Crutchfield, with many others too numerous to list. These are people I see every day, people with whom I trade, who knew Alexander and who know me. I thought, naively, that in this year and a half since Alex was killed that I had won the respect, even though grudgingly, of most of the townspeople. I was wrong.

I am aware that many men are still waiting for me to fall flat on my face. They are going to wait a long, long time. The petition they sent to the legislature was couched in language that Mr. McCoy told me was intended to soften the blow. It said, that the County must have a free bridge, "that the County Court . . . has offered proposals and are now holding out for a bid to build a Bridge—the County is able to construct said bridge with the aid that will be approved by the citizens," and asked the legislature to deny "a charter to any company or individual to construct a bridge."

I am trying to decide how I will counter this development. I am as slow to anger as Alex was trigger happy, but I am seething. I am of a good mind to go to Austin and speak personally to the legislators. I know it's unheard of for a woman to testify in court or in any house where laws are being enacted, but something must be done, and there's not much time. I shall have to confer with Mr. McCoy and Mr. Guess.

I intend to build my bridge.

My loving thoughts,

Sarah Horton Cockrell

August 1, 1860

My dear Friends,

Events of the immediate past weeks must be recorded before I forget the horror of these days, and the impact they have wrought on the town.

And, because I am always inclined to be optimistic, even as I take up pen to write, I dwell first on the good news. The children are happy, healthy and thriving. Aurelia was 10 in May; Bob is 8. Frank was 6 in March and Alexander is 4. They are all bright, wonderful children. And as they learn to read and write, master basic arithmetic, enjoy music, in some cases, begin to study an instrument and show an interest in learning French and, occasionally German, from some of our newer residents, I often reflect on their father's last words to me: "Educate our children." I shall not forget!

During the summer holidays I have tried, more than ever, to devote time to the children, but cannot erase from my mind the challenge facing me if I am going to build my bridge. I have to work hard to keep things in perspective, lest the bridge become an obsession. Every moment when I am not dealing with other pressing matters, I think about the bridge. My lawyers, Mr. McCoy and Mr. Guess are wonderful advisors, but in the final analysis, I am the one who must decide. I pray endlessly.

On the morning of December 12, 1859, I awoke with what seemed to me a clear direction for a first step. Before dawn, I went into my study, lighted the kerosene lamp—the one with the beautiful hand-painted shade that was Alexander's last gift to me—pulled out paper, pen and ink and began! I wrote a personal letter to each one of the state legislators. I stated my case for a bridge, citing that they had given permission for Alexander to build our first bridge across the river, that he had been honorable in every transaction agreed upon and that I would do the same when they approved my request to renew the contract. In a brazen attempt, further to win their support, I said that I would be personally available to testify before their august body at any time of their choosing.

I was scared to death they would take me up. No woman has ever stood in the "hallowed" halls where laws are enacted. Women are supposed to defer to the men in their lives—their brothers, sons or (in my case) their lawyers when they are widowed. No woman has dared to declare personally and publicly her right to control the property her husband left to her. I knew all this. How brazen I felt! But I posted the letters. And waited.

Mr. McCoy was horrified—even though he tried to hide it—when I admitted what I had done, but I could tell that Mr. Guess approved. There was a twinkle in his eye!

Only days after the first of this year the entire town was thrown into a state of mourning at the death of Anne Killen Smith, wife of the Rev. James A. Smith. Even though her death was not unexpected, she had been so much a part of our town—everybody knew her and loved her. We could not imagine how we would adjust to this loss. Mr. Smith—we have become such good friends that I dare call him "Mr." rather than the accepted "Rev."—has been such a wonderful addition to our family that I, who know what it is like to lose a beloved partner, have special empathy for him. I have expressed as much, both personally and in notes to him and his children.

The Smith family has been so successful in Dallas. Shortly after they arrived in 1846, he began to acquire property, eventually 1,000 acres where he grew cotton, wheat, barley, oats and corn. He built a large farmhouse on the property he claimed in North Dallas east of Preston Road for the family, his wife, their five children, Mrs. Smith's mother and the 19 slaves who came to Texas with the family. He supervised his farm by week and on the weekends he preached somewhere every Sunday. He conducted weddings and funerals. The family has been so important in our lives. He conducted our wedding and two years later preached the last rites for our baby Logan. He did the funeral services for both of my parents, and later he was my comforter and advisor when Alex was killed.

Even though she has been ill for a long time and doubtless considered it a blessing to be released from her suffering and go home to her maker, Mrs. Smith's passing is a blow to her family, especially to the Rev. Smith. One cannot be married for 36 years as they had been without feeling an incredible loss when one goes on ahead of the other. I had both a prayer of gratitude and a twinge of envy—gratitude that Mr. Cockrell was a part of my life, and envy because we were together only 10 years. What could Alex have done for us and this town had more time been allotted him?

While we were grieving Mrs. Smith's passing, I got word that I had been granted a hearing before the Legislature and that I was to appear "in person" on Friday, January 27. I cannot explain the fears and misgivings I felt when Mr. Guess called to give me the news. Somehow I thought all my petitions to be heard would have been dismissed out of hand and that I would be handed a victory without ever having to appear in public and raise my voice before our lawmakers in Austin. Even though he privately disapproved of my going to Austin, Mr. Darnell used his influence to see that I had a fair hearing—and his influence was formidable. As a former speaker of the House of Representatives and then as lieutenant governor in the early days of Texas, he had many friends who were still elected officials. He walked me through all of the protocol—what I should expect, how I should present myself, what I should say and not say. I listened to him carefully, then followed both the advice of my lawyers and the instincts of my own heart as I prepared note after note for the hearing.

As I prepared for the trip to Austin, I was aware for the first time how important transportation had become to Dallas. All of the men, including Alex, had been vitally interested in securing one of the new rail lines that were taking some parts of the country by storm. Most rail lines were being laid in the northeast to serve the coal mining industry, but I had already been approached by some of the men requesting that I donate land for a rail right-of-way. Some days when I read the *Herald*, it seemed that a railroad was the only news it printed. But we had no railroad (I am not sure I would have traveled on a train if one had been available. From what I read, the trains were off the tracks almost as often as they were on—simply not ideal transportation.) I would have preferred to go all the way by wagon, but I let Mr. McCoy and Mr. Darnell convince me to take the stagecoach. Since it came through Dallas on the way south only twice weekly, I had to leave almost a week ahead of time to be sure and be in Austin by the day of the hearing.

It turned out, the stage did not come at all at the time I needed to leave, so I rode horseback to Pleasant Run where Mr. Moultrie Miller had a hotel and general store that was also the cross roads of transportation east and west and north and south. When I got there, I missed the stage by half a day, having had the wrong information about its departure. Mr. Guess and my sister, Jane, who were accompanying me urged me to cancel the trip and return home. Mr. Guess said he would go by horseback on to Austin and make the pitch for me, but by that time I was more determined than ever to get to the state capitol and present my case. We hired a wagon and team from Mr. Miller, and all three of us went on to Corsicana where we connected with the coach and made the rest of the trip in style. It took us four days from Dallas to Austin.

I have never been more nervous in my life than I was the next morning when I groomed myself, put on my best little black dress and a small dressy bonnet and, with Mr. Guess escorting me, made my way into the halls of the legislature. I must say I have never been treated more courteously. There is no doubt that most of the lawmakers were in awe. I sensed not so much disapproval that a woman had been allowed in their hallowed halls as a grudging admiration. When I was acknowledged, I made my way to the podium and in as clear and calm a voice as I could muster, I presented my case. Mr. McCoy had advised me not to mention that I had any inkling of opposition, and I didn't. It took me about 20 minutes. There were a few polite questions after I closed my speech. Then I was dismissed with as much courtesy as I had been welcomed. As I made my way out of the hall, every man stood. The Speaker sent a note later to the hotel saying that I would have their decision "in a few days."

Mr. Guess said it was almost certain that I had won them over. I did not know how it had gone, but I do admit a feeling of triumph, though tempered with humility, that I had dared do such a thing. I like to think Alex was applauding! Later I learned that I may have been one of the first women in the country to appear before a law-making body, because it was not until later in the year that Suffragist Elizabeth Cady Stanton appeared before the New York State Legislature to ask that women be given the right to vote.

On February 9, I received word that the Legislature had granted permission for me to build the bridge, and a few days later the legal document arrived. Written in legalese, it has the gold seal of the state affixed and is signed by the Secretary of State in such florid handwriting that I can't even read the signature. But, oh, how that gold seal goes straight to my heart!

The charter is far more liberal than even I had thought possible. It grants "Sarah H. Cockrell and <u>such other persons as she may choose to</u>

<u>associate with herself</u>" the right to "create a corporation under the name and style of the Dallas Bridge Company," and set toll fees which after two years shall be the responsibility of the Dallas County Court. It provides a stiff fine for individuals and conveyances crossing the river without paying the toll, and it stipulates that no other bridge shall be built within two miles of mine. All handwritten, the document is several pages long. I read every word several times.

I wasted no time in calling a meeting of the board of directors. I asked Mr. Jones to chair it. (I know when I have stretched the limits for what is permissible in a woman's behavior!) And I asked Mr. McCoy to be present. Both he and Mr. Guess showed up, and I was grateful to have their presence. The meeting went well and by its conclusion, every board member pledged to purchase stock in the bridge company. Others are waiting in line for the stock to be issued. I hear that even some of the merchants who most vehemently opposed the bridge now want to be a part of the deal. I am entirely agreeable. This is a small way to "turn the other cheek!"

I was so busy with plans for the bridge and other transactions that I had paid no attention at all to my personal life other than trying to stay attuned to my children and their needs. Every night after we eat and they are studying and/or in bed, Mary and I sit down to go over the day's household happenings. That is what we were doing that late night in April when there was a knock at the door.

Mary went to the door and returned to hand me a sealed envelope with my name on it. Thinking it something to do with the business, I laid it aside until we finished with a row of figures and curiosity got the better of me. I gently broke the seal. And this is what I read:

My Dear Mrs. Cockrell:[6]

The many and pressing claims on your time and attention preclude the possibility of a personal interview. I therefore pen a few lines for your perusal with the hope of eliciting an answer that will relieve me from this painful suspence. I entreat of you by that undying love I have for you to give the subject a favorable consideration.

I have reflected on it maturely and prayerfully and the more I think of it the more thoroughly am I convinced that no evil of any kind to us or injury to any one else can possibly grow out of our union and I am the more convinced our happiness would be mutually promoted and secured. Then

---

[6]Original letter is now in archives of the Dallas Historical Society.

*why my dear Sarah should there be any further hesitation.
Why postpone those sweet enjoyments that belong alone to con-
jugal love and domestic affection.*

*My very soul longs to call you mine. Please my Sweet
Loved one to answer me favorably though it should be ever so
briefly. If only that one sweet word YES twill be enough to
complete my happiness and a life's devotion to your happiness will be the least return that I can make. Select your own
time and manner of answering this, but my dearest one, let
the answer be favorable.*

Yours most respectfully and affectionately,

Jas. A. Smith

I was in shock. Reactions, one after the other followed, left me shak-
en, and I must have paled, for Mary laid a hand on my arm and asked if I
were all right. I nodded, continuing to hold the letter in my hand. Then I
read it again. There was no mistaking the words. It was a marriage proposal from the Methodist minister. But for me? I quickly scanned the
envelope again, thinking surely there had been a mistake. When I was
assured that my name, indeed, was on the envelope and when I re-read
the salutation, "My dear Mrs. Cockrell," there could be no mistake that it
was meant for me. My next thought was that somebody was playing a
prank. It was too soon after Mrs. Smith's death, even though she had been
ill for several years, for the minister to give thought to remarriage. My
next thought was maybe he was losing his mind and the kindest thing I
could do would be to ignore the letter and pretend I had never received
it. In that state of denial, I felt sure he would be highly embarrassed when
he came to his senses and discovered what he had done. Then—and God
forgive me for this—I thought, our marriage would be a good way to
secure the property he and his board wanted as an ideal place to build a
new Methodist church.

All the while these thoughts were racing through my mind, I held
onto the letter, trying to recall when and what I had ever done to give
James Smith (and this was the very first time I had thought to address him
in anything except Brother, Mr. or Reverend) the idea that I was romanti-
cally inclined toward him. I had simply been too busy taking care of my
children and managing my business to give any thought to re-marriage.
Even as the consideration was right in front of me, I found the idea almost
repugnant. Marrying again was the least of all my thoughts. And most of
all, to my minister!

Finally, I held the letter out to Mary, swearing her to secrecy even as I did so. She read it through quite calmly, laid her hand on mine and said, "Well?" I shook my head.

What now?

In times of indecision, there is a great deal to be said for having a demanding schedule—and that I had! I was glad all of the children were in their rooms, and, I hoped, asleep. So, I picked up my pen and my ledger and told Mary that we should continue with our work.

The next morning, all brisk efficiency, I knew my first priority was to conclude something I had been considering for many months. I needed to deed the property to the First Methodist Church in downtown Dallas. I considered how I would do this and finally decided that the best way was a little white lie because I did not want the Rev. James Smith to think I was trying to evade his proposal by giving him something. I pre-dated my letter to him the day <u>before</u> his marriage proposal arrived. I wrote out my intentions to donate Lot 5, Block 51 at the corner of Lamar and Commerce for a church, which I knew Rev. Smith and the board had been "coveting!"(isn't it a sin to covet?!). I had Mr. McCoy and Mr. Guess, as my lawyers, attest to my signature. I signed the letter of intention, sealed it and waited until early evening when I knew that the Rev. Smith and the church board were meeting at the St. Nicholas Hotel.

Then, I recognized another irony. The board chairman was Andrew Moore, the same Andrew Moore who had shot my husband and had been absolved of any crime. My, it was forgiveness time! I had Robert deliver the letter to the St. Nicholas after school, asked him to give it to Mr. Darnell and to ask him to deliver it to Mr. Smith or Mr. Moore when they arrived for the meeting and to tell them that his mother had written the letter two days ago! Will God ever forgive me for this story to my son? Robert was ecstatic to be entrusted with an important document, and I watched him grow before my very eyes. I so want to instill in my children integrity and responsibility. Is this any way to start?

The following day, in a curt note signed by both Andy Moore and James A. Smith, I learned that my donation had been accepted by acclamation of the board.

Now what to do about the proposal of marriage? Do I ignore it? Do I "break his heart" by saying no? Do I break mine by giving him an affirmative? Do I simply not respond at the present time and see what develops? I cannot imagine there is a kind way to decline the romantic attentions of someone you greatly admire but have no intention of marrying.

Coward that I am, I chose the least offensive—to me—response. I wrote a personal note thanking him for honoring me in a way that women throughout time have treasured. I told him that, friend as I was to Anne Killen Smith, it would take some time for me to consider any woman capable of replacing her in his affections. I said that my life, as he knew, was overwhelmed with the care of my children and the running of several businesses as his was so full of taking care of his own family including his mother-in-law, the growth and building of a new church and his increasing responsibilities to Dallas. I said we should lay aside any romantic entanglements that might, for the moment, hamper these primary responsibilities. After more time had passed, I insinuated, we could then think of ourselves and what the future might hold for us.

There were a few seconds of awkwardness when on Sunday morning I arrived at church at my usual time—oh, what effort this took!—and took my usual pew, surrounded by my children, all dressed and on their best behavior. Only Mary knew I was shaking. And when I greeted the Rev. Smith at the close of the sermon and extended my gloved hand, he held it only a breath too long, looked into my eyes and nodded. We both knew what this meant. We both knew this was the end of any future romantic involvement. I can only hope that he is as relieved as I am.

One thing that has concerned me from the beginning is my feeling about our minister owning slaves. Alex used to say that it was "unseemly," and Alex "used" those he "possessed" with concern and compassion, as he had taught me to do—to honor the integrity of the Native American, whose land, he said, we had stolen from him, and to teach, respect and set free the Negroes we had "inherited." I had been told, and wanted to believe, that the New England States fostered slavery, and only when they learned the blacks were not suited to their climates and their needs that the slaves were then shipped south. I am ambivalent about what to believe. The only thing I hold as truth is that no one person, under the will of God, should be "owned" by anyone else. And when I "buy" another person, I excuse my own anguish by telling myself that I will be the best "slave master" anywhere. I never divide families. In December of 1859, I "bought" Caroline, a young mother of three children who came to me with Willis, 6, Martha, 3, and Francis, a year old. Since then I have sought the father of these children in hopes that I might reunite the family.

I only wish the situation with my minister and the ambivalence I felt about his ownership of slaves would have been the most difficult problem I had to deal with this year, but, alas, such was not the case.

My pen slows even as my heartbeat quickens. How shall I relate the horror of what happened eight days after the middle of this year?

Our town is in ashes.

On Sunday, July 8, 1860, Dallas burned. It was so hot that day that everything had almost stopped to a standstill. The temperature was well over a hundred degrees. Some say 104, some 105 and some even as high as 110. Church was over. We had all had our mid-day meal. Many of us, including most of the children, were trying to nap—though the weather was too hot for sleep.

Several of the men—some of the leading citizens of the town—were lolling in front of Peak's Drug Store talking and smoking.

Nobody has the entire story of what happened on that sweltering Sunday. It depends on the person you listen to. This, then, is what I saw, what I remember and how I feel about some happenings around the Great Fire.

Mary and I had finished our meal, cleared the table and washed the dishes. I had sent the children to their rooms to rest. Mary and I had gone to our own rooms. I was determined to forget business and concentrate on "keeping the Sabbath Day holy," when I heard a shout from the front of the house. I don't know who sounded the alarm first, but I learned later that a child, peering from her bedroom window, first noticed a swirl of smoke coming from the roof of the Peak Drug Store and shouted an alarm to her parents. At about the same time, one of the men sitting in front of the drug store sniffed and asked his cronies if anybody else smelled smoke. At first, I am told, they laughed. Since almost everybody was smoking, why wouldn't the odor be strong?

In a matter of seconds flames were all around them. Some say the first blaze was spotted coming from an upstairs window. Others say the combustion began in boxes of trash at the left front of the store. The truth seems to be that wherever they looked, their entire surroundings were ablaze.

Up and down the streets the alarm was spread from house to house even as sparks ignited buildings two and three stores away turning the entire block into a blazing inferno. Men raced to their stores and shops pulling out records and as much of the merchandise as their arms could enfold, sometimes tossing it in the middle of the street and returning to the building for additional supplies. Somebody remembered to rescue the mail. It, too, was dumped into the street in front of the post office. In the chaos a male voice shouted for calm, but nobody seemed to pay any attention. But, somehow his calm voice got through and the men, aware that there was no way of saving their own businesses, formed a bucket brigade around the courthouse passing water from all directions toward the center of the town.

The courthouse was spared, though some of the windows exploded and curtains burned. It was the only building on the square that remained standing when the sun set that July day. Supplies rescued from blazing buildings, including the mail, ignited in the streets and for a time turned them into rivers of fire.

Publishers of the *Herald* wrote the most factual and least emotional record of this awful day. Even though their own newspaper was totally demolished, they were consummate professionals who journeyed to McKinney and issued handbills. This is their story:

> *On Sunday last, 8th, inst., the town of Dallas was all but reduced to ashes, and almost wiped out of existence. Such a calamity has never before befallen this community—such an overwhelming disaster afflicted an enterprising and illustrious people, nor so complete a destruction of valuable property ever occurred in a small town. The fire originated in some boxes in front of W. W. Peak & Bros. Drug Store and in less than five minutes the entire building was enveloped in flames. The wind was high, blowing from the southwest, and the thermometer at the time (half past one o'clock) was standing at 105 degrees F. in the shade. The fire was then communicated to the Old Drug store and the building and warehouse of A. Shirek and the Herald office.*

The story continued, listing 24 different businesses and/or buildings destroyed around the square. The list began with (1) Peak's Drug Store, (2) A. Shirek's building and warehouse (3) the *Herald* building, offices and equipment, (4) Smith & Murphy's large brick building, (5) the three-story building of S. H. Cockrell (my own St. Nicholas Hotel—more on this personal loss later); The story said *"At one and the same time the whole west side of the Square was a blazing mass of ruins."* (6) The Crutchfield House; (7) Wester's Barber Shop, (8) the frame for A. Simon's new building, (9) The old tavern stand, (10) The office of B. W. Stone, (11) Young Carr's Saddlery Shop, (12) The large storehouse of Herman Hirsch, (13) Darnell's Livery Stable, (14) A. Simon's storehouse and warehouse, (15) Caruth's old stand, (16) D. B. Thomas's Drug Store, (17) J. W. Ellett's store and warehouse, (18) Sayres Old Drug Store, (19) W.

Brodie's Old Shop and residence, (20) E. M. Stackpoles's store and ware-house, (21) Messr. Caruth and Simon's storehouse, (22) R. R. Fletcher and Company storehouse, (23) J. C. McCoy's law office, and (24) the black-smith shop on the north side of the street.

The story continued:

For a time the fire threatened a number of private resi-dences. There were also several small buildings near, and to the rear of those on the square consumed. In the upper story of Peak's drug store were the offices of Dr. C. C. Spencer and W. S. J. Adams, Samuel Russell and John S. Chapman, lawyers, who lost all their libraries and wardrobes. Also rooms occupied by P. W. Stevinson, Peter Spanburg and W. W. Peak, who also lost their clothing. Jas. S. Smith's small office adjoining it was occupied by himself, Dr. A. A. Johnson and John Good, the last two of whom lost all their libraries.

The old drug store was vacant but had a few of Smith & Murphy's goods in it which were burnt. Over Mr. Shirek's store and in the front room of the Herald office was the office of E. C. McKenzie, who lost all in the room with a trifling exception.

In the Crutchfield House was the Post Office and an attempt was made to save its contents, and portion of the mail was got-ten out but was afterward destroyed in another building. The entire contents of the Post Office were burned with the excep-tion of some of the postage stamps....

The long story continued to give every detail of the conflagration, ending with:

"With this issue, we suspend for a time and hope that our friends will bear patiently with us until our re-appearance on the stage of action."

Now, a month removed from that horrible Sunday, we are all still numb. In our homes and in our churches we have thanked God that no lives were lost and that our residences still stand.

Today I walk in the ashes of what just one year ago was the culmina-tion of my husband's dream, and I recall the night the St. Nicholas Hotel opened. At that time, still in widow's black and sitting quietly at one corner of the grand ballroom while the music and the dancing swirled around me, I thought the hotel, in all its grandeur, was the opening door to an unlimited future.

Today I do not know what to think. I am humbled to my knees. I stand in these ashes. Bow my head. Raise my arms. Lift my prayer to God. And ask,

Oh, Mr. Cockrell, what would you do now?

In grief and in memory,

Sarah Horton Cockrell

PART II: . . . LIKE A PHOENIX RISING

1861

My dear and treasured Dallas Friends,

For the last half of last year I had no time and no energy to continue my journal. When I last took my pen and wrote my version of the Great Fire that devastated our town in July and the pall of hopelessness that shrouded all of our actions immediately afterward, I had not yet seen the end of those dark days.

The town went wild after the fire.

Things were already tense during the days and weeks leading up to the fire. Not only was it the hottest summer any of us could remember—and we all know that temperaments escalate along with soaring temperatures—but the heat raging in national politics equaled that of the scorching weather.

In May of last year the fuse was lighted in a smoldering political war when the Republicans nominated Abraham Lincoln for president. Stephen Douglas, the chief spokesman for the Democrats, and Lincoln had been adversaries for years. Both lawyers, they had started out as friends and served together in the Senate, but divided over slavery and other issues. In the late 1850s and almost until time for nomination of candidates in 1860, Douglas appeared to be a shoo-in as the Democratic candidate. But what appeared to be a waffling commitment on slavery antagonized the South, blocked his nomination and sent the Democratic Party home from its convention without a candidate. Two months later, having divided along philosophical lines, the Democrats split into two factions, one nominating Douglas and the other John C. Breckenridge of Kentucky. The split virtually assured Lincoln's election.

What is clear to me, from reading papers sent to me by family and friends from Virginia, Missouri and Illinois is that neither Douglas nor Lincoln began their debates totally in opposition to each other. Douglas coined the term *popular sovereignty,* which he defined as each state having the right to enter the union as a slave state, or not. Nor was Lincoln, in his early political career, totally opposed to slavery. As early as 1836 while serving as an Illinois state representative, he said that slavery was "both an injustice and bad policy," but added that abolition agitation increased rather than abated the evils of slavery.

From my understanding, it appears that Mr. Lincoln, as president, would do all in his power to conciliate both sides of the issue.

Unfortunately, it seems almost impossible for rigid political lines and hard-core beliefs to reach a point of amnesty. It was as if a line had been drawn. One was either for or against. The situation was either black or white. There was no middle ground. I cannot help but wonder how things might have been different if a group of women had been making the decisions. We—the female sex—are said to be wishy-washy, faint of heart, unprepared to address the harsh realities of life. This has not been my experience. I have had to compromise many times, often to settle for less than I desire, sometimes to give up something in which I strongly believe in order to gain a new perspective and a new advantage later on. But weak I am not. And I do not think women are weak because they know how to keep calm while the world goes crazy around them.

But all this is pure conjecture. The point is that July 8, 1860, changed the life of every Dallas citizen. Those of us who lived it will never forget, though we may not yet know how it will play out on life's stage. What we do know is that pent-up emotions spilled over into yet another scenario too sinister to contemplate.

Three men, all slaves, were hanged on our city street, for crimes of which they were probably innocent.

Emotions were at a fever pitch. On street corners, in bars and taverns, in the middle of city streets, in their businesses and in their homes and along the front of where the buildings used to be—in some cases with embers still smoldering—men gathered and promised vengeance on the perpetrators of the "crime." There were few cool heads and even fewer willing to listen to those who raised their voices for calmness.

On Monday, July 9, a mass meeting was called in the courthouse. Armed guards admitted only those who were deemed "proper" to attend such a gathering. This, naturally, excluded all women and some of the men who had asked for tolerance.

Nat Burford, who had been holding court in Waxahachie, arrived to address the gathering. I am told that he delivered a very rational speech, cautioning the men against violating the law and asking that any hasty decisions be delayed until the legal system took its course. Even as the men listened, their faces were granite-like. A low mumbling testified to their determination that they find somebody guilty and that punishment be swift and complete. A whispering campaign indicted "two visiting preachers" for stirring up the Negroes and fomenting a rebellion among them.

Fifty-two men were chosen to investigate and determine who had started the fire. The report came back swiftly. Three slaves were guilty, three black men led by a "notorious" Negro known as Uncle Cato. He and two others were immediately rounded up and on Wednesday, July 11, hanged on the banks of the Trinity River a short distance above Commerce and west of George W. Baird's home at the foot of Elm Street. All citizens were urged to bring their slaves to the "ceremony" as a lesson to them. Several families complied.

It was further decreed that the two Northern agitators, both ministers of the Methodist Church North, be rounded up, whipped and escorted out of town, and it was strongly suggested that all owners round up and whip their slaves.

This did not happen. Of the 8,665 people who live in Dallas County, 1,074, about 12 per cent of us, are slaves and most of us live in harmony with each other.

I can tell you what this episode did for me. It crystallized my opposition to slavery.

If only the cooler heads had prevailed! By agreement of the 52 men chosen to "mete out justice" we have no record of whether, or not, they came to a unanimous decision, but Judge James Bentley, one of the 52 said later: "It was a hot day when the town burned, so hot that matches ignited from the heat of the sun. Wallace Peak has just finished a new two-story frame building to house his drug store and several men were lounging, visiting and smoking on the second floor of the new building. Piled up near the building were a lot of boxes filled with shavings, and I think a cigar stump or a lighted match was thrown into one of the boxes, and from that the fire started. Several fires had occurred. There was a great deal of excitement about a Negro uprising. Somebody had to hang, and the three Negroes went."

With all of the sadness I endure over the state of my town—Alexander's town—and the possibilities for its future, I must be personally concerned with my own reaction and obligation to its future. The hanging turned out to be a town jubilee. My two older sons begged to be allowed to go, but I would not allow it. I am told there were both women and children present. I cannot imagine it.

With all of the agitation going on around me, with war hovering ever closer and the North and the South split over issues of slavery, it is all I can do to keep my children safe and to decide to what extent I shall rebuild. It is imperative that I consolidate my holdings in order to handle the businesses as conveniently and profitably as possible. It often seems to me that each piece of the business I inherited when Mr. Cockrell died has a life of its own, and there are many times when I feel that I cannot hold the reins of each in my hands and handle all the different pieces. Late last year I decided to sell the sawmill and gristmill. It had become one of the least profitable of my holdings and all of us understand that we must use brick and stone building materials in the future. This feeling was born out when the fire destroyed our city. The sale of the sawmill became final on February 22.

The building of the bridge will have to wait. Even though I received estimates for its erection in May and started arrangements for the building to proceed, what has happened in the past few weeks has drastically re-directed my commitment. But, I must rebuild the hotel. I believe that no matter what happens, Dallas will continue to grow and be a hub for trade, and businessmen will require a place to stay.

I grieve over the St. Nicholas Hotel. Not only did Mr. Darnell lose his position as manager of this most prestigious edifice in the Southwest, but he also lost his livery stable though I am grateful that the animals were all rescued.

The St. Nicholas had only begun, and barely, to make a profit. For the present, I plan to convert the two-story brick building on the southeast corner of the square into a hotel and call it the Dallas Hotel. I had it built five years ago as an office building with retail space on the lower floors. Dallas will continue to grow and must have a hotel. Now, it has none since both the Crutchfield and the St. Nicholas were destroyed in the fire. At some later date I will decide where and what to rebuild.

Even as I count my losses and consider the possibilities for rebuilding any or all of the structures that were destroyed by the fire, I must turn my attention to the future. And I am again amazed at the resilience of the human spirit. Those who suffered the greatest financial losses are often the very ones who are first to announce that they will not be defeated. So even as they began to clear away debris left by the fire on the city square, citizens were making plans to rebuild.

The national political situation is critical. Mr. Lincoln took office as the 16th president in March, but even before his inauguration sparks of a major war were already ignited. Following his election last November, South Carolina on December 17 issued an Ordinance of Secession. A conference of conciliation, the Washington Peace Conference, was quickly arranged but dissolved in chaos. As its delegates assembled, Southerners were meeting in Montgomery, Alabama, to form the Confederate States of America. Georgia, Alabama, Mississippi, Florida and Louisiana immediately joined. On February 18 the new nation inaugurated Jefferson Davis as its president. I can only hope that he is up to the challenges that lie ahead. He's a West Point graduate and had served as a senator from Mississippi before resigning in January.

Dallas County voted three to one in favor of secession. Governor Sam Houston opposed withdrawal from the Union, but called a special election. And on February 23, Texas ratified the secession ordinance. It breaks my heart. We had struggled so long to become a part of the Union, and it seems only yesterday that we succeeded in our endeavors. Has it been all for naught? As a woman, I had no vote—and I had no voice—but this did not keep the city leaders from asking for financial support. I immediately agreed to purchase uniforms for men who join the military.

The first shots were fired in April when the newly organized southern army took over Fort Sumpter at Charleston, South Carolina. President Lincoln immediately called for a militia to suppress the Confederacy. On April 20 Dallas' Captain John J. Good was ordered to march his troops to Austin as soon as possible. A farewell party was hastily arranged. Though renovations are not yet completed, I offered the use of the Dallas Hotel ballroom, and everybody from miles around came to bid the boys good-by. Musicians brought their instruments and the revelry went on almost all night as young couples, husbands with wives, sweethearts and would-be lovers embraced. And, at day break on April 27, they kissed good-by as the troops marched off to Austin.

Railroad fever is, if anything, more intense than ever. If Dallas is to become a major city, it must be a transportation hub; so plans to bring a railroad through town continues to be the most pressing immediate action. But I am certain that rail service, along with the bridge, will have to wait.

Neither the fire nor the rumors of war delayed plans to celebrate past achievements and highlight plans for the future. Most of the leading businessmen in town—and I as the only woman—had already bought stock in the Dallas County Agricultural and Mechanical Association. And in October only four months after Dallas burned, the first fair took place. It was located outside corporate city limits near Mill Creek, formerly called Nussbaumer Branch, and enclosed by a board fence. Centered by a two-story building housing the offices and some exhibits, it extended to either side with seats fronting an arena and racetracks. On the outside of the track, booths held displays of the latest agricultural implements.

Long-horned cattle and razorback hogs were shown in pens erected especially for that purpose. A few fine horses were also on display.

The main building in which the offices were located also held women's exhibits. The ladies showed their arts and crafts—principally needle work, crochet, knitting, piece work, rugs, quilts and blankets, counterpanes and coverlets. I could not take much time away from business to get involved in the fair. But I did find time to go one afternoon and was most impressed with the quilts, such tiny, intricate stitches, such artistry! The blue ribbon winner was Mrs. Alexander Harwood—Sarah Ann Peak Harwood. She had entitled her winning entry "Sarah Ann's Flower Garden," each piece centered with a rose in varying shades from pale pink to deep rose, each surrounded by triangles of solid color to blend with the center flower and each block a six-sided shape set into a larger square. It made me wish I had followed my mother's instructions to learn to sew a fine seam. I get by, but I am simply not gifted with a needle in the way Ma was or in the way most of my sisters learned to be.

In the afternoons and early evenings just before dark, the sporting events took place, an equestrian tournament for both the men and the women and the pony races. John Mays and Jim Barton earned blue ribbons in the men's equestrian tournament. The women's division of the equestrian tournament was not so fortunate to have a unanimous winner. Sisters, the Misses Maggie and Wood Sheperd and Mrs. Colonel Obenchain were the three principal contestants. When Miss Wood Sheperd was declared the blue ribbon winner, friends of Col. Obenchain protested that Mrs. Obenchain was by far the better rider and should have been given the prize. Miss Sheperd was a height of graciousness, requesting that a second contest be held the next day. She and her sister did not participate in this second competition, but several of the ladies were eager to have a repeat contest. I hear that Mrs. Obenchain was sadly disappointed when again she came in second. The judges declared that Miss Fannie Palmer, who had not entered the competition the previous day, was the blue ribbon winner.

The children went to the fair several times, usually accompanied by their Aunt Mary, who liked nothing better than to go and take them.

I did attend the closing ceremonies of the fair. The finale, the lance and ring tournament had been planned for months and promoted throughout the state, so attendance was at capacity. The sport is our adaptation of the ancient Saxon-Norman game of chivalry. Mounted on steeds, players form two teams. Each horseman carries a lance and advances at full speed toward the center of the playing field where he attempts to ring a target suspended overhead. Each team had 12 players who advanced center-arena alternately. Each member had chosen a young lady as his candidate for queen of the fair. The girls, daughters of the most outstanding families in the area, beautifully gowned, formed the queen's court. The Sir Knights was the winning team and Junius Peak the winning individual. He had the honor of crowning his special young lady Queen of the Fair.

John Neely Bryan, Dallas' founder, came home at last. He arrived in the early spring. He had been gone for more than six years. He roamed around in the West, went first to California then back to Colorado and again to California. Like most Dallas speculators, he never struck it rich in gold, and, in fact, worked at menial tasks, mostly for "grub." He lived with the Indians and with other associates he had met in his younger days also, I understand, making new friends along the way. Except for the letters he wrote to my husband, I have no personal knowledge of his meanderings, and Margaret Bryan has always been so protective of her husband that she has, so far as I can tell, not confided to anybody. At one time he and my husband were very close. But after Alex died, I have not heard anything of a personal nature about his travels or about the state of his health. If there were no letters to Margaret and no communication with him until he recently turned up again, he had to have been devastated by the condition of the city he founded.

He arrived on the west bank of the Trinity around nine in the evening unaware that the bridge Alexander had built had caved into the river two years ago. The ferry had closed down for the night, but Margaret heard him yelling across the river, recognized his voice and awakened servants to go to rescue him. Most of the information I have about his return comes through the children. Luther Bryan, Margaret's fourth child, and my Frank are playmates, almost exactly the same age. Frank was born the last of August 1854 and Luther, whose full name is Alexander Luther, five weeks later. The two boys are almost inseparable. Frank says the Bryan children were scared when they got up the morning after their father arrived home and saw this strange man with a beard covering almost his entire face sitting at the breakfast table. None of the children knew him. Luther was born after Mr. Bryan left home, and John Neely Jr., the oldest, was only seven. Lizzie was five and Ned was three. Now they are 14, 12 and 10. Luther, at 7, had never seen his father. Of course, they did not recognize their father.

I wonder not only what Mr. Bryan's return will mean for his family, but also what it portends for Dallas? Will he take a renewed interest in the growth and welfare of the city? Even before he left, his recurrent melancholia often undermined his plans. I recall how hard Alexander tried to reason with him before he left town—even, before that, when he turned over all of the unsold lots in the city to Alex. The boys tell me that he did not know about Alexander's death and that learning about it has sent him into despair. Mrs. Bryan has been planning to move to the property she inherited from her family when her father died, and I wonder if her husband's return will hasten this plan, or scuttle it?

Yours for now.

Sarah Horton Cockrell

1862-1865

To All Who Care About Dallas:

These past three years have been momentous years—bad years. The War Between the States has torn our country apart. The letters to my Sister Jane, which I began as soon as we arrived in Texas and followed them with jottings in my journal, have been laid aside as I have struggled to keep up with demands on my time. The leisure I once had out on Mountain Creek as an unmarried woman to sit and ponder is a luxury I can no longer afford. My life as a widow, the mother of four children and a businesswoman has compelled me to neglect writing. There is no time for detailed daily scribbling or even for a weekly or monthly review of what is happening, but I am loathe to give up writing altogether. I have learned that a review of what has gone on in the past often opens doors to a future I could not fathom. So, from time to time as I can, I will continue this journal.

As I read over what I last wrote, I am astounded that so much has happened so fast—and yet that in one sense it seems that time stands still.

In this spring of 1862, my children, who are all growing up so fast, command more and more of my attention, and managing a large business keeps me occupied day and night. Aurelia is going to be twelve in a few days. Her health is not good, and I worry about her. She was in and out of bed all during the past winter—violent headaches, chills and fever. But she does not let it stop her from her studies and only the most pressing illness keeps her from her music lessons.

The boys, thank God, are sturdier. They are still young enough that I can keep them corralled. Bob, who was ten in January, pushes all the time for more independence than I can allow him. Frank will be eight in August. Some days I think he was born grown up. He is the only one of the children who lingers at my elbow while I am doing the books, and he asks questions about the business that astound me. He is so responsible that I have to remind myself he is still a child and keep him focused on his studies so that he will have the knowledge he needs for future development. Baby Alexander is not a baby any more. At five, he is out of the nursery, and we are converting it to a bedroom for him and Frank, leaving Bob at last to have a room of his own—something he has wanted since we moved into this house. Frank is very protective of his younger brother and the two of them will be much more compatible roommates than are Frank and Bob.

Without my sister running this household, I would be lost. She and Mr. Thompson have been invaluable to me.

Dallas is growing so fast. At the beginning of 1862, I completed renovations on the Dallas Hotel and asked my brother-in-law, Marlin Thompson, to take over as manager. Since my sister Mary (his wife) moved in with the children and me he has been commuting from downtown to Mountain Creek trying to keep the farm going. He is an excellent business manager, and I am grateful that he has accepted this job and that the hotel provided a place of their own.

Most of our young able-bodied men are in uniform and fighting for the Confederacy. All men and boys 16 and over are required to register for the military and an edict printed last week in the *Herald* warned that "anyone engaging in conduct injurious to the Confederacy will be imprisoned." The state government backed up this edict by declaring martial law. And, it is not only the young men who are signing up. John Neely Bryan was one of the first to enlist. He has joined Darnell's Cavalry regiment. He is 50 years old!

Most of my personal information on the war comes in letters from George Guess, the lawyer who helped me on so many occasions. He was among the first from this area to sign up for service and holds the rank of colonel. Getting mail through to the fighting men is very difficult. Most of the time we try to send it by courier because the Confederacy is so new and does not have a dependable system. Mail is not its top priority, though it should be because morale of the men on the front lines and of the families and friends back home is largely dependent on staying connected with each other.

The first letter I received from Col. Guess was dated September 10, 1861, last year. He had just received the letter I wrote to him on the third of August. He asked about his friends here with a special line to my children and asked that I continue to remember him in my prayers, as I most certainly shall.

Out of a Dallas population of 8,665, 15 per cent or 1,300 of them, are in uniform and gone from home. The work normally done by men has been taken over by the women. Aided by the children and slaves, women have planted and harvested the crops, mostly wheat, oats and corn. Wives, mothers and daughters are magnificent—keeping up the home front with all of the traditional chores of women and, in addition, taking on the responsibility of running the businesses. We have daily sewing circles in the churches where we make and/or repair uniforms, knit socks and mufflers, make coats, repair shoes and provide other clothing for our men on the battlefronts. Every home has a garden, and we preserve all the food we can harvest to send to the fighting men. Last week a large shipment, three wagon loads, of supplies left Dallas for front lines in Alabama. We can only hope and pray for a safe delivery.

Dallas has been named a Confederate quartermaster and commissary headquarters. It is far enough away from the front lines that there is little danger of the Union government confiscating supplies, and guards are stationed around the facilities at all times to eliminate sabotage.

With so many supplies going to the fighting men, we are pressed to provide food and clothing for our families. Cloth is almost impossible to find. If it does become available, it is too expensive to purchase. Yardage for a calico dress costs around $100. Needless to add, most everybody is doing without. Shoemakers are much in demand and have turned some unlikely materials, mostly saddle leather and cloth, into shoes and boots.

The *Herald*, which incidentally "went to war" in January and did not publish for a couple of months, urges an organized effort to assist women and children. I have a major role in the relief effort. Never a day passes that I do not receive from one to half a dozen letters from men in the battle zones begging for help for their families here. I do what I can, though my resources are limited. The income from the ferry, from the new hotel and from rental property are the basis for my income, and all of these are tied to whether, or not, people can afford the services.

Even with more than a thousand men in uniform and away from Dallas, the population here has remained stable. Many who can afford to move away from the front lines are living here. I rented my own large house on Mill Creek to Col. Jeremiah Vardaman Cockrell who moved his family here from Missouri. Mr. Cockrell is Alexander's half brother. Several others from Alabama, Mississippi, Georgia and South Carolina have joined families in this area.

The Homestead Act passed by the U.S. Congress in May is also beginning to make an impact, even though we are no longer a part of the United States. The law will not go into effect until January of next year, but we have a trickle of families arriving to take advantage of the promise to provide any citizen or any alien intending to become a citizen with 160 acres of land free except for a $10 registration fee. In order to gain title of the land, they must live on it for five years and improve it. Dallas, doubtless, will not be the beneficiary of many aliens. Most will settle in the Hill Country around San Antonio, which is already peopled with Germans, Czechs, Swedes and Poles. But our connection to France through the former La Reunion settlement will surely lure some additional population.

In February the U. S. Congress created a Department of Agriculture as a branch of the federal government. We have no idea yet how this will impact our part of the world, certainly not in any way now that the country is divided, but who knows what the future will hold?

Even with the war raging, some building is continuing here. William Brown Miller has built a beautiful antebellum plantation home in the Greek Revival style on his property not too far from our Mountain Lake property. The town's expansion continues mostly to that area west of the Trinity River, which bodes well for the future of the ferry and the bridge I intend to construct as soon as the war is over and supplies are again available.

Losses from the fire, and increasing competition from new people makes it hard for some of the older firms to stay in business. Maria Ervay, the bride of Henry S. Ervay, has opened a boarding house in the couples' large home on the southern border of downtown. Mr. Ervay, a developer, built their home with extra rooms to rent to his own employees. Mrs. Ervay decided to provide breakfast and dinner for the boarders, which was approved by her husband as a way of increasing their income. Those who ate at her table spread the word that she was such a good cook and excellent manager that they barely noticed the scarcity of food supplies, and before long she had increased her business to add lunch for the downtown businessmen. I understand the business is thriving.

The death of Will Toomy was my greatest personal loss this year. He was hired by Alexander in our very early marriage and became one of my two most faithful employees. When Alex died, I asked him to take over as general superintendent of all the property. He has been unfailingly faithful, and I shall miss him greatly. I made arrangements to have his body returned to his native Tennessee for burial and have received a beautiful letter thanking me from his old father who told me that having Will home confirmed all that he had told them about us.

Abraham Lincoln, the United States president, made himself even more unpopular, if that is possible, by issuing an Emancipation Proclamation on September 22 declaring "all slaves in rebelling territories to be free" as of January 1 next year. The "ruling" has no effect in the South because we now belong to the Confederate States of America and are not subject to laws or governmental edicts issued in the Union States.

1863. I'm penning this on the very last day of the year, which has, it seems, dragged on and on and on. We are a year older and have been another year into the terrible war. I mark time only by the ages of my children. Aurelia entered her teen years in May; Bob is eleven; Frank nine and Alexander, seven. Many times I am exhausted trying to keep the businesses afloat, provide food and clothing for the children, and meet an increasing load of responsibility to the town.

Raging battles across Alabama and Mississippi daily bring news that one of our own is a victim of this war—killed, injured or missing in action—and every mail brings more letters to me from fighting men requesting food and clothing or help for their families. The money issued by our government is of so little value that some of the soldiers, paid only a pittance, do not even send it home. Women are left to fend for themselves and their children as best they can.

We hear of widespread hunger in the South. Richmond, the capital of the Confederate States of America, suffered a bread riot in May. Alexander Harwood and his wife, Sarah Ann Harwood, live there and much of our first-hand knowledge comes from letters that Mrs. Harwood writes to her parents, Jefferson and Malvina Peak, and other family members. Mr. Harwood is assistant postmaster general of the Confederacy, so if any mail gets through, hers has a good chance of arriving safely.

In November Mr. Lincoln was re-elected for a second term as president of the United States with more than half of the popular vote and 212 of the 233 electoral votes.

The United States continues to expand and the battle rages between territories that do not allow slave ownership and those that do. Congress approved statehood for West Virginia which two years ago split off from Virginia over slavery. Nevada then was approved as the 36th state. It is interesting that the Union, in counting its states, does not acknowledge those of us who have left the Union and formed our own government. In addition to West Virginia and Arizona, two other territories were created and legally acknowledged—the Idaho Territory from parts of Dakota,

Nebraska, Utah and Washington, and the Montana Territory from Idaho. Families continue to move to Dallas both to escape the war in other southern states and to take part in what we think is a bright future for our part of the world.

My children are clamoring for roller skates, a new fad that is sweeping the country. I have not seen the contraption but am certain that roller-skating will never succeed here. What few sidewalks we have are covered with planks and are so uneven that anyone daring to try to traverse them on wheels attached to their feet are certain to be injured. There will be no roller skates for the Cockrell children! You can be sure of that.

1864. As this year ends, I have the energy for only a few lines to mark its passing. There are so few good things to remember.

We are war-weary. In the spring a new leader named Ulysses S. Grant took over as commander of the Union forces. Until the middle of the year, the South was victorious in several battles, but after that we have continued to lose the war. Even worse, the countryside of the beautiful Southland has been ravaged—homes burned, cattle and food stolen, inhabitants left destitute. On March 3, there was a major march on the Confederacy's capitol in Richmond. Most of the Southern ports have been blockaded; no reinforcements can get through. Help from France and England is no longer available. General Sherman marched his Union army from Chattanooga, Tennessee, through Georgia razing everything along a mile-wide path to Savannah, which is now occupied by Union forces.

Our summer was sweltering and so dry that the Trinity River looked like a small creek. Drinking water is precious. We hoard every drop. I most miss being able to bathe every day. We have done the laundry only every two weeks and sometimes not that often. We have not dared to water our gardens so there are very, very few flowers to brighten the landscape. The crops dried up in the fields. What cotton we were able to produce and harvest found such a limited market that there was little use in trying to pick it. It's good that we had such an abundant crop last year and preserved so much food, which we are using frugally, because the harvest this year is minimal. There is nothing much on the shelves of the stores, and even if there were, nobody has money. Confederate money is worthless; the gold value of paper money has fallen to $4.60 per $100. It would take a bushel basket of Confederate dollars to purchase a pound of sugar.

The hot summer was followed by the coldest winter anybody can remember. What little water remained in the Trinity froze almost solid. My kids joined everybody else's in Dallas in a frenzy of ice-skating. It is good that, at least, they have this diversion because Christmas came and went with barely a nod of recognition. There is no money for celebrating, but Sister Mary and Aurelia brightened our spirits by decorating the house with cedar, pine and holly.

1865. I have vowed to do better this year at keeping up with what is going on. In re-reading my entries from last year, I was embarrassed to see that everything I wrote sounded like doom and gloom, but I need to add that even in the worst of times, good things do happen. Most important, the Cockrell family is well when so many of our friends and neighbors are suffering from colds and pneumonia. There have been a number of deaths among the townsfolk.

Now, on the fifth day of February, we are in the midst of a cold, wet winter. When I recall the drought of last summer, I remember to be grateful for the rain, but it is difficult to be thankful when we are shivering!

A few days ago (on February 1) the United States Congress made President Lincoln's Emancipation Proclamation freeing all slaves official. Since I, as a woman, am not a participant in any of the local discussions, I don't have a clear idea what the reaction here has been, but it seems to me that almost everybody has been aware for a long time that the South is losing the war and that ownership of Negroes will no longer be allowed. We have owned a few slaves from time to time, but it has never seemed so to me. Our people who are black live on our property, work for us and are paid a salary. My family never owned slaves; we were too poor. For one time in his rambunctious youth, Alexander hunted down runaway slaves and returned them to their owners, but he lived to regret it and by the time of his death was totally reformed. As a businesswoman I have been chided to take a firm stand for slave ownership, but as a devout Methodist woman, I have heard horror tales of injustices that disturb me greatly. I am glad that the issue is legally settled.

There has been very little on the issue in the *Herald*, Dallas' only newspaper, but occasionally I receive newspapers from Philadelphia, Washington and Richmond and from them I have learned that there is great unrest among women's groups because it appears that the newly freed black men will be given the right to vote while women are still held in legal bondage. So far I have not suffered greatly because of my legal restrictions because, as a widow, I have many freedoms that married women do not enjoy. But it only seems fair and right that all women of legal age should enjoy the same privileges as their husbands, fathers and brothers.

Later. It is only a matter of days, I feel sure, until the war will end. In South Carolina, Union forces are occupying both Columbia and

Charleston, and now the siege is on to take Richmond. Only pockets of resistance continue. We have just learned that the Confederacy's president, Jefferson Davis, has been captured and imprisoned.

We have no idea of what the future has in store for us, but are immeasurably heartened by the words of Lincoln in his inaugural address. He is quoted in the *Herald* as saying, "With malice toward none, with charity for all . . . let us strive on to finish the work we are in, to bind up the nation's wounds . . . to do all, which may achieve and cherish a just and lasting peace."

Mr. Lincoln has not been popular in the South, but he seems sincere in his desire to reunite the country as quickly and favorably as possible. This hope for reconciliation was greatly enhanced on April 9 when General Lee and General Grant affixed their signatures to the terms of surrender. It was Palm Sunday, a warm and sunny afternoon when the two generals met in the William McLean Parlor at Appomattox Court House in Virginia to put an end to the bloodiest war in American history. The meeting was entirely cordial, according to reports, and the terms unbelievably generous. As a token of his surrender, General Lee offered his unsheathed sword to General Grant, who refused to take it. Lee's 28,000 men, most hungry, some starving, many sick and wounded, were allowed to keep their horses and guns and told to go home. Neither man considered the settlement a great victory for the North or a shameful defeat for the South. In battle they had been unflinching. In victory and defeat they behaved as the gentlemen they were.

On Monday, the day after Generals Lee and Grant signed the armistice ending the war, the last battalion of the Confederate army surrendered at Shreveport, Louisiana.

If we thought the ending of the war would be the beginning of great progress for our country and for Dallas, these hopes were shattered on the night of April 14 when President Lincoln was assassinated while attending a play at Ford's Theater in Washington. A 27-year-old actor, John Wilkes Booth, who knew the theater well and doubtless had plotted his escape, climbed the stairway into Lincoln's box and shot him in the head. He then jumped from the box, breaking his leg, leapt onto the stage shouting *"Sic temper tyrannis"* (The South is avenged) and made his escape.

It was not until near the end of the month, on April 26, that a Washington posse discovered Booth hiding in a barn. He was killed by a gunshot—either by his own hand or by those seeking to arrest him.

We have been very ambivalent about Lincoln. He seemed lenient in victory and again harsh in judgment. Under his presidency we had no idea what the future held for us. Now we will never know. But I personally felt that he was our best protection against marauders.

Vice President Andrew Johnson, who is little known, has succeeded Lincoln in office. A native of Tennessee, he is not a wealthy man, is a Union loyalist, against slavery and against secession. We tremble because in this vacuum of leadership, jostling for position will be fierce. Only time will tell whether he has the potential of great leadership or whether he will succumb to the masses that seek further to plunder the South.

June. By summer it became clear that President Johnson is his own person, in control of the government, and plans to follow the policies outlined by his predecessor. Even though he has been bitterly denounced by rabble-rousers who demand retribution from the South, the president has been firm in his resolve to reconstruct the nation with the former Confederate States reunited into the fold as full partners. It seems that the President is determined that governance of the states should come from the people who are governed. His appointments are exemplary. Though loyal Unionists, they all seem to be reasonable men who will carry out the President's policies.

Gordon Granger, a general in the Union army, took over the military control of Texas on June 19. There's a lot of grumbling about his edicts, but they seem reasonable to me and do not include any orders not already agreed upon in General Lee's surrender. He made four points: (1) That secession is null and void, and Texas is again a state of the United States of America; (2) That all Confederate state officers must relinquish their control; (3) That all prisoners are paroled, and (4) That all Negroes are free.

Andrew J. Hamilton has been appointed provisional governor of Texas. So far, we don't know what that bodes for us. We are told that state-named officials will appoint all of our city and county officials, and this is already happening in cities to the south, namely San Antonio and its environs. I am sure they will get around to us before long.

A steady stream of returning soldiers are coming through here, many of our very own, and we do everything we can to cheer them on their way to their families. I have made rooms available in the new hotel for some that needed overnight accommodations. Some of the men are in rags. Many are ill. The Lost Cause is sending back many men who seem to have lost their way. The light has gone out in their eyes.

One night a few weeks back, a young soldier came into the hotel at dusk just as I was about to go home. He looked so forlorn that I lingered. After Mr. Thompson provided him a room, assuring him that there would be no charge, I walked over and told him that a hot meal would be waiting for him in the dining room when he wanted it. Mr. Thompson looked aghast. The help had gone home and the dining room was closed, but I knew Mary would have dinner on our table and there would be enough to share. I asked Mr. Thompson to see that water was taken up to the boy's room so that he could wash up. The kid disappeared up the stairs and I hastily made my exit, found my family waiting for me when I got home, quickly packed a portion of our dinner and sent Frank back to the hotel with it. Frank didn't come back for more than two hours, but I didn't worry. I knew he was listening with rapt attention to any and all stories that the young soldier had to share.

We have suffered less than most other of the seceded states. No battles have been fought on our soil and no Union armies have ravaged our countryside. The factory established in Lancaster to manufacture and repair artillery and supplies with Maxime Guillot as superintendent has never been attacked. Our Quartermaster Headquarters to distribute supplies and food has been unbelievably safe. We are also aware that we are the center of a rich, abundantly producing food supply—when the weather permits. Our numerous Gulf ports and our proximity to Mexico allowed shipments to continue through our city when most of the other outlets in the South were closed, either captured or under siege.

We have continued to grow. Many people dislocated from their native states and cities who came here for sanctuary during the war have decided to stay. A few others are filtering in all the time, including some of the returning soldiers who, while passing through, experienced the first really friendly responses in many months, and have vowed to return with their families. Some will come; some will not. But, in all, the future growth of the city is assured.

The arrival in our town of the Reverend William Ceiton Young with his family gives me great hope that the Methodist Church we have long desired will now be built. Since I gave the property at Commerce and Lamar to the church some years ago, the war has intervened and no building has taken place. Now, it is time. We have met in homes or in public buildings with one minister or another, the Reverends Smith and Hughes among them, filling the pulpits. We could never be sure that we would have a minister when we met each Sunday morning. The Rev. Young moved here earlier this year from Paris, Texas. A former circuit-riding minister who covered vast territories, he served as a chaplain in the Confederacy under the command of a Dallas officer, Gen. W. L. Cabell. When he arrived in Paris earlier this year with his family, he attended the annual conference where he was persuaded to accept our appointment in Dallas. It was a great day when they arrived, and he filled the pulpit for the first time. Not only is he a good preacher, but his family is very special. His wife is the former Mary Susan Carolyn Pipkin, the daughter of the Reverend and Mrs. John F. Pipkin. That alone will make the family a marvelous addition to our Methodist ranks. Though very young, they are already parents of three children. And, if this were not enough, he is also accompanied by his mother, Marilla Ingram Young, who instilled in her son the best of Methodist values. Great preacher! Great family! And one other bonus. He has pledged to raise the necessary funds to build our first major Methodist church in downtown Dallas. He has already approached my brother-in-law, Marlin Thompson and me. There will be no turning back this time. Both the church and the bridge will be built in due course. The church first!

December. As the year winds down, I look back with gratitude for the enduring blessings and hope for a brighter future.

We are growing so fast! The day when I knew everybody in town is over. Along with exemplary people like the Youngs, there are many ruffians and charlatans. I am loathe to allow Aurelia and her friends to leave the house unescorted any more, and I worry about the boys every time they are out of my sight.

The freed Negroes are forming communities of their own. Within the last few months three small settlements have been established, one just to the west of downtown around the fair grounds called Deep Ellum[7], one on the farthest area north of the city called Little Egypt and one a little farther out called Elm Thicket. There are smaller pockets of freedmen throughout the county. Though some white folks look for trouble from these communities, I see no cause for concern. It is only natural that people of a kind band together in communities for protection and companionship.

In other states the situation is much tenser. In Pulaski, Tennessee, a group of young men with apparently nothing better to do have formed a group they call the Ku Klux Klan. Named for the Greek Kuklos, meaning circle, it started out as a social club with the aim of "recapturing the camaraderie and excitement of the war years," but the high jinx quickly got out of hand. Secret membership, strange rituals and eerie costumes terrorize the new black neighborhoods and frighten all whose aim is for a smooth transition into a new era. I hope that the young men of Dallas will have sense enough not to get involved in such an organization, and I have warned my three sons of its danger.

Yours for a brighter future,

Sarah Horton Cockrell

---

[7] Deep Ellum is a term that was not used until the 1920's.

December 30, 1866

Mrs. Margaret Bryan
White Rock
Dallas, Texas

Dear Margaret,

Since you moved so far away out into the area you inherited from your parents, we never get to see each other, and I miss you so much. I keep thinking that I will find the time to come see the new home you have built there. The children tell me it is marvelous, big and roomy, far removed from the double cabin you and Mr. Bryan built and that we moved to when we exchanged houses some years ago.

Our children keep us connected. Frank had such a good time when he spent the week with your Luther during the summer. Thank you for having him come visit. He misses his playmate as much as I miss having you as my close neighbor. I cannot believe our two boys, our babies, are twelve years old this year!

Thank you, too, for sharing your Lizzie with us these past two years. She is a gracious and beautiful young woman and seems like my very own. She is the sister Aurelia never had and though she is three years older than my daughter is, the two are the greatest of friends. They have enjoyed being in Miss Mullen's school together. Both are good students and enjoy music. Aurelia misses her very much since she moved back home this past summer.

Aurelia's health is greatly improved since she is beyond the age of childhood diseases. For most of her life she has caught every malady going around and seems to have suffered the worst symptoms of everything from whooping cough to measles to chicken pox. This is the first winter of her life that, so far, she has not had either a bad case of influenza or pneumonia. I think that having Lizzie as a friend and companion improved even her health!

Now that Lizzie has gone home, Aurelia misses her terribly and spends hours alone in her room reading or at the piano. She fills pages of her journal with poems and inspirational sayings along with her own writings. Last evening I found a sheet of paper she had left in the front room listing the names of all 58 of those enrolled in Miss Mullen's school.

The names are a Who's Who of prominent Dallas families and include your daughter and others you know, among them Kate Bowser, Georgia Claypool, Laura Crowdus, Bettie Floyd, my nieces Lizzie and Sallie Horton, Kate Knight, Belle and Kitty Patterson, Florence Peak and Friona Webb.

You must have been frantic about Lizzie's safety last spring if you heard about the terrible flood before you heard from us that we were all safe. I know Lizzie told you about it, and Frank doubtless gave his version. It was one of the most frightening experiences of my life. It came on so suddenly and we had no warning. When we went to bed on May 8, there were heavy rains but no indication that the river would overflow its banks and make prisoners of everybody living within its range. Flooding started at midnight and continued relentlessly the rest of the night until we were completely cut off from the outside world except for the road to McKinney. When the water started to come into the house, I got everybody upstairs and felt sure that we were safe. I even tried to get the children to go back to sleep. It is a good thing they didn't because within two hours floodwaters began to course through the second story. Some of the men had been rescuing stranded people since midnight, and we escaped that way. We spent the rest of the night in the hotel with about 40 others who had also been forced out of their homes. All of us kept anxious vigil the rest of the night hoping that water would not reach that high up. As you know, it didn't.

It's being called the Big Washout, and it was that and more. A story in the *Herald* on the day after the flood said, "it will in future years be remembered as the day of the greatest crisis in the Trinity River ever known at this place. Occurring during the heavy spring rainy season, it holds top place as the most disastrous in local history." There was only one human fatality, that of a young Negro boy named Austin who worked in Henry Ervay's livery stable. Austin was in the stables when the floodwaters swept him away. His body was not discovered until two days later. He was a former slave of Obadiah Knight, who said the kid was doubtless trying to rescue some of the animals when he was swept away—such was his loyalty.

I feel sure Lizzie told you about the Dallas Female College founded by the Methodist Church as a boarding school for girls that opened within the past year. You will recall that I was a strong advocate and supporter of the school from the moment of its inception. It is located on Bryan Street between Pearl and Crockett and is the first major educational institution in the city. I'm glad it's a boarding school so that girls from the surrounding countryside can attend. Doubtless families would find it impossible to enroll their daughters if they had to come from long distances.

Aurelia hopes to enroll there next year. We were hoping that Lizzie would be interested, but I think she may decide that marriage is her choice.

I am so glad the war is behind us. Robert, who will only be fifteen next month, was already eager to get old enough to sign up and fight in the war. And if the battles were still raging, I have no doubt that he would have found a way to get involved. He is my restless child! Since there are no schools of the caliber of the Female Institute for boys, some time within the next year I will make contact with Alexander's family back in Missouri to assist me in finding a school for him. Not a day passes that I don't remember my husband's dying wish that his children be educated.

I almost lost the notice of the American Equal Rights Association founded in New York because it happened on May 10, two days after the great flood here which dominated the news in the next several issues of the *Herald*. The organization is an outgrowth of the Women's Rights Society. As you know, I have never been involved in any of the women's activist projects. I do not know of any women's activist groups here and wouldn't have time to be involved if such existed. But, sometimes I wish things were different. I waste so much time maneuvering around barriers to get something important done, time that could be used so much better. It took a full week, probably more, of my time when I went to Austin to defend my proposal to secure the legislature's permit to build the bridge.

I can't help but be a little offended that my name does not appear on the list of board members. I am, the major stockholder, and it's my vision, my time and my money that is making the project possible. I know! I know! I did it! I made the appointments, and if I had been determined to flaunt convention just to prove a point, I could have done so. But getting the job done is far more important than winning another personal battle. Too, I was still so bruised from the bashing I endured in getting permission to build the bridge that I did not want to hurt myself further by insisting that my name be listed on the board. So, again I am the "phantom" project manager.

I am so glad that Mr. Bryan is well enough to be interested in the progress of the city again. When I read in the *Herald* that he had called a meeting of city leaders and outlined proposals for securing a railroad, I knew that he must be much improved. You are surely relieved, even when I know you worried about his health in August when he headed the delegation he appointed to the railroad convention in Tyler. I know that progress has been made because I have been approached to donate right-of-way through some of my property to build the railroad. Of course, I will oblige.

Next time Mr. Bryan plans a business trip into town, please come with him so that we can visit. I miss seeing you and talking with you. Time limitations make it difficult to seek new friends and even if I found them, no one would be as precious as you.

My love,

Sarah Horton Cockrell

December 1867

Notes for posterity to my Dallas friends:

As this year draws to a close, I'll make only a few observations for posterity. I've spent most of the day tending to business details, checking up on the property and getting prepared to pay the taxes. I've taken everything out of the little trunk I use as a repository for important papers, tossed out old records, gone over receipts for work completed, comprised a list of the unfinished business and the bills I need to pay—and made an estimate of everything I have committed myself to do

Though all is going well for me personally, there is a seething state of unrest surrounding us that impacts everything. In the spring, a radical Republican congressman from Pennsylvania named Thaddeus Stevens successfully led Congress to overthrow all leniency to the Southern states and put us all under military rule. In one fiery speech in Congress, he advocated giving each freed slave 40 acres and a mule out of the confiscated lands of the slaveholders. This could not have possibly worked, because most Southerners did not own slaves. I seriously doubt that there were a sufficient number of 40-acre plots among those that were slave holders for each freedman to have received his promised 40 acres. The new radical approach to reconstruction totally dismantled Lincoln's plan of amnesty for the reunification of the United States, policies being carried out so well by President Johnson.

In March, General P. H. Sheridan was put in charge of the District of Texas and the District of Louisiana. He had full power to remove any and all duly elected state, district and county officials and replace them with men of his own choosing.

On July 30, E. M. Pease, by military appointment, became governor of Texas. The appointments, dismissals, jockeying for power were a dizzying charade that few of us could follow, because on any given day, we never knew which man was in charge of what.

For the most part, Dallas County fared well. Men appointed to fill county governing positions were lenient in following restrictive orders and some appointees are quite popular. Though all the appointed individuals opposed secession, they are not radicals. Big A. Bledsoe was named county judge and Sam S. Jones, county clerk. N. R. Winniford is our sheriff and A. J. Gouffee, treasurer. County commissioners are Isaac Webb, John M. Rawlins, Samuel C. Phelps and Lewis B. Long. There is not a radical among them. Many are peace-loving men who long to put the divisions of the past behind and create a new and better society. While this makes our lives much less complex than conditions existing in other southern states, the very idea that the people do not elect officials and that they can be displaced by military rule for any infraction plagues us. This is not the country we pledged to honor and protect when we became a part of the United States of America, and it is not the vision Abraham Lincoln promised us in reunification.

We were all especially uneasy in the summer when we learned that a provisional government was to be established in our very midst. The block between Commerce to the north and Jackson to the South, Lamar to the west and Poydras to the east was designated a military headquarters. The "confiscated" lot is owned by John C. McCoy, our leading attorney and my personal lawyer, whose home is located on the northwest corner. It is a prime city block shaded by cedar trees. Mr. McCoy moved, leaving his residence vacant, when the federal troops occupied the entire lot. Numbering somewhere between 40 and 50 men, they arrived on July 30 under the command of a Captain Horton (no relation to me). It turns out that Capt. Horton is a quiet, low-keyed fellow who keeps his troops under control. At first when any of them ventured out onto the streets, citizens avoided them, but their behavior has been exemplary and gradually they are being accepted. Sometimes, we almost think they are a part of us! Capt. Horton has been invited into the homes of some people and is said to be gracious and accommodating.

For me personally, and for many of my friends and associates, far more disturbing than the presence of Captain Horton and the soldiers he commands was the sudden appearance in the early spring of Quantrill's Raiders. They rode into Dallas—hundreds of them, or so it seemed at the time—though we learned later that only a small percentage of the Raiders stopped off here. Quantrill, himself, is a handsome young man, about 30 years old, who walks as if he owns the earth. He is a former school teacher, turned radical at the outset of the Civil War, who began to collect friends and associates to battle Union troops. They first made headlines in 1862 when they were credited with being primarily responsible in the capturing of Independence, Missouri, from federal troops. This made them so popular that, on the spot, all 450 Raiders who took part in that battle were mustered into the Confederate Army, and Quantrill was awarded the rank of captain. Since then their numbers have grown. Jesse James and his younger brother, Frank, and Cole Younger who have been arrested several times for robberies are among the members. We never knew exactly how many or which ones of the Raiders stopped off in Dallas.

I was at the hotel when Quantrill tethered his horse at the entrance, came in and asked to register for a room. I didn't have any idea who he was, but he made quite an impression as he sauntered across the foyer followed by an entourage of several of his men. He was unerringly polite and cordial. Fortunately, Mr. Thompson was at the desk. Captain Quantrill requested all of the rooms not occupied and registered, using his real name, William C. Quantrill. As soon as he and his men went upstairs to their rooms, Mr. Thompson filled me in on our guests' identities. I must admit that having him and his men in town—and in our hotel—right across the street from the military compound was enough to turn my hair gray!

The news of his arrival spread like wildfire. Before night, the men were strolling up and down our streets as if they had lived here forever. They sauntered in and out of the stores, highly favoring the saloons. The Missourians among us remembered the viciousness of the battle in 1862 and alerted Captain Horton who gathered his troops and with six shooters ready, prepared to defend the city. Quantrill stationed his men on the west bank of the Trinity ready to fight. Fortunately, Captain Horton did not give the word to advance. A few of the Missourians, some related to the visiting "enemy" or at least intimately acquainted with some of the men, intervened to keep the peace. After a tense several minutes, the Quantrill men wheeled their horses and rode out into the country where some of them remained for several days on Joe Reed's ranch.

Even in these uneasy times, our country continues to grow. On the first day of March Nebraska was admitted to the union as the 37th state and on March 30 "we" completed negotiations with Russia to buy Alaska. Secretary of State William Seward promoted this purchase relentlessly, in the face of great opposition from several Congressmen who said the $7,200,000 purchase price was exorbitant. Our papers were full of charges and counter-charges. For some, the purchase has come to be known as "Seward's Folly." My opinion is that the purchase is one of the best business deals in the history of the United States. The price comes to only two cents an acre! And the area is rich in furs and fish. In our own neighborhood, a new town called Grand Prairie has been incorporated.

In August I was granted permission to continue operating the ferry across the Trinity with fees only slightly differing from what we had in the past. The charges for individuals walking across the bridge are five cents per person, children under twelve free of charge. For a man and horse, we charge ten cents; for a horse and buggy, twenty-five cents and for a wagon with one span of oxen or horses only ten cents. Each head of cattle is charged at a nickel and each sheep or hog, two and a half cents. The fees do not add greatly to my income, but they are consistent and sometimes, in these difficult economic times, provide the food for our table.

I have renewed the license to build the bridge and early next year expect to concentrate on its construction.

For the foreseeable future, I do not plan to rebuild the hotel. The remodeled office building is serving our needs fairly well. When we opened it following the fire that burned the St. Nicholas, we called it simply "The Dallas Hotel." Mr. Thompson, my brother-in-law who manages it, thought we should have a more enticing name, and we've re-christened it the St. Charles. It is not full much of the time but again helps to meet my economic needs.

Within the next few years, I anticipate my expenses to increase dramatically. The children are growing up, and I am making inquiries about schools for the boys.

Friends tell me that Aurelia is unusually bright and that I should also consider sending her to a boarding school in the East. When I talked to her about going, she was very reluctant, saying that she would be happy to stay at home and attend Dallas Female College. I know that she feels protective of me and her younger brothers and that she is hesitant to leave us, and I must admit that I can hardly bear the thought of having her away. I continue to be concerned about her health. Though she is much improved, she is still susceptible to colds and to ear and throat infections. She promises to study on her own; I have no doubt that she will do so because she has always been a reader. I order every new book that I think may interest her. She has all but exhausted all musical training offered here, and I would like for her to have the opportunity to study piano with more advanced teachers. When we determine the best schools for the boys, perhaps I will arrange for her to travel with Bob to the college of our choice and, that way, find out how resilient her health is and whether, or not, she and I can bear being separated from each other. She has always been so dependable. I promise myself that I will not lean too heavily on her, but it is a temptation to impose because she is so available and so ready to take on any responsibility I ask of her.

At 17, Aurelia is a stunning beauty—at least in the eyes of her mother, and if the glances of the young men are any evidence, in the eyes of others. She is taller than I am and like her father in coloring and in body build, but she moves with the grace of a ballerina. And she is totally without guile, doesn't seem to care or even to notice the homage paid to her by an increasing number of young swains who seem determined to win her favor.

Col. Guess, who recently returned from his long service in the war, his health severely impaired by the rigors of war and his incarceration in a prison camp, is especially fond of Aurelia. He admonishes me almost daily about becoming too dependent on her—even while he often acts like a doting father! He is one of the most avid of those pushing me to consider a boarding school for her. He is afraid, he often wrote in his letters, and even more now that he is home, that Aurelia will fall in love with—as he puts it "a no-account scoundrel—and marry someone unworthy of her."

As you can see, I am preoccupied now with my children, even while I am always concerned about securing our holdings. Central to my thinking is that I want to enhance the inheritance I inherited from their father and pass on to Aurelia and Bob and Frank and Alexander the gauntlet passed to me by him on the day he died.

Almost equally, I long to leave a legacy to this city. When Alexander bought Dallas from John Neely Bryan, he had a dream—a vision that it would become the most important city in the South. If he had lived, there is no doubt that this dream would have been accomplished, for he was a man of vision, of conviction, and of purpose. He had everything laid out in his head. I am so grateful that he shared this vision and so many plans for making his dreams realized and made me a complete partner and confidante. I doubt there is another woman in this country that, having been left a widow, has been so blest. Even so, everything has been hard enough to hold onto, to balance, to know what to do, to trade, to expand, to build, to sell. Often, after a long evening of going over the books, I kneel in prayer beside my bed, I ask two questions: "Good Lord, what do I do now?" and then, "Alexander, forgive me for making mistakes and send me a message about what to do with this or that piece of property. And how to control your oldest son!" Amen.

Faithfully,

Sarah Horton Cockrell

August 30, 1868

My dear precious daughter, Aurelia,

A few days ago I read a tiny article in the *Dallas Herald* that broke my heart.

Colonel George W. Guess had died. The tiny article, tucked away on a remote page was the strangest possible way to report the passing of a person who had figured so prominently in our city. The death was revealed in a letter from one, David Rhine, writing from Memphis, Tennessee. He wrote: "Dear Sirs, I have cut from this morning's *Memphis Avalanche* a clipping about the demise of G. W. Guess (and forward it to you) knowing that he will be lamented by many." That was all, followed a few days later on August 1 with the clipping, which read: *"Col. Geo. W. Guess, whose death on the steamer Victor from sun stroke, was mentioned Sunday, was a prominent lawyer of Dallas County, Texas and a high Mason. His remains were interred in Elmwood Cemetery yesterday."*

The two small items raised all kinds of specters—grief that one who had mattered so much in my life on so many different occasions was gone, pain that I had dismissed his distrust of others in Dallas as borderline paranoia, anger with myself that I had not listened more closely and questioned more deeply what he was trying to tell me the last time we were together and resentment that I would never know how it all would have ended.

It is in this mood that I write to you, my Daughter, thoughts and feelings that I must get out but that I do not intend for you to ever read. My purpose in writing it is to rid myself, so far as is possible, of the ghosts that haunt me. And there is nobody, not a living soul to whom I can bare my most intimate thoughts or turn to for comfort. As I have done so often in the past in moments of despair, I turn to the pen. Throughout my life, which has often been a lonely journey, the exercise of writing everything down gives me perspective and balance. Countless times, letters to others (which are often never mailed) and prayer are sources of strength that give me the ability to continue the work I am called to do.

There is a chance that the colonel's letters I have saved which are arranged by date, tied in ribbons and stored in my trunk may one day come to your attention or to the notice of others after I am gone—and if so, this letter will be among them. I was not able to destroy them, either as they arrived from the battlefields and from the prison camp during the war or later after the colonel had returned to Dallas. And certainly not now, though I plan one day to toss them all on a burning pyre along with other memorabilia.

I address these words to you, My Daughter, because you meant so much to Colonel Guess. There was a time when I thought he had romantic tendencies toward you and was only waiting until you grew up to express his feelings—not once realizing that those deep feelings were directed toward an entirely different woman.

But I get ahead of my story. . . .

You remember that Colonel Guess came to visit us two days before he left Dallas on the fateful trip from which he will never return. He had been in our home many times, at first on business and later as a personal friend both before and after he was released from service in the recent horrendous war where his health was destroyed. After dinner that night we sat in the parlor and talked. You were in and out of the room. Once, you will remember, he asked you to play something for him and you did. As you left to retire to your room he remarked that he had always thought of you as the daughter and of your brothers as the sons he did not have. He had said the same to me previously in the letters he wrote.

He was melancholy at moments that night, explaining that he was leaving Dallas on a prolonged trip to North Carolina, the state of his birth, and Tennessee where as a very young man he had met and married Mollie Miller when she was only a little more than a child. He talked about her and about the son they had lost, in ways he had never shared previously in all the years I had known him.

He had graduated from law school in Tennessee and practiced in Memphis before John C. McCoy invited him to Dallas in 1858 to join his law practice. George and your father met in Mr. McCoy's office shortly after the couple arrived and only a few weeks before Alex died. Your father had told me all about the young couple; said he was most impressed with the young lawyer and asked me to befriend Mrs. Guess who not only was very young and very homesick but was ill and expecting a baby. A few days later your father said that the young couple was having a hard time finding a place to live and he had rented them one of our small houses until they could buy land and build a home.

I immediately took food and extra blankets to Mollie. I have never known a more fragile person. She had "celebrated" her 18th birthday on their trip to Dallas. On that first visit I knew that Mollie Guess was in an advanced state of tuberculosis.

I did not meet George until Alexander died. Quite late in the evening after your father was shot, and I had lived through the horrors and confusion of that evening and, I thought, had said good night to the last departing friend, there was a knock at the door. Jane answered and came to tell me that a young man named George Guess was at the door and said it was important that he see me for just a moment because he had something he must return to me personally. Even in my state of confusion and grief, I was curious and asked her to have him wait until I dealt with the children who had just arrived home from where they were spending the night out on Mountain Creek with friends and cousins. He must have waited almost an hour; I had really forgotten that someone was waiting to see me. When I remembered and went into the sitting room, he and I both apologized—he for interrupting me on such a sad occasion, and I for forgetting that he wanted to see me.

He had Alexander's watch. He told me that Alex had handed the watch to him for safe keeping just before the encounter with Mr. Moore. Neither he nor I have any idea why Alex did this, but we surmise that my husband expected the young lawyer to keep a time record of what transpired. I was impressed that night with the sincerity of the young lawyer, who not only expressed his condolences, but seemed genuinely, saddened by Alex's death. He told me there was absolutely no reason why the altercation should have ended in gunfire.

Throughout the days that followed, even during the birth of his son, George Junior and soon after the death of Mollie, Mr. Guess was often quietly at my beck and call. I understood why Alexander had found him so appealing. As a younger recent law graduate in Mr. McCoy's firm, I often found him more knowledgeable and helpful than my older friend. He was in court every day during the trial, took a leading role in some of the proceedings, and it was usually he who came to the house during the trial to discuss anything that required my input.

He met all of you and was overwhelmingly grateful when I helped him find a wet nurse and caretaker for his infant son. The truth is that whatever I could do for others kept my mind off my own troubles.

When the jury cleared Mr. Moore of all charges, neither of my lawyers could believe that such a thing was possible, but it was Mr. Guess who continued to care for me personally along with offering legal advice. For many weeks I saw him almost daily either at his office or in our home while we were winding up details that left me in charge of the Cockrell estate.

Gradually I saw less and less of my young friend until two years later when his son was sick. As soon as I learned about the baby's illness, I went to visit and knew right away that he had contracted the dreaded disease that had taken his mother's life. George doted on Georgie and when the baby died shortly after his third birthday, it was my turn to offer words of comfort. The two tragedies cemented our friendship as nothing else could, and I became more and more dependent on the legal advice of the younger lawyer.

I was especially indebted to Mr. Guess for the way he handled my business when I was seeking permission to rebuild the bridge. Mr. McCoy, a gentleman of the old school, believed that women should handle all their business through the males in their family with the advice of their lawyers. He was horrified when I insisted on going to Austin and personally presenting my case to the legislature. He all but demanded that I not consider such a thing. However, Mr. Guess supported me. I felt sorry for him because he was quietly going behind the back of his mentor, the older lawyer, to pave the way for me. To keep him in the clear, I took full responsibility in working with Mr. McCoy about my decision. In fact, it was my decision, but it was Mr. Guess who cleared the way for me, got the appointment for me to speak, made provisions for transportation and, at the last minute, insisted on accompanying me. I shall never forget that.

You remember that Mr. Guess came to our home for dinner shortly after Texas voted to secede and told us that he would be going into service as soon as he could assemble a regiment. He felt it was the right of all states to dictate their own future. I remember listening to his very persuasive arguments. I remember the response from your brothers, especially Robert, who insisted that he was old enough to sign up in Mr. Guess's regiment. (Robert was nine years old!) All men and boys seem to glory in the trappings of war. You sat silently, never uttering a word and when I looked at you, both of us mirrored our reluctance.

Within a few days Mr. Guess had assembled his troops. Within a few more days he was on his way to training camp, having recruited a group of young men who would follow him into war.

What could I do? I promised that I would do everything in my power to support and protect the women left behind. I would provide uniforms for all the men in our county who signed up for service. But, even while musicians were blaring military marching tunes, war drums were thrumping and the speeches of hotheaded orators were touting the glories of war, I dreaded what lay ahead. And as I looked around on that day when many of our finest young men marched from the city square toward Austin for military training, the faces of the women and girls reflected a deeper knowledge: killing each other is not the way to settle human differences.

The first letter from Col. Guess was written on September 10, 1861, and posted from military camp in response to my letter of August 3 shortly after he left Dallas. It was very formal, addressed to "Most respected Madam," with a few details about his training, adding "you promised you would pray for me . . . I ask you to continue to do so."

He was so grateful for every little kindness. In June of 1862 he wrote: "Your box containing the coffee was received. . . . I am very grateful. . . . May God bless you and your dear little children and keep you safe from harm and danger till I return. . . . My return must depend upon the peace of my country. . . . My remains may be brought home before that time."

It was in this letter that he first alluded to a belief that someone in Dallas was deceiving him. In a veiled comment I dismissed as the delusions of someone suffering from battle fatigue, he wrote "I have heard something since I left home which pains me . . . which I will communicate to you at some future time . . . to those at and about home who take pleasure in slandering me as soon as my back is turned, I have nothing to say. They have my sincere pity. You, at least, know me well enough to give a contradiction to all slander." He signed it "Most truly yours, George W. Guess."

Three days later, in a better frame of mind, there was no hint of dark secrets lurking. "I am still in command," he wrote from Red River County near Clarksville, . . . the weather is intensely hot. . . . News from Richmond (is) that we are still driving Yankees before us. God bless you and love to the children. I am truly yours, Geo. W. Guess."

From time to time no letters got through, but in November of 1862, I received a long—four tightly written pages—letter thanking me profusely for the coat, pants, shoes, socks and gloves I had sent to him. The gift created "ties of affection between us. As to you being my friend, I have never, ever doubted it and my own feelings are unchanged toward you . . . they are as strong and warmer (than when we last met). You know "I hold you in the greatest esteem."

Twenty-one miles from Paris, Texas, on February 8, 1863, he wrote to me: "My dear friend, Why cannot I hear from you? Have you all ceased to care for me? Believe me, my feelings toward you are just the same as when you last saw me. It does me good to be in sight of my adopted state. I am 131 1/2 miles from Dallas. I have a good notion to ask for leave to come up and see you. The weather is miserable . . . up to 9 inches of snow. Tell Aurelia I would love to see her."

Can you begin to see, my child, why I thought that you could be the object of this great man's affections? Even though he was 21 years older and already a man when you were born, I entertained these thoughts because his sweet Mollie was so much younger—13 years—than he.

In the late winter of 1863, I sent a large parcel to Col. Guess in Indian Territory, one of many I had posted that had not gone through. This one did and on March 6, 1863, he penned a response: "My own dear friend, I have no words to express my emotions on receiving your two long letters and cannot begin to tell you how much your gift to this starving man is appreciated. Ham! Cake! The tea cakes (as you know, I like tea cakes better than anything), butter, fruit, coffee, pickles, preserves and the candles. Well, my dear friend, God bless you for this unusual assurance of your feelings for me alone." Writing that he misses "all my friends" he adds that he is very homesick, "I fear I am melancholy." Again the distrust he believed from former friends surfaced. "It is one a.m. I have been writing reports. I wrote you only part of what I felt as to the outrageous slander which had been perpetrated against you and (me) but I know that one of your purity could not long sink under such falsehoods."

I do not know what "outrageous slander" had been voiced or written to him, but you can be assured that our relationship with each other was totally circumspect.

It was only at this time in our correspondence that I began to believe that Col. Guess's letters of appreciation and admiration were directed toward me—and not toward you. I was surprised, relieved (because I want so much for you to have a husband and a family with an honorable man near your own age) and, I admit, flattered. And, it was the first time I knew I must consider what my response would be should he ever give voice to sentiments other than friendship.

His letters continued to arrive, with consistency if not constantly. Many, many of his to me and many of mine to him were lost en route. The best way to assure delivery was to send letters and packages by special messenger, but there were not always horsemen going to or returning from the camps. And certainly none came from the battlefields.

On May 2, 1863, writing again from Texas, 5 miles from Clarksville, he told me that "I am missing you" but said that his hoped-for furlough was not possible. "I wish I could come live with you about a month and eat some vegetables out of your garden. I might then get into some better health." It was the first time he had mentioned that his war experiences were deteriorating his physical condition. He added, "I have lost my pony. I was offered $250 for him the day before he got away."

By midsummer he wrote from Camp near Tibadeaux, La., that he had received from me a letter written on Christmas Day! He wrote "You said in that letter what you had never said in any other. Would to God I had known one or two things that were in that letter six months ago! But is not too late. God Almighty, bless you for your dear generous and your kind affectional feelings and (may I say it) your love for me."

I truly cannot remember what I wrote on Christmas Day, but I must have expressed my continuing devotion, which he interpreted as an admission of love. While I would never have been the first to speak, I admit that I was beginning to care for him in ways that I had not felt since your father died. Then, to be sure that he was on safe grounds (and perhaps I had been, too,) he went on to say "I love you more dearly because you love the memory of my darling wife." In that we were mutual. I cared for Mollie as a daughter; he cared for Alexander as a father figure. But where were we as a couple in all of this?

And, six days later, this: "My dearest Madame. . . . As to my losing confidence in you, I have never done any such thing in one single instance . . . I have loved you and trusted in you and I do so yet and in whose love I place all confidence." It was a long letter, expressing confidence, caring, appreciation, affection, but still no avowal of "forever after."

The war was not going well. With the few newspapers to which we had access, I could read between the lines and know that the South was losing, but we all knew—or pretended to know—that the tide would turn in our favor at any moment.

And then another blow fell.

In a letter dated October 12, 1863, and written from "In Prison, New Orleans" the very long and heartbreaking letter read, in brief. "I write from this vile prison . . . taken prisoner on September 29. Yours ever, Geo. W."

As the war was winding down, on February 15, 1865, writing by candlelight at "4 o'clock a.m." with "the chickens crowing loudly" in the background, George wrote in words what he had long said between the lines. "My own dear, kind (what shall I say) Sweetheart. You won't be offended at this . . . will you? I mean every word of what I say, but I am afraid to say it. I love you, my sweetheart. I have another sweetheart, Mrs. Baird, my sister. Aurelia is my dear sweet daughter. I live to see you and (to see) your dear little ones grown up to be men and women, to see my dear Aurelia married to some good man. Tell her she is not to fall in love with some no-account simpleton." In the four pages of his letter he reiterated several times his love and devotion. "I want you to believe I still love you and yours" . . . and he closed with "and now my dearest one, I must bid you good-by."

It was next to the last letter I received from him before his return to Dallas. The last one was written "On the Day Lee Surrendered. . . .

April 9, 1865" and was very brief. "My health is very, very poor. I hemor-rhaged from the lungs and head twice in the last few days."

Not even this warning prepared me for the man who arrived back in Dallas during the summer of 1865. He was only a remnant of his former self. He had aged 20 years.

I heard that he was home, but he did not come to see us as he always had in the past. When I ran into him at the hotel days after his return, it was almost as if I was seeing a ghost of a former friend. Both in looks and manner, he was a changed human being. I both looked forward to and dreaded a personal encounter. A note came a few days afterwards deliv-ered by a courier—asking permission to call. This formality puzzled me, for always before he had considered us such good friends that he felt free to drop in at any time. I had insisted on this informality since the days when he had become not only my lawyer but also a confidential friend. I knew his health was not good, but I was not prepared to learn that he was also struggling with what he termed mental incompetence.

I asked the courier to wait, read the note and immediately sent back a response that he was not only welcome in our home, but that I insisted that he come for dinner in two days and that not only I, but the children were eager to see him.

He arrived punctually, on the day and at two minutes past the time I had designated.

Fortunately, my four children were successful in bridging the awk-wardness that entered our home with his arrival. I, who had dealt with so many problems of one kind and another, had no idea how to greet this man who had declared his undying affection for me. And, I knew I was still dealing with unvoiced reservations of my own. On the one hand, I knew I was ready to make a commitment; on the other, I knew that I must consider not only my desires, but also the wishes of my children, for whatever the future held we would be in everything together. My four children greeted him with all-out enthusiasm, alleviating any awk-wardness. Aurelia told him how much she had appreciated all of the ref-erences to her future that he had expressed through the years and told him that indeed she had learned to play some of his favorite tunes and would be eager to entertain him with piano selections after dinner. Robert wanted to know all about the battles. With this I saw a cloud drift over our guest's face and successfully diverted the conversation to other topics promising Robert that at some future time when they were alone, Col. Guess would be glad, I knew, to talk to him about his war experiences. Frank was eager to tell him about the books he had been reading, that he had decided to become a lawyer like his uncle and namesake in Missouri, and Alexander wanted to know when they could go hunting together. I had prepared my children for the different appearance our guest would present, but it was their exuberance that paved the difficult first moments.

Then it was my turn. Taking both his hands in mine, I said simply, "Welcome home. Home to the one place where you have always been welcome and that you will continue to be welcome for the rest of our lives." Or words to that effect.

We all relaxed. The dinner was delicious, prepared under the guidance of my sister, Mary, before she went back to the hotel to her own quarters with her husband, who was the manager. The candlelight lent a mellow glow to the courses, served by Caroline, our faithful maid, who had been freed from slavery by the Emancipation Proclamation. I had "bought" Caroline in 1859 along with her children, Willis, Martha and Francis. At that time Caroline was 25, her children six, three and one. Now Caroline was 32, Willis 13; Martha, 10, and Francis, almost 8. I "bought" them as a family so that the mother and children would not be separated. Willis was a year older than Robert and they had become hunting buddies. Martha was Alexander's age and "Baby" Francis was everybody's baby. My children had taught Caroline's children to read and write.

But I am digressing. After the piano solos, the diverting musings on war issues, the needs of my two younger sons to seek out their companionship of former years, George Guess and I were left alone in the parlor. Both of us were nervous. After a circuitous route, he declared his undying love for me with reservations about what the future might hold, both for him as a "shadow" of his former self, and for me as the town "matriarch" and mother of four children. Both of us, I firmly believe, were relieved, when we agreed that only time would determine our future destiny—whether together or apart.

Time passed. We saw each other often, but neither of us spoke about the future. He was busy rebuilding his law practice. I was busy with my business and with the children. His health improved. I'd like to think that a large part of the improvement occurred at my table where I served fresh vegetables, milk, meat, and the lavish cakes and pies that were his weakness. He no longer shivered with war remembrances, at least not in my presence. He had longer and longer lapses between memories of the battles he had fought. He gained weight, looked sturdier, and became more the man I remembered at that long-ago farewell.

We talked often. The businessmen of Dallas, the decision-makers were again accepting George Guess as a part of their inner circle. George was beginning to put to rest the ghosts of war and devastation that haunted him. I was beginning to acknowledge that my future might well entertain a new man in my life after the never-to-be forgotten Alexander Cockrell. I was 47—past childbearing years—but still feeling in the prime of life. He was 37—with years of experience that I could not, in my wildest imagination, fathom.

We continued to see each other often. We continued to communicate. We continued to acknowledge that we were very special to each other. And then came the night of July 17, 1868. We had dinner together that night at my hotel, but at his invitation. I knew that whatever he had to say at that time and whatever decision I made would determine the future for both of us, and in a very large sense, the future for my children. After dinner, by candlelight, he said his love was constant and undying, that he wanted me to be his wife. He said that his lack of finances and the state of his health had kept him from speaking sooner, but that he was much improved and feeling better every day. He was speaking now, he said, because he was going away on a prolonged visit to his native North Carolina and to Tennessee where he had studied law and had begun his practice. He would reconnect with family members and, perhaps, tie up any loose business ends, though he felt sure the war had wiped out any assets he might have inherited. He did not expect nor want an immediate response but dared to hope that upon his return he would be in much better health and that we could have a future together.

I was relieved. As I bade him goodnight, he held both my hands, declared his undying affection and left me standing. After a moment, I closed the door. Chastened. My emotions in turmoil. So much to think about. So many decisions!

The next morning, a sweltering midsummer July day, Colonel Guess left on the stage headed east toward the Mississippi River where he would board a steamer headed for Tennessee.

There have been so many endings in my life. I have learned to accept and move on, at least most of the time. But it is hard. So very hard.

Your loving mother,

Sarah Horton Cockrell

1869

Notes for the future:

At last, I am making a start toward the rebuilding of the bridge. It seems a lifetime ago that it all began. I am a totally different person from the woman who battled an all-male world, received permission from the legislature on February 9, 1860, to organize the Iron Bridge Company and begin construction. A war has intervened. There has been no money for anything other than necessities. Engineers and construction workers have been preoccupied with destruction rather than construction. My children are growing up. My hair is streaked with gray.

It would have been so easy to give up and let somebody else take over this part of renewing Dallas. But, somehow I just can't. I may be more cautious than the woman of ten years back, but I am, if anything, more determined. And now that so many people are moving here, it is imperative to have a link between the city west of the Trinity and those of us to its east and to provide a better passageway for the continuing migrations to the West. The ferry has held up well, but it is totally insufficient to handle the increasing traffic.

I called a meeting of the board of directors, and they unanimously agreed that it is time we got started on the construction. Even under the best of conditions it may be two or three years before the bridge can be completed. Iron and steel is still in short supply and dependable workers even harder to hire and retain. I was able to keep most of the men who served on the board from a decade ago when I first started this enterprise. The new and expanded board consists of J. W. Crowdus as president; G. M. Swink as secretary; A. C. Camp. James H. Bryan, W. H. Prather, J.K.P. Record and J. W. Haynes. I am not on the board, but they do allow me to sit in on the meetings and, of course, I write the checks!

Through the years I've studied everything I could find on bridges and had about decided to go with a similar bridge to the one Alexander constructed earlier, but my studies and the advice of others has convinced me that a wire suspension bridge is better. We hired the best civil engineer we could find, W. H. Wentworth, to locate the site and to supervise the construction. It pleases me that he chose to build the new bridge in the exact spot that Alex chose to build his wooden construction many years ago. We estimate the total price will run around $50,000 to $75,000. A toll booth will be located on the east bank. Businessmen are still clamoring for a free bridge, and that would be nice if we could afford it, but we must recover a portion of our cash outlay.

Construction will begin as soon as materials arrive. It will begin at the foot of Commerce Street and extend for 300 feet across the river to its west side. Its beginning and its ending are both on property that has been in the Cockrell estate since Alex began buying property. Mr. Wentworth guarantees me that it should last "forever." I am not foolish enough to believe it!

With the sanction of Mr. Wentworth, I have placed an order for the material with Moseley Iron Works in Iola, Kansas. He says the company is the best, and we do not want to compromise in any detail with quality. As soon as the material is completed, it will be shipped by riverboat down the Mississippi to New Orleans, and there by barge through the Gulf of Mexico to Galveston were it will be loaded on freight cars and brought to Corsicana where the rail line ends. Then it will be loaded on ox-drawn wagons and brought to Dallas.

Mr. Crowdus told me that some doubters are snickering behind my back about the folly of the widow woman who ordered a bridge from a mail order catalogue and thinks she can build it in Dallas. When I think about it rationally, I agree with the doubters. Then I recall everybody doubted that Alexander could build a first-class hotel in this frontier city. I finished what he started.

In an effort to appease the doubters—and to make way for the opening of our new toll bridge at some time in the future—I have ordered elimination of ferry tolls for both pedestrians and horseback riders. Since that is the conveyance of preference by most who cross the Trinity, I am hoping it eases the animosity of the nay-sayers to my new toll bridge. And frontier city it is! So many things have happened in the past two years that I have not had the time—or the patience—to write about, so let me catch up just a bit.

Transportation is on everybody's mind. While I've been concentrating on getting the bridge built, the male business leaders of the town are working to make this a rail center, and I solidly support them. I've given everything they require in the way of free land for the rails to be laid across property I own. And I watch with great interest every effort to bring trains into and through town. We must have them. While new citizens are arriving weekly, families still must travel by wagon, a slow and tiring process that takes months.

Some are still determined to make the Trinity River navigable. It would be wonderful if we could have a waterway from here to the Gulf Coast, but I don't see that happening—at least not any time soon. We do not have the money or the expertise at this time to turn our river into a major waterway that can accommodate shipping. Since 1866 when the Texas legislature voted to incorporate the Trinity Slack Water Navigation Company, several efforts have been made to put boats on the Trinity. Within the past two years, 35 boats have been launched. But only one, Job Boat No. 1, made it all the way up the Trinity to Dallas, and it did not last long. Last year ambitious businessmen built a steamboat determined to prove that the Trinity is navigable. Eighty-seven feet long and 18 feet abeam, it was launched a week before Christmas Day, on December 17. Named the Sallie Haynes for the daughter of Dr. and Mrs. John W. Haynes, it was christened by Sallie herself who broke a bottle of sparkling wine over its beam before it steamed away on its maiden voyage. Wild celebrations ensued and editorials flooded the *Herald* predicting the dawn of a new day for the city. A long poem in the paper on February 6 this year summed up the city's exultation at becoming a navigable waterway from the Gulf Coast to Dallas. It said in part:

> *As for wagons and oxen we will have no use*
> *We will turn our mules and horses loose—*
> *And just so long as Old Time remains,*
> *We'll bless the builders of the Sallie Haynes.*

The poet was more ambitious than accurate. On its first trip to the Gulf Coast the Sallie Haynes and another boat coming up the river toward Dallas met at Trinidad in Henderson County where the channel was so narrow that they could not pass each other and had to exchange cargoes and return to their starting points. The Sallie Haynes made several other attempts to prove her supporters accurate before hitting a snag ten miles southwest of Palestine and sinking. Several other boats were launched during the past two years, but none has been successful. And I predict that others will reach a fate similar to the Sallie B. before, if ever, there is a waterway sufficient to sail to Galveston.

I wish that some effort and expense would go toward improving transportation within the town. Our streets are deplorable, mud holes when it rains and dust bowls when it doesn't. Pedestrians compete with horsemen and wagons for space. It is not safe for women to walk down the streets. There are times when the roistering is so intense that I do not feel safe going from my home to the hotel alone. I don't dare let my children go anywhere by themselves, though Robert is determined to be independent and has sneaked off several times. Even when I discipline him severely, he goes off again at the slightest opportunity. He inherited his daring nonchalance and charisma from his father. I delight in seeing him emulate the vision and passion that marked his father's life, but I do want to keep him safe! I wish he had just a little of my caution.

The small town where everybody knew each other is fast disappearing. Hordes of individuals come through here every week, some settling and others continuing westward. Sometimes the noise is so loud at night that nobody can sleep.

The amazing growth has also brought positive changes. Our streets may not be safe, but we have ten new ones named Sycamore, Oleander, Harwood, Bryan, Live Oak, Masten, Billington, Martin, Murphy and Stone. We have several new businesses, among them Louis Wagner's grocery and liquor store on the southeast corner of Main and Jefferson at the corner of the Courthouse Square. The Wagner family lives over the store. They are recently arrived from Europe and are welcome additions to our town.

Late last year the First Methodist Church was completed on the southeast corner of Commerce at Lamar on the property I donated to the church several years ago. Though only a small wooden building, we are glad to have it. At Christmas shortly after its dedication, special services were held and a beautiful new hymn, "Oh Little Town of Bethlehem," was heard in Dallas for the first time. Aurelia played for the services. I am so proud of her and was thrilled to hear the music of this wonderful Christmas hymn and its story. The music and lyrics were produced by two men, Louis H. Redner, organist, and Philips Brooks, rector, both of the Holy Trinity Episcopal Church in Philadelphia.

Our first public water supply was opened this year, and several homes, including mine, now have indoor water piped from Browder Springs. It is amazing to turn on a spigot in my kitchen and have clear water readily available for us. We are cautious with the amount we run because I never want to use it up and have to go back to digging a water well.

Our first bank has been created by W. H. Gaston and A. C. Camp and is now open, but I am afraid to trust anybody else with my money. So until it proves the promises that have been made, I will continue to bank in my little trunk even though I don't feel good about having so much money in the house.

Freedmen's towns continue to grow in different areas of the city, two to the north of the city, one in South Dallas along Ten Mile Creek, another the Thomas Hill Community in Oak Cliff, the Jones Community in Grapevine, Elm Thicket to the northwest, Deep Ellum to the east of downtown and the largest, Freedman Town just north and within easy walking distance of downtown. Even though, legally, black citizens are free to live anywhere they choose, they seem to prefer to congregate together. Doubtless, safety is a major factor.

In April of last year, posters were displayed during the night in many conspicuous places reading, "K.K.K.[8] Demon's Den. Dark Day. Cloudy Moon. Time Out. Dumb Ferret." This, in large letters that made no sense, was signed "Shrouded Brothers, Dallas Division, No. 28, and led viewers to this: "The Great Past Grand Giant commands you. The hour to act has come. The knife and pistol to use are given. The Foeman's chain must now be riven. On the eleventh of this mortal's month go forth to the harvest of Death. Come from the shadow of the grave and dye your hands red with the blood of your victims. D.C.U.L.A. Beware: The PIT yawns to receive you. By Order of the GREAT GRAND CYCLOPS"

The Klan and its message was quickly repudiated by the *Herald*, which termed the perpetrators "ignorant and superstitious . . . threatening turbulence and revolution."

The threat of violence by the Klan did not keep Negro men from voting for the first time. On March 30, the Fifteenth Amendment to the Constitution became law guaranteeing the right to vote to "all without regard to race, color or previous condition of servitude." Women are still denied the ballot, though Wyoming Territory has enacted a law giving women the right to vote. Susan B. Anthony, one of the most vociferous and persistent advocates for women's suffrage has bolted from the American Equal Rights Association which she helped to form three years ago and formed the American Woman's Suffrage Association to devote full time to campaigning and lecturing for a Constitutional amendment that will give women the right to vote. Her newspaper, *Revolution*, founded last year, has a motto that reads, "Men, their rights and nothing more; women, their rights and nothing less."

Sarah Horton Cockrell

December 31, 1870

Miss Aurelia Cockrell
Walnut Grove, Missouri

My darling child,

The year draws to a close, and I sit here in the twilight of a new year—the year in which you will officially become an adult. I have thought of you as grown up for so long and have depended on you so much that I can hardly believe you are still only 20 years old. I have often taken for granted the responsibility you assumed so young in life to support me and to help me in raising your brothers. I forget to tell you how much I appreciate you and how guilty I sometimes feel for expecting so much of you. Without your help and that of your aunt it would have been much more difficult for me to support this family. I appreciate all you have done and all you continue to do, and I love you so much.

Life is not the same with you away. Sometimes I am so lonely to see you, to hold you in my arms and to have a long talk with you that I am almost ill. In fact, during that long time after you left and only one letter came, Frankie and Alex thought I was sick. After your letters finally began to arrive, your brothers declared that "Ma is singing again! She heard from Aurelia!"

If I had known how long it would be before you could return home, I would never have let you go. I had hoped, (and I think perhaps it has worked) that your health would improve once you were away from Dallas. But your trip to Missouri with Robert left me without two of my precious children. It seems like an eternity since I waved good-by to the two of you in July and sent you off on the stage to Sherman where you spent the night with your Uncle Vardeman and Aunt Jane Cockrell, before traveling by train to Missouri. I had been in such a quandary about getting Robert situated in school because the state of our family business here—what with the problems I've had with the bridge and the moving from one house to another, which had me all but overwhelmed. I knew I could not let Robert go alone, and when you said you wanted to go with him, it seemed the best possible solution.

I knew that once Robert was enrolled in McGee College, he would be away for at least a year, but I thought you would be home within six weeks to two months.

Your letters have been sporadic, arriving only now and then with long gaps between. For almost two months, I heard nothing after the first letter you wrote on August 1, the day after you arrived at your Uncle Reuben and Aunt Polly's home in Walnut Grove. I was so glad to learn that you and Robert had arrived safely eight days after leaving on July 23. Then, I heard nothing more for almost two months, and I was almost frantic with worry. Finally, your letter of September 15 arrived along with the detailed accounting of expenses.[9] I know that I am not receiving all of your letters. It is so very frustrating. I only trust that mine to you are getting through better, and I think perhaps they are because the letters I do receive from you lead me to think that you are aware of what is happening here.

It is so hard to determine what is going on there. I know that you are homesick, but I also fear that something is happening that you are not able to tell me. I hope you are not missing us as much as we are longing for you. There is a vacuum in this family that only you can fill and that will be vacant until you return.

Your first letter indicated that you were welcomed into the home of your Aunt Polly and Uncle Rube and were having a lovely time getting to know your cousins Lizzie and Maggie. But I gather there have been several occasions when you have felt that you were not very welcome.

Your letters to Dallas relatives and friends are so few and far between. I could not believe it when you wrote in your letter of October 15 that you had written six letters to me, four to your brother, Frank; two to your brother, Alex, and five to others who live in Dallas, including one to your Aunt Emmerine that she did receive and has answered.

Mitch Gray has been by here almost every day. He doesn't say much, but I know he comes to find out what we have heard from you. When I asked, he said he had not received a single letter. I know that you are writing and I cannot believe so many letters are lost.

Your suspicion that your letters might have been intercepted makes sense. I have been most concerned over what little you have said about your cousin, Polk, and his numerous shenanigans. Since he had the reputation of playing loose with the affections of several of the young ladies in the vicinity, you have been wise, indeed, to avoid being alone with him. The fact that your letters have come through since Polk settled down is evidence, though certainly far from proof that he may have simply failed to mail the letters entrusted to him. I am sure the death of his brother, Virge, only shortly back from a trip to Texas and planning to be married to Fannie Garth on Christmas Day, sobered Polk considerably. Then, you told me in your letter of December 16 that Polk and Mattie Crisp are soon to be married.

---

[9]See appendix page 281.

This relieved my mind considerably because I was very worried about his having taken up with Robert. Your brother tends to be a bit wild anyway and having the influence of an older cousin whose reputation is not too good made me terribly uneasy.

I suppose I should not be surprised that you feel more comfortable with your Aunt Polly and Uncle Rube than you do with your Uncle Frank and Aunt Anna in Warrensburg. I am appalled that some of your relatives do not help with some of your most trivial basic necessities. When your father was murdered and I asked your Uncle Frank to come and help me in his defense, I got only platitudes of support. Nobody came to assist me during the trial. Nobody in his family ever helped.

I would never have sent Robert to his uncle asking for his support in seeking out a college for my son if I had not promised your father that I would ask his family to assist me in choosing schools for our children. That I intend to do . . . and I am eternally grateful for your help, my loving daughter, in making sure that this is possible.

I cannot believe that your father's relatives are so frugal that they would not provide you with thread and a scrap of material to repair your own and Robert's wardrobe before sending him on to college. It appalls me that your aunt would not even give you thread or a couple of buttons, but instead told you to go into town and purchase your own, as if going the seven miles into town was easy. Not only did you not have the thread and buttons you needed, but also you had then to depend on your relatives to provide transportation to town. When you tell me that your Uncle Frank's law practice is so successful that he brags he sometimes makes as much as $150 in a single day, I am further baffled at their behavior.

I have done my very best—distance and the uncertainty of the mail often intervening—to respond to every financial need of both you and your brother. And I trust that you will let me know immediately when and if you need more money, and I will send it to you as fast as possible. There are many people in this world that dote on the dollar and are miserable when they do not instantly collect what they think they deserve. I get the feeling that your Uncle Frank may not think much of his Texas sister-in-law's ability to provide for her children. Maybe he thinks I sent you and Robert to Missouri to foist you off on your father's relatives. I don't know what to think. Doubtless, the fact that we have provided hospitality to so many for so long makes us out of touch with the realities of people in other parts of the country.

Your more recent letters indicate that things are improving. I wanted you to think of your Uncle Rube and Aunt Polly as your substitute parents until I could have you back here in Dallas, but I learned that there have been times you felt almost abandoned. I was so upset when you wrote that your aunt and cousins left you alone to make social calls when you were ill. I would never have treated one of their daughters that way.

I am glad your Uncle Frank and Aunt Anna treated you to a St Louis trip in mid-December. Perhaps they are discovering that you are really a refined and special young woman and are trying to make up to you for their lack of attention in the first weeks after you arrived. Your letter just arrived telling me that you received the money I sent to you in time to buy the things in St. Louis that you had mentioned several times you needed or wanted. I am glad you finally got the watch, chain, a set of furs, a silk dress, shoes and a hat and buttons for your sleeves while you were there. When you left home last July, we agreed that you would purchase these items for yourself, but you spent so much money on Robert and his needs that only now have finally made the purchases—half a year later when you surely are about ready to come home.

I do not understand why your Uncle Rube will not let his daughters escort you home when I have offered to pay their way here and return. At first you wrote that your cousins were eager to make the trip to Dallas and that you hoped to be home by Thanksgiving at the latest. When yellow fever was raging last summer, I understood why it was not possible for you to travel. But when cold weather put an end to that barrier, it seems to me that the Cockrells could have found some passage for you to get home. I do not understand their reluctance to let Maggie and Lizzie come home with you. Perhaps they think we live in squalor here, but I would think since there was so much going and coming among family members during the war, and that the Vardaman Cockrells have moved to Texas, their minds would be at ease about us. Also, I know that you are the personification of courtesy and friendship. So, I know not the reason for their sudden change of mind about letting their daughters come here.

Even as badly as I want you home, I cannot bear the thought of your making the trip alone. Your threats that you will do just that if there is no way for you to get here leaves me miserable. As much as I want you to be here, I cannot give my permission for you to travel alone.

When Christmas came and went without having you home, it was terrible. Not even your brothers felt in a mood to celebrate. At 14 and 16, they are at an age when I thought they would not be so affected by your absence, but they miss you almost as much as I do.

As to Robert, it is difficult to know how he is doing at McGee. He rarely writes, and when he does, it's usually mere notes saying that he is well, I am not to worry and, inevitably, asking for more money. I am still hoping that he will apply himself to his studies and that he will mature and become independent and much better able to handle his finances. Next year it will be Frank and Alex's turn to go away to school. I can barely think what I will do when all four of you are no longer at home with me.

I do not think it unreasonable to expect Robert to live within an allotted budget, but unlike you he has always expected more and spent more than is wise.

I know that I am frugal; I have always had to be. When your father was with us he was far more generous than I, often spending money on wild ideas that I thought foolish. Usually it turned out that he was right in the business decisions he made. I pray that Robert, so like him in so many ways, will also be fortunate in handling his finances.

Remember the trouble I had with Robert over his college wardrobe? I insisted that he make a list of what he needed, gave him a budget limit and sent him to make his own clothing and supplies purchases. When the bill came in, it was considerably over what we had talked about. I let him keep some of the items that did not appear on his original list, but I also had him return some of the things to the store for credit.

It does not surprise me, therefore, that Robert has spent, and not accounted for, the money he had when he left Dallas. His lackadaisical attitude toward money makes me doubly grateful for your careful accounting. When I received your September 16th itemized account of the money you spent getting to Missouri and getting Robert into college, it reminded me so much of the way I keep books. I was astonished that, after all the things he had purchased in Dallas, Robert still felt that he needed more clothing and supplies. I know that neither of us could imagine the difference in the climate, into which he was moving, so if he had only needed to purchase additional warm clothing, I would have understood. But more pocket-handkerchiefs, drawers, collars, a hat, socks, a cravat? That I did not understand. Thank you for sending the list.

My understanding with your Uncle Frank was that he was to deliver Robert to McGee, pay for his tuition and board and provide him with spending money in accordance with what he considered appropriate after consultation with his faculty sponsor. I have received nothing from Mr. Cockrell, only details from you and a letter from the Rev. J. B. Mitchell, president of McGee advising me that Robert is duly enrolled, and they are glad to have him as a student. It did help me to learn from Mr. Mitchell's letter that Robert lives in the best dormitory on campus and that he is rooming with a young man who is studying for the ministry. I don't know whether the roommate will be more of an influence on Robert than Robert is on him! It would relieve my concerns considerably if your uncle would write to me.

You say that your uncle is thinking of running for senator. Doubtless he will be successful if he decides to go into politics. Wonder what he then will think of his "poor" Texas relatives! I'm glad you gave Frank and Alex's pictures to your grandmother and even glad you refer to her as Grandma. At the same time, I wonder how your father would feel about this. When his mother died and soon afterward his father married Nancy Ellis, Alex no longer felt at home there. He always said, when he talked about it all, that his step-mother was mean to him, but perhaps it was just that she was a child herself, not much older than he and totally incapable of coping with a step-son who doubtless was a handful. His mother died when he was four. The troubles began when his father remarried and he and Nancy started a new family. Jeremiah Vardaman was born in 1832 when your dad was 12 and his life became even more tense. Two years later in 1834 when your Uncle Frank was born, your dad packed up and left home. He was 14 years old. He had very little to do with his family afterward, but as he was dying admonished me to get in touch with his family in Missouri and ask for their help in educating his children. I know there had always been a longing to be re-connected with the family, or he would not have named our Frank for his half brother. The fact that Grandma Nancy asked for the picture shows me that she regrets some of the things that happened in the past and now wants to have my children claim her as a grandmother.

I subscribed to the *Herald* the day you left and had it mailed to you in Missouri so that you could keep up with the news back here, but you have given no indication that you are receiving the paper. I will fill you in:

The census figures for 1870, though not official yet, indicate that Dallas has a population of 13,314—a 65 per cent increase over the 8,665 people who lived here in 1860. Mr. Henry S. Ervay who was appointed mayor in April has had a full share of problems with lawlessness rampant. The coming of the railroads and the extra stages that emanate from here and arrive here daily, plus the booming economy have brought a full quota of rowdies—gamblers, hustlers, drunks and prostitutes. We don't talk about it in polite society, but I can tell you that we now have three Red Light districts—Freedman's Town along the railroads at Main, Commerce and Elm, another north of the courthouse along the Trinity River called Frogtown and a third south of the courthouse from Young and Lamar southward to Boggy Bayou. I tell you this so that you will be warned ahead of time what areas to avoid when you get home.

My efforts to get the new bridge under construction keep running into trouble. My charter calls for a wire suspension bridge, but further study and the advice of Mr. Wentworth, the civil engineer I hired to oversee the construction, has convinced me that an iron bridge is superior, so all of our plans have been adjusted accordingly and now, I hope, at last construction will get underway as soon as the material arrives.

You will remember that in June, a month before you and Robert left, I made a donation to erect a building in downtown Dallas to house a college? The two-story building is well under way. It will be called the Dallas Female College and will be administered by the Trinity Conference of the Methodist Church. The Rev. W. H. Scales, under whom you studied and who is now teaching both of your younger brothers, has been named head of the school. Maybe you will want to enroll there?

Our new home is more significant than the bridge or the new school building. I thought we were almost ready to move into it when you left here in July, but we ran into many problems I did not anticipate. It took me a long time, as you recall, deciding what to do about a bigger, safer house. I knew that building one from the ground up would be costly and time-consuming, so I decided to move the large two-story white frame house from the mouth of Mill Creek here to the northwest block of Commerce at Broadway. It is such a big house—was built by your father to house employees of the Cockrell sawmill.

There were many headaches involved in moving, reconstructing and enlarging the house, and many times I wished that I had just started from scratch. I am now very happy at how things are working out. I had hoped that we would be moved into it before you left for Missouri, but as you know, we weren't quite ready. We finally moved in on August 6, and I have been busy ever since adding on, repairing things that were damaged in the move. I've added an "L' with two extra bedrooms and a front gallery. The two small rooms were made from space that had been wasted under the roof. Sealed and papered, they are now charming extra bedrooms for the countless relatives and friends who make our house their home when they are in the area.

It is good that I have the extra space because our house seems to be full to overflowing all the time. Two weeks after we moved, in addition to Polly and Lou, your two brothers and I, we had your Aunt Emmarine and Uncle Joe Reed and Will Bradshaw for several days. Since then we have had a constant flow of folks, most recently Mrs. Bryan and three of her children, Lizzie, Ned and Luther. All of them were sick when they arrived. While I gave them shelter and care, I started looking and soon found a house to rent for them. Before Mrs. Bryan was able to help, Lizzie and Ned had moved their things from White Rock back into town. While they were here in November, Sallie Johnson came for a visit and then Jim Reed brought his wife, Radak, in from the country. She is very ill and not expected to live much longer. I have moved my room to the second floor and put her in my bedroom because she cannot climb the stairs. Someone sits up with her every night. We try never to leave her alone. I am disgusted with Jim; he has been drunk a great deal of the time. He comes reeling in and spends a few minutes with his sick wife, then staggers out again. He is destroying his very lucrative law practice. Why are some men such fools?

Friends at church were joking the other day that I do not need to continue to try to run the hotel, or to hire anyone else to do it because I run a hotel in my home. They are right. Even so, I want you to know that your room is all ready, and I am quite selfish in keeping it free for you! One of my great delights was in trying to anticipate your desires and decorating it with you in mind. Your aunt is quilting the beautiful pattern you pieced last year to have it ready when you return.

Speaking of the hotel, I am not sure what I want to do about it—if anything. Marlin Thompson ran it successfully for a long time, but just walked off one day and went to work on the railroad. He said he could make more money there. Now he is working in Brenham. I don't know what got into him. If your Aunt Polly (Mary Horton Thompson) knows anything, she isn't saying. She was ill off and on for several weeks; I think it was from worrying about her husband. She has now gone for a few weeks to be with your Uncle Jim Horton, who has been distraught since your Aunt Jane died. Mr. Thompson came in recently and stayed several days, but only dropped by twice to see his wife. I think he is angry at me about something, but to save my life I don't know what it is. If he would just talk to me we could work through almost any problem.

This has been a good year for crops. Our corn and cotton produced in abundance. The garden was excellent. The tiny cabbage plants I set out in the spring before you left produced a bumper crop. I processed 300 large heads, made them into sauerkraut. Had two barrels full. I put up a barrel of pickles from the cucumbers that were just beginning to produce when you left. I dried most of the apples you mailed from your Uncle Rube's, and we have had a feast of different desserts from them. I was amused that your Uncle Rube sent word for me not to grumble because I "live in paradise" without having to pay road, school, railroad, income and state and county taxes. If they call this paradise, there is something very skewed with their thinking.

I am glad you are having a good time at last. Now that you are just beginning to get to know people and to be included in all of the social events—three weddings attended in one week!—it is long past time for you to come home. I told Mr. Gray about your saying that a young man was planning to give you an oyster and wine farewell party. He didn't respond, but I could tell by his face that he wonders if you are enamored with someone else. I wonder, too.

We must get you home! I love you too much to imagine that you would even think of living in Missouri permanently.

Your loving mother,

Sarah Horton Cockrell

June 20, 1871

Dallas, Texas
February 1, 1871

Mr. and Mrs. Reuben Fulkerson
Walnut Grove, Missouri

I hasten to inform you that Aurelia arrived safely home yesterday and to thank you for all you did for her while she was in Missouri. I know that her health gave you concern at one time and another, and I very much appreciate your attention to her and to Robert. When she left home last July, I thought she would be back within a few weeks. In my wildest imagination, I would never have thought it would be a long half-year before I would see her again.

If you accumulated any expenses for either of my children while they were there that I have not covered, please let me know and I will send you the money immediately.

Aurelia wrote to me on January 16 that she had taken leave of your family and was then at the home of Cousin J. Longacre in Kingsville, Missouri. From her letter, I know that she was pressingly homesick for several weeks prior to being able to leave you. I trust you will forgive her if she became a difficult guest. She left Kingsville by stage and arrived through Indian Territory to Sherman where she spent the night with her uncle and aunt and then came on to Dallas. Had I known she was traveling a part of the way unescorted, I would have been so worried. I am glad I did not know until she arrived back in Dallas!

I cannot begin to tell you how happy I am to have her here. I miss Robert, too, but not nearly as much as I have missed Aurelia. From the time she was a small child she has been so responsible, such a joy to have, so eager to be helpful. I have depended on her far more than I deem healthy. Her father died when she was eight, and she became independent almost overnight, taking care not only of herself, but helping me with her younger brothers as I have had to spend so much time taking care of the business that Alex left for me to handle. I hope that one day Robert, Frank and Alexander will grow up to assume more of the responsibilities that I have so long depended on Aurelia for.

We are all well here. I do not hear much from Robert. I only hope that he is applying himself diligently to his studies and that he has an opportunity to come home for the summer.

Truly yours, from your sister,

Sarah Horton Cockrell

✳ ✳ ✳

Dallas, Texas
March 15, 1871

Mr. Robert Cockrell
McGee College
College Mound, Missouri

My Dearest Son,

Your letter arrived yesterday. We were all so glad to hear from you even though I am distressed to learn that you are homesick and thinking of dropping out of school. Do not do such a thing. You have had a very good start toward the college education your father so desired that you have. His relatives in Missouri, especially your Uncle Frank and Uncle Reuben, have made such an effort to see that you are well situated and, of course, I have sent money both by Aurelia when the two of you went to Missouri last July, to your Uncle Frank to reimburse some of your expenses and a draft directly to the college president, the Rev. J. B. Mitchell.

From all reports, you are well situated there, rooming with young men who are serious about getting an education. I daresay that all young people, at one time or another, feel that college is a waste of time. When you are young, a few years seems like such a long time, but believe me the years will begin to go faster and faster as you grow older. And if you do not equip yourself now to handle a job and advance in a career, you will later pay for your folly.

Your father left us well situated economically, and I have been able to retain his businesses and to enlarge on most of our holdings. For that I can only be grateful to the counsel of Mr. Guess, who was my lawyer and friend until his death, and to other good business associates and advisors. I do not intend to squander any portion of what we have been able to accumulate and this includes paying out good money for college courses for my sons when they do not merit the expenditure. All of your life I have admonished you to be more careful with your money and at the risk of making myself again very unpopular with you, I will continue to advise you to stop spending. There is a fine line between what you need and what you want, and you do not seem to know the difference. I want you to have everything you need. I will provide tuition, room and board, books and supplies, clothing and medical expenses and to see that you have a limited spending allowance as long as you live up to your promise to me that you will apply yourself to your studies and not be wasteful.

I know how tempting it must be for you to take the job you have been offered as a cowhand herding cattle up the Chisholm Trail to markets in Missouri. Doubtless it all sounds very romantic to you to have work in the open country you love so much, and indulge your love for horses in an all-male atmosphere. Why don't you consider trying to get a job for the summer months? You might try applying for such a job from there, or you could wait and if you come to Dallas for the summer, apply from here. But under no conditions will I condone your dropping out of school.

Aurelia has been home for a little more than a month and this house is again a place of rejoicing. I knew that she and Mr. Gray were good friends when she left to go to Missouri, but I had no idea that they were serious about each other. Aurelia has still not said anything to me about her future plans, but I would not be surprised to learn that they plan to be married. Mr. Gray, who dropped by almost every day to see me on some sort of business or other, has now dropped all pretenses and has made it quite clear by his actions that he is courting your sister. They have attended several parties and musical programs together, and I understand that he plans to escort her to church on Sunday. I had hoped to have Aurelia at home for at least another year, had even dreamed that she would enroll in college. Reports on the new college for young ladies here are all to the good, though the school is yet too young to have gained any kind of recognition beyond the immediate surroundings. Late last year a new college, Texas Christian Univesity, opened in Fort Worth, and I hear that it is excellent. Though it primarily is a training school for potential ministers in the Disciples of Christ faith, it also takes a limited number of young women and is said to be a good source for those interested in music. Aurelia has a wonderful talent for the piano, and I have always wanted her to have more training in music. She has long since advanced beyond the stage of what is available here in Dallas, so I had decided to be willing to let her room with someone in Fort Worth and go to school there if she were interested. Dr. and Mrs. Carroll Peak are very involved in the civic and social life in Fort Worth and would be able to make recommendations for us. Also, Mrs. Juliette Peak Fowler, Dr. Carroll's sister, who now lives back in Dallas, began her married life in Fort Worth and knows a lot about the possibilities there.

I have talked to Aurelia about these possibilities and have asked her what she wants, but she has not made any response other than to say she is interested right now in many different possibilities for the future.

Both of your brothers are studying with Mr. Scales, who has been named the new director of the Methodist College but has not taken over that position yet. Frank will be 17 in August and in the fall will be ready to join you in college. It is even possible that Alexander may be ready to attend college, too. He writes and speaks very well for a 15-year-old. Both boys seem mature for their years, and I would not be reluctant to have all three of you away at school together even though it would be terribly lonely here.

All of the relatives send their greetings and ask why you do not write to them. I have explained that you seldom write to your own mother. Try to do better, Son. You know I love you very, very much.

Love from your mother,

Sarah Horton Cockrell

✷ ✷ ✷

Dallas, Texas
July 15, 1871

Mrs. Margaret Bryan and
Miss Lizzie Bryan
Montezuma, Pike County, Illinois

My dearest Margaret and Lizzie,

Your letters of June 26 arrived yesterday. After feasting my eyes on them and re-reading them several times, I have shared them with everybody, those you mentioned by name to be remembered to and others who have been asking about you.

I am grateful that your trip to Illinois is proving so profitable, but I can't tell you how much you are missed back here. You, my dear Mrs. Bryan, have always been like a sister to me, and you, Lizzie, like another niece since the moment you were born. Having you away from Dallas is almost as painful as those seven months I recently endured when Aurelia was in Missouri. You did not mention your health, my dear Margaret, but Lizzie says in her letter that you are much improved even to the point that you have had an outing in the wagon with your relatives and that you arrived back home looking much refreshed. Would that you continue to improve and that you come home to us very soon.

I saw John and Sarah, your son and his wife, in church last Sunday. It was good to see them. They seem to be well and happy. We see quite a lot of your Luther. I know you miss him, because I also have a son "missing" right now and never a day goes by that I don't think about Robert. I also know that you want the best for Luther, and I agree with Lizzie that the best is right here where he is now living. As Lizzie says, he is the overseer of the two Bryan farms and has an excellent house right in town. I try to see that he eats properly and have offered him a place at our table any time he will join us. Sometimes he does.

Your Luther and my Frank will both be 17 this year. I can hardly believe! Though the boys are like brothers, Luther seems to have more in common with Robert and Alexander than he does with Frank, who is so studious. I guess mothers never have everything just right! I worry about Robert—that he is too carefree and easy-going— and I worry about Frank that he is too studious and responsible. And I worry about Alexander because, as the youngest child, he has not had a lot of responsibility. His older brothers, and, especially, his sister have always protected him, and his Aunt Polly, who came to live with us when he was a tiny little boy, has shielded him.

Lizzie, you mentioned that you hope Luther will go back to school this fall. I hope so, too.

Luther is a handsome youth, large for his age, well coordinated, can turn out work like a fully mature man. I also understand that he is quite popular with the young ladies and more than one looks on him as a good catch, as well they should! Not many young men have so much going for them—the son of Dallas' founder, whose mother's family were the original residents of this place, a young man who will inherit property as well as an illustrious name and history and yet is not afraid of hard work. I can only hope, along with you, that he will have sense enough to forego marriage and commitment until he is old enough to understand what he is undertaking.

It must be a source of great pleasure to have both Ned and Lizzie with you. Ned is as solid, studious and responsible, as is my Frank. I am so glad he was willing and able to escort the two of you to relatives in Illinois. In both of your letters you mentioned that "Ned is reading." He may well be the best self-educated man ever to live in our area. Give him my best regards.

I have saved my best news for last. Aurelia was married to Mitchell Gray on Thursday, May 11. From the time she arrived home from Missouri, Mr. Gray was an almost constant presence in our home. I soon understood that she would forego my desire for her to continue with her education in favor of matrimony. She was a beautiful bride. She did not want a wedding dress, instead opted for the beautiful blue silk that she had bought in St. Louis. Her long dark hair framed her face and was caught in a loose halo effect and laced with baby's breath. Her obvious happiness and the glow on Mitch's face as she came down the stairway into the parlor where they repeated their vows before the Rev. Scales was enough to ease my disappointment for her future. I am sad to have her gone again. I wanted her home so badly those long seven months when she was in Missouri, and had her home only a little less than four months before she was whisked away again.

Following their wedding, we had a feast to which we invited what seemed to me half of Dallas. We entertained almost a hundred people. We missed having you among our guests, and Aurelia was disappointed that Lizzie was not here to be her honor attendant. Aurelia and her new husband spent the night at the St. Charles Hotel before leaving on the stage the next day for Groesbeck where he is the business manager of the town's leading store.

I had a note from Aurelia that they had arrived safely and were boarding at the Beaumont Hotel in Groesbeck and then a long letter dated June 5 with more detail. She described Groesbeck as "quite a little city," which, she said surprised her. She was very pleased with their living accommodations. She said their room was the last one at the back of the house next to a Dr. and Mrs. Tobin, who were married two days before they were. When they moved in, they found the room very poorly furnished with a bed, which had a terrible mattress and lumpy pillows, a wash stand, a small table, two small chairs and a rocking chair. When she and Mr. Gray moved their three trunks and two valises into the room, it still looked bare. He went right out and bought a good mattress, two feather pillows, sheets and pillowcases.

As much as I was glad to hear that she was happy about their living accommodations, I was much more pleased to have her write, "I must tell you about Mr. Gray's goodness and my happiness." I am convinced she has made a good decision. You said you had not heard from Aurelia; I hope a letter has reached you by the time this arrives. Doubtless, she will give you many more details about her wedding and her new life as a married lady.

Please write me a long letter soon and let me know that you are continuing to enjoy life in Illinois. And don't forget to come home!

Your friend, sister and aunt,

Sarah Horton Cockrell

* * *

Dallas, Texas
June 20, 1871

Mr. Frank M. Cockrell
Harrodsburg, Kentucky

My dear brother,

Your letter of June 9 was received along with the bills for Robert's tuition, books and other expenses. I am sending a draft to cover these bills, plus the $25 you leant Aurelia when she left your house, plus $50 which I entrust to you to hold in account for any other expenses that Robert may have. I trust, also, that you will take from this money any personal money you have coming to you for your own transportation and other expenses pertaining to Aurelia and Robert. You have generously given your time and interest to my two children and I would not for a moment have you also obligated to cover any of their expenses.

I am distressed to learn of your wife's illness. I wondered about the postmark on your letter and am glad to know that you are in Harrodsburg with Anna while she is recuperating at her parents' home. It is good to know that she is well enough to go for outings in the buggy. You say that she sometimes is cheerful, that she thinks she will soon be fully recovered and can go home and at other times is deeply depressed. This is only natural when one is ill. It is so sad that her physician and the new doctor he brought for consultation agree that her chances for recovery are not good. You asked for my prayers. Of course, you have them. My thoughts and prayers join yours that she fully recover and be able to return to her home with you.

I am glad that your Willie is at McGee along with Robert and trust that they will be good for each other. Surely having a cousin enrolled in the same school will help Robert to overcome his bouts of homesickness. From all I hear, it appears you are making a wise decision to send both Willie and Johnnie to McGee next year. Having one's children close to home is such a blessing.

I felt I had hardly had Aurelia home long enough to begin to enjoy her again when she married and moved to Groesbeck. Her health seems much improved. I am glad you have received the wedding cards, and I am passing along to her the greetings and congratulations you sent from yourself, Anna and Mollie.

You might be interested in knowing that the bridge we are constructing across the Trinity River goes very well. Mr. Wentworth, the civil engineer from St. Louis we selected to oversee the project, is here and is daily in consultation with the workers. My board and I ordered the ironwork from the Moseley Iron Company near St. Louis. It took a long time to get everything delivered. We paid $65,000 for the ironwork, had it shipped by boat down the Mississippi River to the Gulf of Mexico where it transferred to a freighter and was delivered to the Galveston port.

From there it was shipped by rail to Houston where it was reloaded onto another freight car and shipped by rail to Corsicana. The rail line ended in Corsicana, so we had it loaded onto ox-drawn wagons and brought to Dallas. I am very pleased that the construction site is in the exact location where Alexander built the first bridge. The stone work and foundations are nearly completed and then begins the ironwork. We plan to have the bridge ready for opening early next year.

I am very pleased with the board we have been able to assemble to oversee details pertaining to the bridge. The names probably won't mean anything to you, but I assure you they are men of stability and integrity. Dr. J. W. Crowdus serves as president; George M. Swink, secretary; John B. Bryan, treasurer; A. C. Camp, C. H. Beauchamp, W. H. Prather and E. P. Bryan. I do not serve on the board—everybody knows it would be unseemly for a woman to be an acknowledged partner in a business deal—but the gentlemen seem quite agreeable to allow me to make most of the decisions and to sign the checks.

Thank you so much for inviting Robert to spend the summer vacation at your home. I would love to have him home, but the trip here and back is both expensive and dangerous. And if he can find work there for the summer, as you think he can, I know it will be best that he remain in Missouri. I had one letter from him threatening to drop out of college and go to work herding cattle up the Chisholm Trail from Texas to market in Missouri. I know it all sounds very romantic to him, but I told him I absolutely would not hear of his dropping out of school.

My best to Anna and your daughters.

Affectionately, your Sister,

Sarah Horton Cockrell

* * *

Dallas, Texas
December 10, 1871

Mrs. Aurelia Cockrell Gray
Beckham Hotel
Corsicana, Texas

My darling daughter, Aurelia,

It is with the greatest of joy that I learn you and your husband plan to be in Dallas for Christmas. Frank and Alexander are almost as thrilled as I am for they have been fattening a fine turkey for our Yuletide feast since October.

What a year you have had. Your long newsy letters have almost—but not quite—kept me from missing you so much. I am kept so busy with the bridge and other business that the fast-approaching holidays have crept up on me.

I am thinking that I should begin to write my will. While I consider myself still a young woman, I have to admit that in my early 50s I am far more than halfway through "this veil of tears," and I want to do for you and your brothers what your father did for me—leave the business as clearly defined as possible. Mine will be a far more difficult task because there are four of you to consider where he—and I've always felt so blessed for this—left everything to me. Not many men do that for the wives who survive them.

But, back to you and your plans. As usual, your careful noting of expenditures leaves me both pleased and amazed. I was so surprised that you felt you should, or wanted to, give me a complete run-down of the money I gave to you as a wedding present. You surely know that I had no desire for an accounting of the way that you spent the money. I am, nonetheless, delighted to know you have made it go so far.

I am especially pleased that Mr. Gray has bought you a sewing machine for the handsome price of $81.25, and that you are enjoying it so much. This is something that you will need for the rest of your life as you increase your family in the years ahead. I have sent you muslin and ribbons for the tiny garments you say you are making. When you are home for Christmas, you and I will have a very heart-to-heart mother-daughter talk about this! In the meantime, you do know that I have always known I would love to be a grandmother, even while I have been overwhelmed with rearing you and your three brothers.

Now, I am most concerned about your health. Several times you have mentioned that you have sick headaches and that you continue to have risings in your head. I had hoped that when summer came and you moved from the Beaumont Hotel in Groesbeck to Dr. Iglehart's home, with its much more comfortable accommodations and where the meals were much healthier, that your health would blossom. From time to time I have had indications that such was the case, but it never seems to last. Is there an excellent doctor in Corsicana and are you seeing him faithfully?

Often when you write to me, to one of your friends or relatives in Dallas, unless there are personal things, we share your letters. It makes us all feel closer to you, as if you are a part of the chatter we enjoy around a cup of tea or a meal. I was especially charmed with your description of the women you had met in the Beaumont Hotel in Groesbeck, mostly newly married couples and brides who were left alone to get acquainted while their new husbands went to work. Your letter to Lou about the eight bridal parties you had attended made me smile. I was amused to learn that all the ladies, brides mostly, in the hotel go down to breakfast in their wrappers and do not get dressed until mid-morning. I cannot imagine such leisure!

I was overjoyed that on your trip with Mr. Gray to Galveston you bought a new linen suit. It sounds beautiful, and though it will be far too cold and unseasonable for you to wear it while you are here, I hope you can bring it so that I can see it. You said in your letter to your cousin that you were "exceedingly pleased with your new home," adding "Mr. G. is wonderful." That is enough to make this mother happy about your choice of a husband and to help me not have a single regret that you chose marriage over continuing education.

I am delighted that Mr. Gray is able to bring his books home in the evening so that the two of you can work on them together. It is such a joy to be able to help one's husband in this manner. The idea takes me back to the work I did with and for your father when we were newly married.

I think I have forwarded to you most of the clothes, blankets, other bedding and supplies you have requested in your letters. If not, you can look around the house when you are home for Christmas and take what you need. It is entirely possible that in the move from one house to this while you were gone to Missouri that I may have stored or mislaid some of the things you need. It is also probable that some of your personal things may be stored and forgotten when you married and that you will want to go through boxes and drawers and retrieve your precious possessions. In your letters to me, you have asked so many questions that I am never sure I have given you the information you want. I trust that you have been in correspondence with Lizzie Bryan and know that she was married to a man named William Nathan Dillon on October 12 in Pike County, Illinois. I have few details, but hope this does not mean that her mother will continue to stay with her so far away. It would be nice if I had more information. I am concerned about Lizzie, for I cannot help but feel that her marriage, so closely following yours and so far away from home, might have been a mistake.

It is wonderful that you so much enjoyed meeting your husband's family and that you felt so warmly welcomed by everybody. Nothing makes for a happier marriage than to feel truly a part of your spouse's family. I never had the opportunity to know any of your father's family when I was a bride and now that so many years have passed and so many things have happened, I find it difficult to embrace them. It is often said that if a young girl wants to know how a potential husband will treat her, all she must do is look at the way he treats his mother. For many years I have had the chance to observe your husband on many different occasions and have always thought him a wonderful young man. It is a joy to your mother's heart that his mother now seems to feel the same way about you.

I am glad that Mr. Gray was able to hire an excellent two-horse buggy, which made your 16-mile trip quite comfortable. I could not believe that it had been two years since he had seen his parents. His twin sisters sound very nice. You said that one sister, a Mrs. Price, is the mother of four children, but you didn't say whether, or not, Mrs. Warren is also a mother. Are the twin sisters older or younger than your husband? You also mentioned that he has two younger brothers, one married with children and the younger 17 and still a student. This makes his parents, who you described as very old and white-haired but jovial and lively, several times grandparents. And you have yet to meet his oldest sister who is married and lives in Palestine. I am sure you will be equally welcomed to the family by her.

I know that you were just beginning to feel much at home in Groesbeck, attending church and making friends when you moved on to

Corsicana, but I must add that now you are settled there I feel much relief. Having a Federal general among you in Groesbeck—with something like 500 Negro soldiers stationed there, many arrests of citizens, fear of having your houses raided for no reason at all, the closing of the bank and of some businesses—left me trembling for your safety. When you wrote in October that orders had been issued that no one was to leave town, I despaired of your ever getting away. I am glad this order was soon rescinded. Doubtless many of the residents were trying to move and that accounted for the long time—four-to-six weeks after making your first plans—that you were required to remain in Groesbeck after you were packed and ready to leave.

I am glad I did not know your ordeal in moving until it was all over, for I would have had a few more hairs turn gray. I shivered along with you in that dark, frigid depot as you waited one of three women among a countless number of men, for three hours for the train to arrive because of the ice and sleet. The very memory of it makes me want to wrap you in the warm blankets that are so plentiful here and hold you in my arms until you stop shivering.

Your husband is a saint! When he promised me that he would take care of you, I didn't have any idea, and I know he couldn't know what he was undertaking. That he took off his own coat to wrap you in, kept himself warm enough to lift you onto the train when it finally did arrive and held you through the four hours it took to go from Groesbeck to Corsicana is a gift beyond measure.

I trust that by the time this letter reaches you, you will have sorted out your living accommodations in a manner both pleasing to you and comfortable for you. I certainly understand why you did not want to board at Dr. Love's home because of the distance to Mr. Gray's work, but the room sounds so much better than where you are now staying.

It would be wonderful when you come for Christmas if you would plan to stay here at home for a few weeks until the coldest part of the winter is over and your health has improved. Your present condition and your headaches cause me great concern.

That brings me to share a bit of what is happening in Dallas so that you will not be too surprised at some of the changes.

You won't recognize the bridge. The ironwork is going up at a rapid pace, and we should be able to open the bridge on schedule early next year. Our new courthouse is already open. In October we got our first real fire department. Called the Hook and Ladder Company No. 1, it has 14 volunteer firemen with W. C. Conner as chief. It's located on Austin Street.

The water for fighting fires is available from two cisterns, one located on Houston at Main and the other on Market at Elm. So far we haven't had to avail ourselves of its services for anything more serious than a couple of brush fires, but it's comforting to know we have it. The Great Chicago Fire that raged for two days in early October hastened our opening. And then, most assuredly, many of us remember the Great Fire that all but destroyed our own town a little more than a decade ago.

A new little city has gone up to the east of us. It's called East Dallas and was founded by William H. Gaston, who has opened a bank in town. It's growing rapidly.

The German residents of the town, most of whom came here with the La Reunion settlement and now live east of town between our downtown and the new town of East Dallas, continue their innovative ideas. The ladies of the settlement have organized the Dallas German Ladies Aid Society. They are busy almost every day sewing, quilting and cooking, and selling their food and crafts, then using the proceeds to help people in need. It sounds like a marvelous idea to me, but I can't imagine how they find time to be in an organization outside of the work that has to be done in every home.

I seldom hear from Robert, more often from your Uncle Frank who assures me that Robert seems to be thriving at McGee this year. Both of your Uncle's boys, Johnnie and Willie, are there with him now. Nevertheless, I am strongly considering sending Robert, Frank and Alexander to Virginia to school next year. I think it is time that I counted on my own wisdom in choosing a school for them rather than continuing to depend on your uncles to make that decision.

Please write and let me know when you and Mr. Gray plan to arrive for the holidays. I will have everything ready for your comfort. I am counting the days.

With all of my love, your mother

Sarah Horton Cockrell

1872

Dallas, Texas
January 20, 1872

Mrs. Mary Thompson
C/O Mr. James Horton
Mountain Creek, Texas

My dear, loving sister, Polly,

I pen these few lines hastily to tell you how much I miss you, and so that Luther Bryan can deliver them to you when he rides out to the farm today.

I trust that you are well and that Jim is recovering from the death of Jane. Grief comes to all of us, much too soon. I have been there and am well aware of how difficult it is to pick up the pieces of one's life and find some kind of comfort along the way. Sometimes I think a living grief, such as you are having, is ever so much harder than death. At least when a spouse dies, one has no choice. But, when a good person simply walks away without explanation, there does not seem to be an easy answer. Mr. Thompson was such an exemplary citizen, husband and father for so many years. He was a model employer when he managed the hotel—honest, responsible and courageous—as he was the day Quantrill's Raiders walked in. I shall never forget his courage and his courtesy as he greeted William Quantrill. That he should suddenly decide he did not want to be married any longer and walk away from his vows to you, the church and this city is beyond what any of us can understand. I want you to know that, even though I do not comprehend what happened, as I am confident you don't, I will do anything to support you as you restructure your life. The last time I had any news from Mr. Thompson, he was working on the railroad, which is due to open in the summer. When my Frank encountered him recently on Main Street, Mr. Thompson seemed delighted to see him and sent word that he was well and happy. Who is to understand what goes on in the minds and hearts of anyone except us—and sometimes even that is a mystery.

I hope that our brother Jim has sufficiently recovered from the loss of his wife that he is willing to let you return home. While I certainly approve and applaud your need to spend the winter with him, I feel that you would be happier back in the city.

And what a city it is turning out to be! The 1870 census, recently released, after a ponderously long year, shows an official population of

13,314 (we know there are more, but somehow some citizens were not counted.) We go on record as having three banks, two cotton gins, and a flourmill and are noted as "the world center for leather and buffalo hide trade."

Having Aurelia and Mitchell home for Christmas was wonderful. To see the young couple together reminds me so much of my own early marriage, the only difference being that Alexander had to prove himself with my parents, and I fell in love with Mitch even before my daughter did! She laughs about that, but I think it's true. I recognized Mitch's sterling qualities while Aurelia was still so young that she needed to explore other options for her life. As much as I resented the seven months she spent away from home with her father's family in Missouri, I know that it was good for her—and for me. She has always been so conscientious about money and duty. It delights me that she is learning that love and family is by far the most important thing in life. She is radiant in her blossoming motherhood-to-be. I have to pinch myself to believe that I will be grandmother come early summer! I still worry about her health. She says that she has found a wonderful doctor in Corsicana where they recently moved, but I would be much happier if she were here with me until the baby comes. Mitchell left the decision up to her, and she was absolutely convinced that she wanted to go back to Corsicana with him. She said that nearer her lying-in period she might be agreeable to "coming home to mother," but for now she wanted to be with her husband. She has begun to help him with the bookkeeping of his job. Does that sound like someone else you know!?

There is much more to tell, but Luther is standing around. His horse is saddled and ready to take off, so I leave you only with these additional ideas:

Hurry home. Frank and Alexander ask every day when you are coming back.

Tell Jim that I grieve with him and trust that, through faith, he will soon begin to recover from the loss of Jane. He should know what a lovely "sister" she was to all of us from the time they were married.

Love to you, my dear sister,

Sarah Horton Cockrell

* * *

106 Commerce Street
Dallas, Texas
February 25, 1872

Mr. Francis Marion Cockrell
Warrensburg, Missouri

My dear brother, Frank,

Thank you for your recent letters and for your concern that I have not been able to visit you in Missouri. I had hoped to make the trip this past summer, but after the death of your dear wife felt that it would not be a convenient time for you. So much has been going on in my life and in the young city to which I am committed that I have had little time to write.

I am so grateful for your hospitality to Robert, both last summer and during the recent holidays. And I am especially grateful that you continue to oversee his education. I know that my late husband would be pleased to know that his brothers are concerned and involved in helping me to carry out his final wishes that his children be educated.

Aurelia and Mitchell were here for the holidays. It is my abiding joy to note how happy she is even though her health still seems precarious. She wishes to be remembered to you with fondness.

I am sure you will want to know what is happening in the business world that Alex entrusted to me.

The bridge is scheduled to open on March 2. Mr. Swindells at the *Herald* has promised a long story on opening day, which I will clip and send to you later. It should include all of the details, some of which I have outlined in prior letters. I am the principal shareholder. If things work out as I hope they will, this should provide a consistent income to support myself and allow me to finish paying for my three sons' college education. Far more important, the bridge will open transportation to the west, not only to the part of Dallas County where my family settled when they came here in 1844 and where Alexander and I began our married life, but on westward to the Pacific Coast. Our first rail line, the Houston and Texas Central, traveling north and south, is due to open this summer. A second rail line, the Texas and Pacific, is even as I write completing plans for an east-west artery. The two will intersect right here in Dallas. I am almost as pleased about the rail lines as I am about the bridge because I have given right-of-way property for both. I know that your part of the country is more settled and has already experienced the bounty that excellent transportation affords, but I perceive that we are not far behind. Within the next year the trains should provide service from your part of the world to ours and perhaps I could entice you to pay us a visit.

The rest of my business, at this moment, is going extremely well. We had a good cotton crop and raised enough corn to supply, not only our needs, but to share with our neighbors and to provide food for the live-stock. I am slowly improving the farm out at Mountain Creek, have added a herd of cattle since we now have the means to feed them through the winter. You will remember that is the farm where Alex and I started housekeeping. I have retained it because I am sentimentally attached. In the past it has been something of a financial drain, but now that family members are managing it and have produced a couple of seasons of bountiful crops, it is beginning to be profitable. Vegetable gardens and a small fruit orchard provided us a variety of foods, both for daily con-sumption and to preserve for the winter. Frank and Alex have tended chickens and turkeys and are quite good at hunting deer and squirrels, so we have not lacked for food. My downtown properties are also thriving. The hotel is not always full. I had considered selling it, but have decided against it. The railroads will bring an increasing number of visitors and speculators, and they will require even more rooms. The major problem is keeping a good manager. Since my brother-in-law left I have not found anyone that I can fully trust. The downtown office building is totally rent-ed. I have sold some of the property that abuts the rail lines but will retain the major portion.

My son-in-law is encouraging me to invest in milling, and I am strong-ly considering it. If he will move back to Dallas and run it for me, I just may open a flourmill within the next year or so. I think it is a good busi-ness proposition, but equally important, it would bring Aurelia and Mitchell home. I have no idea what careers Robert, Frank and Alex will choose. I know that Robert loves the outdoor life, and I am hoping that in the future he will want to manage the farm. Frank, the studious one, says now that he wants to study law. At this point, Alex just wants to play! I don't suppose it matters what I have in mind for my sons. They will pretty much do what they choose. That's the trouble with young folks! You raise them to be independent, and they grow up to do what you've taught them!

I know I've rambled on, but thought you would be interested in how I am managing the business that your brother and I started together. At his death I was devastated as to how I would look after four children, make us all a living and manage the property. It's turned out far better than I ever imagined.

Give my regards to Mr. and Mrs. Fulkerson when you see them. My love to your daughters and regards to all other relatives. Tell them to write. I would like to meet each of you and want you to know that all of you are welcome in my home at any time.

Most cordially yours, your sister,

Sarah Horton Cockrell

✳ ✳ ✳

March 30, 1872

Mrs. Margaret Beeman Bryan
Montezuma, Illinois

My dear Margaret,

You asked me to write and tell you about all of the festivities surrounding the opening of the bridge, and if you have not heard from other sources what happened, you must be wondering why I haven't written. It has not been possible for me to write even to my dearest friends, for the world as I knew it ended on the day that should have been the most triumphant of my life. I am still in shock.

We buried Aurelia on the day the bridge opened.

By the time we learned about Aurelia's death, it was too late to postpone festivities surrounding the bridge opening. Dignitaries had already been invited and some had even arrived in Dallas. And so it was that I sat in deep mourning with Frank, Alexander (Robert could not make it back from Missouri in time for the funeral) and a stunned Mr. Gray in the first pew of the Methodist Church to hear the Rev. Stokes eulogize my beloved daughter while only a few blocks away at the foot of Main Street, the bridge I had so long worked to bring into being was dedicated and the first travelers passed over during a subdued celebration that went on all day.

We buried Aurelia as near to her father as I could find a space in the Masonic Cemetery just south of downtown. There is talk of a new cemetery being created north of town and as soon as it comes into existence, I plan to buy lots there with enough spaces for all of my family, and move my husband and daughter. I would like also to bring Logan's body to lie beside his father and sister, but am loathe to move my tiny son from the grave which his father personally chose.

I do not have all of the details of Aurelia's death and doubt if I ever will. Not even her husband knows what happened. As you know, she had been suffering from headaches and infections for years. We could barely get her over one illness until she came down with another, but after her wedding she seemed to be dramatically improved. Occasionally, when I got her long and loving letters, she would mention excruciating headaches, but they always were of secondary consideration as she wrote of her happiness in her marriage and the work that she was doing with her husband. When they were here for Christmas, she had just seemed to blossom. She was so happy over the impending birth of a baby, brought some of the infant garments she had been sewing on her new machine and talked at length about their plans for their family. She was so happy, she said, that she would like to have at least six children, but her husband was not so sure. I listened with love—and sometimes with envy—as she poured out her heart to her mother, something she would not have felt at all comfortable doing in letters.

When she and Mitch were preparing to return to Corsicana in early January, I tried to convince her to remain at home through the birth of her child, which would have been due in late April or early May, around her 23rd birthday. When it became apparent that she would not consider being away from her husband for such a long period (and his work would not allow him to remain in Dallas with her), I promised that when the time came, I would somehow get to Corsicana to look after her and my first grandchild.

We were all so happy, so expectant the day they left to return to their home. I was jubilant because we had begun to close the deal to open a flourmill in Dallas, which Mitchell would oversee. This meant that in a few months, I would have my lovely daughter, her husband and a grandchild back home!

The last long letter I have from Aurelia was written in early December last year brimming with excitement over their move, their new home and their planned trip to Dallas for the holidays. I had only a brief note after they arrived home in January telling me of their safe arrival. I don't know where that letter is. We have passed Aurelia's letters around through the family and to friends who were eager to hear about her, so some of them have been lost. I wish I had kept every letter she wrote.

On the night of February 27, 1872, Aurelia went to bed early, Mr. Gray tells me, while he was completing the ledgers. He knew she was not feeling well and had encouraged her to go to sleep. She had not complained, but he knew from the meager supper she had eaten and from the drawn look on her face that she needed to rest.

He completed his work, closed the ledger, left the room for a few minutes, returned with a glass of fresh water for her and put it on the bedside table, then blew out the lights and retired. During the early part of the evening, he checked on her a couple of times and found her quiet, so he turned over and went to sleep. Around 3 a.m. he woke suddenly with an ominous foreboding, turned to check on his wife and found her too still, too quiet. And lifeless. She was already beginning to cool. The life had gone out of her, said the doctor, sometime around midnight.

He sent a rider to deliver the shocking news to me. I immediately penned a hasty note to Mr. Gray that the funeral and burial would be in Dallas, and I would at that moment begin to make plans for the services and the burial.

When they arrived on March 1, everything was in place, everything planned. I told her young husband that he was free to change anything he desired, but that I had tried to honor every wish I had heard Aurelia express. He, like I, was in shock. All of us moved through the next few days in a trance.

The opening of the Iron Bridge was the last thing on my mind.

I have no medical knowledge, and have not, of course, been able to talk with her doctor in Corsicana, but I think something in her head just burst. I don't have a name for it, or an understanding of it, but I feel sure that the headaches she had been suffering since she was a young girl must have meant that there was some growth, some pressure on the brain that eventually burst and took her life.

I feel so all-alone. My sons are wonderful boys and will all grow up to make me proud, but Aurelia was like me—the same consideration for the feelings of everybody around her, the same dedication to detail, the same careful steward of money and finances, the same reverence for life, the same belief that service to others is the principal motivation for one's life. There are times I do not think it possible to go on without her—and yet, I must.

And, added to the burden is the death with my daughter of her child, who would have been my first grandchild.

There are not many people, my beloved Margaret, friend and "sister" to whom I could write my heart out this way. You are one of a very few who will understand and not judge me. How I miss you!

At the last hearing from you and Lizzie, she said she had not heard from Aurelia. I hope that my daughter wrote to her some time before February 27. Even if she did not, Lizzie knows how precious was their friendship.

The "obituary" of Aurelia's death was printed in the *Weekly Herald* (March 9, 1872, page 2, col 6), a tiny little reminder: *"Departed this life in Corsicana on February 27 after a painful illness in the 22nd year of her age, Aurelia, wife of M. Gray and daughter of Mrs. S. H. Cockrell of this city."* In a second paragraph it added: *"The deceased, reared in Dallas as she gained her maturity, had ripened in the affections of the entire community."*

I have had an eight-page letter of condolence from F. M. Cockrell, Aurelia's uncle in Missouri, who has been responsible for getting Robert into McGee College and who, with his late wife, was one of the families whom Aurelia visited last year. He has recently lost his wife. His letter is filled with platitudes meant to comfort me. Nothing does. It will take time. From bitter experience, I know that.

So, you can see why I have not been enthusiastic over the opening of the bridge, even though I waited for 12 years for it to happen. Since I was not there, I have no way of reporting what happened. I am enclosing the long story that appeared in the *Herald* on Saturday, March 2, 1872, page two, columns 2 and 3.[10]

My dear friend, please know that you are much in my thoughts. I have missed you—especially over the last month. My late husband's half-brothers keep admonishing me to make a visit to Missouri; I doubt now that I ever shall. They are welcome to come here if and when they wish. I think I will send all of my sons to Virginia to school next year.

For myself, my life is over for the moment. I hope that someday I will care to live again, but for now, I exist. Mourn. And wait.

My dearest love,

Sarah Horton Cockrell

* * *

106 Commerce Street
Dallas, Texas
November 1872

Washington and Lee University...
Lexington, Virginia

My dearest sons.... Robert, Frank and Alexander,

How I miss you. Even though I know it is best that you are away from home and together at college, I find myself still peeking into your bedrooms to see if you are up in the mornings, even though, by this time, I

---

[10] See complete *Dallas Herald* story, appendix page 277.

should be adjusted to having you away. It has, after all, been almost four months since the three of you moved away. I hope you are looking after each other. Robert, as the oldest and the son already experienced at living away from home, I want you to take extra care of Alexander. He is only 16. I hope that the educational preparation you all received in Dallas has prepared you for your university studies.

You do not write home often enough. May I suggest that you take turns corresponding with your mama? It won't strain you too much for each of you to write one letter a month. I can live with a letter every 10 days, but would be much happier to hear oftener. I have received and paid the bills for your tuition, room and board and some of your books. The bank deposit I made in your names in Lexington shows a bare balance. As I told you before you left, I count on each of you to be cautious about spending.

Since your sister's death, I have had to rewrite my will and take care of other pressing business. Since you left I have received my certificate of bridge ownership, 80 shares of stock in the company at a hundred dollars in gold per share, making me the largest of all the stockholders. The $8,000 I paid for these shares put quite a dint in the family's finances and is all the more reason that I prevail on all three of you to spend money wisely. I am certain that this investment in the bridge will prove to be one of the wisest business decisions I have ever made.

Our little city is exploding in growth. Every day, it seems, there is new evidence that Dallas will be a major city in this part of the world. Just this year there have been several major advances beginning with the opening of the bridge in early March followed by the arrival of the first train in July at about the same time that telegraph service became available. Mayor Henry S. Ervay sent simultaneous wires to the mayors of Austin, Brownsville, Galveston, Houston and San Antonio reading ". . . the people of Dallas send greetings to their sister cities over which you, respectively, preside. We are this day placed in telegraphic communication with the whole national public, thanks to arrival of the Iron Horse. Verily, in the language of holy writ, what wonders God hath wrought." Within hours the mayor received responses congratulating Dallas and its citizens from all of the cities for acquiring telegraphic service.

The Iron Horse, Dallas' first wood-burning locomotive steamed over the new Houston and Texas Central rails into town on July 16, eight days after telegraphic service was instituted. It completed a 15-hour trip from Houston at 16 miles per hour! As you recall, convicts were recruited to work furiously to complete the tracks on time. I am glad they were allowed to remain free long enough to be a part of the celebration when the train arrived. The *Herald* reported that more than 5,000 jubilant citizens were on hand to cheer the arrival of the train.

I was not among the celebrants—since your sister's death I have not been able to celebrate anything—but nobody who was present that day will ever forget it, and the stories expand as time passes. Mr. William Brown Miller, one railroad advocate who gave both time and money to the project, rode in from his farm about five miles west of the Trinity. He had saddled his most spirited horse and was about to ride off when little Minnie, his 6-year-old daughter, begged so hard to be allowed to go see the train, that he pulled her up in the saddle in front of him and off they rode. He related that the noise of the locomotive and the shouting of the crowd created such a disturbance that his horse panicked, and it was all he could do to keep him from throwing both him and his little daughter.

Robert Seay, a young lawyer who moved here last December, wrote glowingly about the arrival of the first train.

"Well, the H&TC is in. We called it a holiday and set out to celebrate. Sam Duncan, Tom Marsalis and I, with some others, hired a hack and started to the depot, a mile east of town. Hardly realized so many people in this little place, but long lines of them, horse-back, in buggies, on foot, streamed in long lines from every direction, converging in one spot like ants in a drop of honey. We were in too great a hurry and our driver, excited like the rest of us, turned too short and we were all spilled out in the road as hack turned over. Nobody badly hurt (though I find I have a stiff neck) so, picked ourselves up and righted the hack. Fortunately the horse was too gentle—or too old—to run away, so we hurried on.

About 9 a.m., some sharp-sighted folks, gazing south, yelled "there it comes." First a wisp of smoke, and then the outlines of the engine shaping up, growing larger, whizzing toward us. The crowd went wild. Men whooped, women screamed, or even sobbed, and the children yelped in fright and amazement. As to that, there were some grown folks there who had never seen a railway train before, and I think the chugging of the log-burning furnace and the hissing of the steam startled them a little.

But to all of the grownups, it was a day never to be forgotten. Then the oratory broke out everywhere, railways officials congratulating Dallas upon getting a railway into Dallas and Dallas officials congratulating the H&TC upon having such a fine town to come into, sometimes having a dozen orating at one time—until they were too hoarse to talk any more. Then we tackled the barbecued buffalo steaks and prairie chicken, and I don't know what all. I had a grand sick headache that night, as I always do, after seeing thrilling, interesting things. But, all's right this evening. Everybody is. We are not only on the map but we are on the railroad now. Hurrah for Dallas!"

Even before the H&TC rail tracks were completed from the south and now heading north toward McKinney rails were being laid for an east-west line, the Texas and Pacific. To secure this line, Dallas passed its first city bond election in July, to the tune of $100,000. Of the 227 qualified voters in the city, 192 voted and not a single man opposed issuing the bonds. If women could have voted, the numbers would have been much greater because we are all so weary of having to travel by stage. Other concessions have been made, including the closing of Burleson Street and renaming it Pacific Avenue. And many of us have donated property. As you remember, I gave land for both rail lines.

Just think! Now we will soon have rail service both north and south and east and west. We can get to McKinney in two hours where it now takes us five or six, and we can get to Houston in 15 to 16 hours where it now takes almost a week!

While the trains make it so much easier to get from town to town, transportation within the town has also advanced. In the early fall, street-car lines opened on Main Street from the courthouse to the railroad station. It has two cars, each capable of carrying as many as 17 people.

Almost every day a new business of one kind or another opens here. The latest, and by far the most interesting, is a retail establishment called Sanger Brothers opened by Alex and Philip Sanger who arrived almost simultaneously with the railroad. They seem to have a prodigious eye for future development and a compelling need to provide services that people need. Theirs is almost a Cinderella story because five of the brothers—Alex, Isaac, Lehman, Philip and Samuel— arrived in the United States from Germany in the early 1850s. Both separately and together they established retail stores following the expansion of the rail routes in Texas, their most recent until they came to Dallas in July, being one that Lehman built in Millican. Here, they rented a 30 by 70-foot building on Main Street opposite the courthouse. In its first few weeks of operation it became apparent that it would be highly successful, so they are now constructing a 50 by 80-foot building of their own. I shop there at least once a week because they stock **everything**, and I don't have to traipse all over town for food, business supplies, or even dress yardage and notions. In the last few weeks I have bought such disparate items as a ham, a plow for the farm, two yards of ribbon, a sack of flour, assorted canned foods, and 10 yards of calico. You have no idea how convenient this is, especially when the streets are unreceptive to ladies and the rowdies around town make shopping an adventure not to be desired.

That is the one thing I do not like about the arrival of the railroads. It has brought so many derelicts to the community. No lady would dare venture out of her house after dark. This works a real hardship on me because, as you know, I have often gone back to the hotel after the evening meal to check books, to work out problems with staff members or just to observe what is going on in my business there. Now, I dare not go unless there is a gentleman to accompany me and this does not occur often since the three of you are away.

The arrival of the Sanger Brothers and other citizens of the Jewish faith plus an increasing number of Catholics have expanded our town into one of religious variety. It reminds me of the time when the Swiss, French and Germans came to establish LaReunion. The growing Protestant faiths—Methodists, Baptists, Disciples of Christ, Presbyterian (with, I am sure, citizens of other religious persuasions)—has now grown to include Catholic and Jewish congregates.

During the summer, eleven persons formed the Hebrew Benevolent Society, elected Moses Ullman as president and Alex Sanger as vice president and rented the Masonic Hall on the south side of the Commerce to hold Jewish religious services. They have purchased a lot on the south side of Commerce where they are erecting a two-story brick building.

The Catholics, some of whom arrived here with the LaReunion settlement, have organized into a parish and dedicated the Sacred Heart of Jesus Cathedral. I understand that they are calling a priest, whose name is Father Joseph Martiniere, to lead the parish. That is about all I know. Even though I am Methodist to the core, I know that our little city is vastly enriched by the variety of people who have arrived to make it their home.

What think you (or, do you think of politics at all? YOU SHOULD. It shapes so much of what is possible for your lives) of the reelection of President U.S. Grant? I cannot believe that he was re-elected after all the scandals that surrounded his administration. Speaking of politics, were you aware that Congress passed a law guaranteeing equal pay for equal work in all federal employment? A woman named Belva Anne Lockwood campaigned for that change. It doesn't mean a lot yet because there are so few women working in careers outside their homes, but I predict that in the future it will be a very important development. I have heard that Sanger Bros. plans to employ women clerks! Isn't that amazing? I was very distressed to learn that Susan B. Anthony was arrested in Rochester, New York, for trying to vote in the general election on November 5. Many of us rejoice that Victoria Claflin Woodhull dared to announce as a candidate for president. She knew, and we knew, that she didn't stand a chance of being elected, but it's a start. And all of us who believe in privacy were appalled when Congress making it a criminal offence to import, mail or transport any article for the prevention of conception or causing abortion passed the so-called Comstock Law. Where are women's rights in all of this?

Not, that you, my sons, are interested in what you have long considered to be your mother's eccentricities!

I know I have gone on and on and on. It has been so long since I wrote you a long letter that I simply let myself go in this. I do not think you will pay a lot of attention to what your mother has to say, but I hope you will—at the very least—read this. You need to know what is happening in this growing city, which of course I hope you will return to and make your own. I miss you and I . . .

Love you, my sons, your mother
Sarah Horton Cockrell

1873 and the following years

Journal notes:

The years are speeding past. I have just "celebrated" my 54th birthday (January 19) without so much as a greeting, a letter or a cake. Aurelia always remembered, and she wrote such long and loving letters. I can't expect the same of the boys. And now that all three are away in Virginia in school, I keep busy making money so that I can afford them! I have lived in Texas for more than a quarter of a century (28 years last November). I have watched it grow from a village of half a dozen businesses around a make-believe court house square on streets all but impassible most of the time (sandy ruts during droughts, tar-like mud goo during rainy seasons). In my more than half a century of living, I have seen wars and pestilence, famines and fires and floods. I have been blessed with a good marriage to a man of vision who made me a full working partner, and though he signed legal papers with an "X" was the smartest person I have ever known—smart enough to leave a will that made me the total owner of everything we had acquired at a time when most men left widows bereft. I have been a widow for almost 15 years. I have birthed five children and lost two of them, our first-born as a baby and last year my beloved daughter just before she made me a grandmother.

I have seen the good times. I've been extremely fortunate in almost all of my business relationships. Good men, for the most part, have supported my efforts—just so long as I did not present myself as a pushy woman. The St. Nicholas Hotel, though it lasted only a year before going up in smoke when Dallas burned in 1860, was my first major accomplishment. Nobody in Dallas thought that a widow woman would dare take over such a major project. I was determined to prove, most of all to myself, and then to everybody else that Alexander had left his holdings in good hands. There have been so many business ventures that turned out well, culminating last year in the dream-come-true of my lifetime when the bridge opened.

Since I have described my life mostly in letters to family and friends and since there are now so few interested in my long missives, I will use a journal to record the stories that I do not want lost to posterity. Who I am and what has happened in my lifetime may have no value to anybody in the future, but I have wished many times that I had learned more about my parents' stories, and I want to leave our legacy and the history of our town in my lifetime to future generations.

I have not yet, nor I think I ever will, get over the loss of Aurelia. I had made my peace with the death of my parents, my first-born and even my husband, but Aurelia was so young and vibrant and had so much promise that a part of my life ended the day I buried her.

And yet life goes on.

The railroads continue to dominate the news. We cannot over-estimate the value of this most significant advancement. When the Texas and Pacific train steamed up Pacific (formerly Burleson Street) on February 22, its arrival as an east-west carrier connecting with the H&TC going north and south made our town the only transportation crossroads in this part of the country. The property that I, along with countless others donated to bring the railroads here is an investment in our future that seems to have no limitations. It is turning Dallas into a commercial city. The area in which my family settled when they first came to Texas has also benefited by having rail service, thanks to my brother, James, who acquired 4,000 acres around Eagle Ford and donated the right-of-way for the rails and land for a depot there.

I am not happy with the riff-raff that has followed the railroad to our town, but I am very happy that it has also brought numerous new families including some of the best merchandisers in the country.

Our Main Street between Austin and Market has so many saloons and gambling houses that no decent person would dare traverse the area after dark. There are almost a hundred professional gamblers in town at any one time. Many business men say that closing down the saloons and gambling halls would ruin business and hamper the town's progress, so there is constant friction between the law-abiding citizens and those who will take any opportunity to make money. I see it as the battle between God and the devil.

Mayor Ben Long has been almost powerless when it comes to controlling the evil elements, to make the town a law-abiding place where it is safe to raise families. I am so glad that my sons are away from here at this time because the temptations are so prevalent that even the best of parents find their sons falling into depravation. When the mayor tried to regulate the gambling halls there was a three-day stand-off with the gambling hall owners barricading themselves in the second story of a downtown building and openly defying any attempt to bring them under control. The mayor and his deputies were powerless. The siege ended when the two sides agreed to a compromise that, I think, left the ruffians in control because lawlessness continues unabated.

The new Sanger Brothers that opened here last year has moved into its recently much-enlarged building in downtown Dallas where it is providing an assortment of merchandise equal to anything one might find in the better stores in St. Louis or even New York City. Its owners, Alex and Phil Sanger have very innovative ideas. Mr. Philip Sanger has gone to New York at least twice on buying trips, and I hear that they are planning to open a buying office in that city to help them keep up with all the latest styles and trends. Most amazing of all, they have hired a woman to clerk in the store! Now, that is progress! When you think about it, having women as employees makes perfect sense because we, the women, do most of the planning, if not the actually buying, of food, clothing and supplies for the family. I am told that when this new lady clerk works late, the Messrs. Sanger have made arrangements for a delivery wagon to see her safely escorted to her home.

Europeans, mostly Swiss, who came here two years ago at the urging of Mayor Long, after he had made a trip back to his native Zurich, add a special flavor to our little town to make us think we are truly becoming cosmopolitan. These new citizens added to the Swiss, French and Germans who moved into Dallas after the failure of LaReunion, are very industrious and though they have congregated into one area, are very open and accommodating, sharing their industry with the rest of us and eager to learn what we have to teach. Not surprisingly, the major road leading from near downtown into their settlement has been named Swiss Avenue.

Early this year Louise Dusseau Jones took her daughter, 17-year-old Guillelmine to France to visit her family, who were among the first settlers of LaReunion. Her mother had shortly returned to her home in Lille. Louise was not well when she left Dallas. Her health worsened and she died in France in June. Her husband, Sam Jones, immediately sailed for France to return his daughter to this country and left her with relatives in Tennessee. My sons are Guillelmine's friends, and I know that Robert, especially, was saddened to learn about her mother's death.

With all of the unsavory characters arriving in our area, it is heartening, indeed when an upstanding family moves here and such is the case with a nice family from Tipton County, Tennessee—the Cullum family. Both our town and our Methodist church are enriched with the arrival of the Rev. Marcus Hiram Cullum, his wife Elizabeth Jane Davis Cullum, and their sons, daughters, in-laws and grandchildren—14 in all including Jacob, Lou, William, Isadora, Cal, James Isaac Jones, Emma, Frances, Lora, Ashley, Marvin, Willie, Daisy and Viola. They have settled north of Dallas and just a bit south of where the Cochrans live.

Mr. William Henry Gaston, the businessman who with A. C. Camp established a bank here in 1868 and who has lived with his family on Ross Avenue, has bought 40 acres to the far east of town where he is building a showcase Greek revival-designed home on the northeast corner of Swiss and St. Joseph. Wallace Street, named by Mr. Jefferson Peak for one of his sons, has been changed to Gaston Avenue. I've never really trusted banks, but my lawyer tells me that I must begin to make friends with them! I don't trust banks because they have never seemed too stable to me. For instance, the Gaston-owned institution has a colorful, but what appears to me not a very stable history. Mr. Gaston and Mr. Camp established the bank with $40,000. Their counter was a used dry goods box and their own pockets were the safe deposit vaults. The bank was known as Gaston & Camp until W. H. Thomas became a partner and its name changed to Gaston, Camp & Thomas. Now Mr. Camp is getting out and the bank will become Gaston and Thomas. This constant change does not seem very stable to me.

We have the beginning of a cultural center with the opening of Field's Opera House located on Main Street between Austin and Lamar. On opening night the new center presented the very popular Crisp Sisters, Jessie and Cecelia, in *Richelieu* by Bolivar. I made myself get dressed and go, though my heart was not in it, but I'm glad I did just to see first-hand the rave responses of the overflow audience, most of whom seemed starved for the cultural advantages they had enjoyed before they came to Dallas The opera house itself is a small auditorium on the second floor of a building owned by Tom Field on the south side of Main Street between Austin and Lamar and across the street from the new Sanger Bros. Dry Goods store.

The commercial flour mill that Mitch Gray and I planned before Aurelia's death, was incorporated early this year and is now in full operation producing 75 barrels a day. We sought additional financing to be able to build the mill and open it for business and were very happy to have Mr. H. C. Kimble as a third incorporater and business partner. We named it Todd Mills for Mr. Todd of Todd and Stanley, the St. Louis firm that built it. It is the first commercial mill in this section of the country. It's located between Broadway, Water and Pacific at the intersection of the Texas and Pacific Railroad and the Trinity River. We do not grind grain for farmers, but instead exchange a given amount of flour per bushel of wheat that is brought to us. Some farmers leave a portion of their flour for future use and we issue a receipt for additional flour to be delivered to him on demand. I am very pleased with Todd Mills as a business development and as an extension of the industry in this city, but my personal interest in the endeavor ended with Aurelia's passing. I had counted on the project to bring my daughter and her husband back to live in Dallas. Mitch and I would create it together and he would be the manager. I should be pleased—and I am—that in planning, opening and running the mill Mr. Gray has shown the first spark of interest since his wife died. He is an excellent manager, and I count him as one of my own children. Maybe one day when my sons are through college, one of them will be interested in helping him run it.

Our new business neighbors are Paul H. Samisen Sr. and S. M. Leftwich who have bought the bankrupt brick company just down the way apiece and have installed the first brick-making machine in Dallas. Until now all brick has been hand-produced. On their best production day they turned out 5,000,000 bricks, all of them from clay, which they hauled from the river bottom property, which I own. They pay me for each carload of our farm land mud. This further adds to my income. To me, it's just money. My heart and soul lies with my family and my friends—and with the successful growth of this town.

We have a new courthouse. It's a gleaming white two-story structure on Main Street much larger than the wooden building our county offices formerly occupied. The builders brought white stone quarried from the Chalk Hill area six miles away to build it. The first floor is 66 by 110 feet; the second floor slightly less.

We also have the beginnings of city water and city illumination. The Dallas Hydrant Company, a private concern, is piping water through wooden mains from Browder Springs to the tower, which is located at Main and Harwood.

The Dallas Gaslight Company, with offices on Elm Street in the Schroeder and Davis Wholesale Grocers, is lighting up our downtown. Wooden mains pipe gas to consumers, most of whom are located in businesses. The city is installing 102 gas lamp posts downtown that will soon be functioning. I think I will add gas fixtures here at home as soon as they are available.

Our first city directory has recently been published by Lawson and Edmondson. They write in their preface that they encountered "many obstacles, lack of interest, streets in a peculiar condition, some existing only on paper and many terminating abruptly." But I think the directory is unusually accurate and useful, and I am astonished at their accomplishment. There are 2,320 entries both residential and business. I am listed as a "Widow."

Yours for posterity,

Sarah Horton Cockrell

1874

Journal notes:

I wish I had the words to express what our city looked like and how I felt on the night that the first gas lights illuminated our town. It was like magic! All up and down along the main streets, after a gas-lighter had made his way, touching his torch to the 120 newly installed units up and down the city blocks, the word was passed that our city would now be alight!

And it was! Every able-bodied resident and business owner and visitors from the country for miles around stood on the streets and gazed with awe as the lights went on. We had heard about and read about such magic in other parts of the world, but we had never imagined that we, too, would be able to join the crowd. What a miracle! Lights!

Almost as if in celebration of this major event, our *Dallas Herald* has become a daily newspaper. J. W. Swindells, its publisher, proclaims that since our growth is so phenomenal, we must be counted among the elite in publishing. How will I ever find the time to read everything I should. So many books are being published now that I cannot begin to keep pace.

And now, just a few notes about what's going on in Dallas:

The Episcopalians have built a new church, St. Matthews Cathedral, on the northeast corner of Commerce at Church, across the street from Temple Emanu-El. Early Gothic in design, it is a lovely addition to our city. Many parishioners, however, are disgruntled because the noises from the nearby Santa Fe Railroad interrupt worship services. The Rt. Rev. Alexander C. Garrett, the first bishop of the Episcopal Diocese and the first bishop of any church to be assigned here, has arrived. His district covers 12 stations, 100,000 square miles in North Texas. He comes to us from a distinguished career in England, Canada and other U.S. Cities.

Obadiah Knight, whose wife is Serena Caroline Hughes Knight, one of the seven sisters who came to Dallas in its first decade, along with members of his family, has established a new settlement on 1,000 acres to the north of the town. It is called Oak Lawn. The Rev. Marcus Cullum, who moved here last year with his family, lives in the community and has created a new church in the area called Oak Lawn Methodist.

Todd Mills, our new flour-producing operation here, is successful beyond my expectations. Mitch Gray is so pleased. When he's home from school, Frank helps out and is listed as the co-manager. Frank says he plans to become a lawyer; I encourage him to remain in college even though it is so comforting to have him home. He is so level-headed and such a help to me in all areas of business. He says he feels torn—that he could gain so much business experience just by being involved in all of our holdings in Dallas. But I tell him that he will be even more beneficial to our future when he has a law degree.

I was disappointed that Robert dropped out of college; he completed two years at McGee College and one at Washington University, but would not agree to go back to school for another year. Alex did go back, but he, too, wants to leave college and go to work.

Speaking of education, we have a new school for girls here, Ursuline Academy, founded by the Catholics. Six Catholic nuns of the Ursuline

Order arrived from Galveston on one of our new trains on January 28 to establish the school. Led by Mother St. Joseph Holly, a native of Austria, the six, though united by their faith, are very different from each other. Sister St. Paul Kaufmann was the first girl born in Galveston. Sister Mary Patrick Flaherty is a native of Ireland; Sister Mary Francis Xavier Vindrier of France; Sister St. Bernard Dowd, from Ireland and Sister Philomena Gerngros, born in Germany. The school opened with seven students, only one more student than teachers, but grew rapidly and as I write this, the enrollment has doubled. Only one small room, heated by a wood-burning stove, provided space for classes and all other activities. Soon after the school started, Sister St. Philomena, who was ill, returned to Galveston, but the other five persevered. Within the past few weeks a permanent building is rising on a small plot on Masten and Ervay streets. Tom Crutchfield, owner of the Crutchfield House, has been a great help in fund-raising. His daughter was a boarding student in the Ursuline school in Galveston, and he is eager to help the Dallas school succeed.

Public education is also progressing. Recently the Supreme Court upheld Kalamazoo, Michigan's right to levy taxes to support a public high school. One of the citizens had brought the suit declaring that the city had no right to tax him to pay for an educational system when he had no children eligible to attend. Thankfully, the Supreme Court ruled otherwise.

Another boon to education began with the recently created Chautauqua Movement at Fair Point on Lake Chautauqua, New York, when the Rev. Joel Heyl Vincent, a Methodist bishop, and Lewis Miller, a farm machinery maker from Akron, Ohio, opened a training center. The first session trained Sunday school teachers, but the movement now includes training sessions for people in many different disciplines. Would that I could attend!

And, in France, several artists who were not allowed to display their work in the established salons, have banded together to form a group called French Impressionists. We are told that some of them will become world-famous in future years. The founding members are Pierre Claude Monet, Paul Cezanne, Edgar Degas, Edouard Manet, Berthe Morisot, Camille Pissareo, Auguste Renoir and Alfred Sisley. They immediately gained favor among artists and art critics. Only the future will tell how they succeed.

For me personally, the most significant happening of this year of 1874 was the death of my brother, Enoch, on November 23 and his funeral the next day. The story in the paper said he was interred in Mrs. S. H. Cockrell's "private cemetery," but this is not accurate. There is a new cemetery being created just north of the city to be called Trinity Cemetery[11], and I am one of the first to buy a block of burial plots there. Though it will not be opened until early next year, I got permission to bury my brother there and soon afterward moved the bodies of Alexander and Aurelia there. It is a secluded and wooded area and has enough space to expand, not like the small cemetery downtown, which is contained, on all sides by private property.

It is never easy to give up a family member. Enoch and I have always been close, even more so as the years have gone by. He was only two years and five days younger than I. He was the most personable and out-going one in the family, made friends easily and quickly. When we were young just after we came to Texas and before any of us were married, Enoch was usually the family member who became acquainted with strangers easiest. He brought countless people home to introduce them to us. In the past few years he and I have collaborated on several business deals. I knew I could depend on his knowledge and integrity.

I shall miss him dreadfully.

Until another journal entry, I am

Sarah Horton Cockrell

December 30, 1877

Mrs. Margaret Bryan
Dallas, Texas

My dear "sister" Margaret,

Since I learned about Mr. Bryan's death in September, I have intended daily to come to see you or, at the very least, write to you. I know that your husband's death came as a shock even though he had been ill for some time and had grown worse since you and your sons were compelled to institutionalize him in the State Lunatic Asylum in Austin last February, both for his safety and your sanity. You and I both are now widows. I remember so much about the earlier years—what good friends our husbands were, how they brought us together and helped to cement life-long connections between our children, what vision they both had for

---

[11] After going bankrupt, Trinity was reorganized in 1898 and renamed Greenwood Cemetery.

our city before his untimely death felled my Alex and mental demons robbed your John of his brilliance. I remember the times when both of us were quite upset with those same husbands, when Alex bought the remainder of property rights of Dallas and the ferry from your husband and then both insisted that you and I change houses. That was a tense period for both of us because neither of us wanted to move. You loved your house on the banks of the Trinity, and I adored my White House high on the hill at Mountain Creek. I cherish the special bond that exists between you and your daughter, Lizzie, because I, too, enjoyed a similar closeness with Aurelia. I know that it was very difficult for you to leave her in Illinois when you returned to Dallas, but at least you know she is alive and well and that eventually you will be together again. Never a day passes that I do not miss Aurelia.

Once I walked to Trinity Cemetery to Aurelia's resting place where I have also moved Alexander. Banker W. H. Gaston created the cemetery on a 33-acre site north and a little east of town. It was a long walk from my home on Commerce Street. Since then, occasionally, when one of the boys or one of the hired hands is available, I have them take me to the cemetery in the wagon. I do not like to do this because I am not comfortable with an audience. I have been only once to the cemetery since we buried my brother Enoch there, two years ago in November. Since then I have lost another brother. James died on April 24, 1876, but he is buried near his home at Eagle Ford.

I was very disappointed when both Robert and Alexander dropped out of college. I felt like I had failed their father.

But you and I have both learned we cannot control our grown-up children. We can provide the opportunity and, I hope, the example. But they will become their own people and follow their own paths no matter what we may have wished. I had once hoped that one of my sons and your daughter would fall in love, get married and produce grandchildren you and I could share. But that was never in their minds. I am sure that your Lizzie looked on Robert, Frank and Alexander as brothers, and I know that my three boys consider her a sister.

Robert has turned into a very responsible young man, and I am very pleased at his choice of a wife. Last year he and Guillelmine Jones were married. You will remember Gillie as the only child of Sam and Louise Dusseau Jones and that Louise took Gillie to France to visit her family, became ill and died there. Sam went to France and brought his daughter home[12], leaving her for a time in Tennessee with family members, but she wanted to come home and soon returned to Dallas where she was a very popular with the young set. She and Robert had been childhood friends,

---

[12]Sam Jones wrote his daughter a letter outlining the history of the family. The original is in the unpublished papers of Joseph M. Wilson. See letter in appendix page 284.

and I was not at all surprised to see him immediately begin to compete with the other young Lotharios for her favor.

Eleven months after they married, Robert and Gillie had a baby daughter, who was hardly with us, only 16 days old, before she died. We buried her at Trinity Cemetery. I was so pleased that they named her Aurelia Effie for my Aurelia and saddened that there are now two Aurelias sleeping in the new cemetery.

I really had a scare back in the spring when a letter from Frank informed me that he had been challenged to a duel. He even sent along a copy of the "challenge," but he did not have the foresight to let me know immediately that he was all right. I enclose a copy of the duel challenge so that you can see I am not making this up:

Lexington, VA
March 20th, 1877

Mr. Cockrell
    Sir:
    Hearing you have said you want to know who wrote in a Sunday School book your name coupled with that of Mattie's, you can bring your second and meet me tonight at the Fair Grounds at 8 o'clock. I will show you who to call a sonofabitch.
    I will try and kill you. Damn you.
        Yours until we meet

The challenge was unsigned. In an accompanying note, Frank said that he was challenged to fight with pistols, didn't know his challenger's identity, but thought it was either Johnson or Saunders, neither of whom I had ever heard of. He said he did not think anything would come of it, but that he would meet his "assailant" as indicated and hoped that everything would come off without bloodshed. He then sent me a list of how his personal possessions were to be distributed "in the event I get killed." For what seemed like an eternity I was in anguish even though I kept reminding myself that his college, Washington and Lee, would let me know if any harm had come to my son. After two weeks I got a letter from Frank with no mention of the altercation. I was so relieved that I cried tears of joy, but when I see that young man, he will be severely chastised. I had not dared communicate with the college, for Frank had assured me that if everything went well, he did not want anybody to know about the challenge. I was afraid if I said anything to university authorities; Frank's outstanding record there would have been in jeopardy. He added a note to his younger brother, "take my advice and keep clean of such scrapes." I didn't share any of this with anyone, not even Robert and Alexander until it had all been resolved. I am still appalled that my solid-as-a-rock ever-so-responsible son could have got involved in anything to cause anyone to want to harm him.

We do have telegraph service now, beginning on October 1, 1875, but delivery is spotty and erratic so I knew I could not count on getting a wire if Frank had been injured.

Since you were away in Illinois for so long and upon your return did not tarry in town long enough to observe its expansion, I include just a bit of the changes that have taken place. There are now 38 states in the Union, the country spreading from coast to coast. Colorado, located in the center of the country and somewhat west, is the last, admitted on August 1, 1876. Prior to that Oregon joined California on the West Coast, becoming the 33rd state on February 14, 1859; to the South, Nevada became the 36th state on October 31, 1864, and Nebraska, the 37th on March 1, 1867. It makes me wonder if, in my lifetime, every part and parcel of this country will be settled and if the United States will spread from coast to coast and from Canada on our north to Mexico on the south. When I consider the wilderness that our family traveled through only 33 years ago from Virginia to Texas, the expansion seems impossible.

While our country expands, our city explodes. The 1870 census counted the population of Dallas at 13,314. In 1875 we had more than doubled that number, and there seems to be no end to the migration throughout the area with many, many people stopping here to make their permanent homes. The number of new businesses also increases every week. From my home here on Commerce Street, I have a ringside seat to observe the growth.

The Dallas Elevator and Compress Company on Houston Street at the railroad is one of the newest and grandest, reportedly the biggest in Texas. Sometimes it runs into the night and the noise disrupts my sleep. The cotton compress is not the only disrupting noise. Often revelers at all hours of the night keep up a steady racket. Robert has put locks on my doors with a stern admonition that I lock myself in every night since, a few months ago, a man, too drunk to know what he was doing mistook my home for his boarding house and staggered into the house.

Several estate-type homes are being constructed in our area. Two years ago Alexander Harwood built a beautiful house at 4117 Swiss Avenue for his wife, Sarah Ann Peak Harwood and their two children. It features a rounded roof, or dome-shaped cupola at the top of the second story. The kitchen is at the rear of the house. Inside, the windows reach from floor to ceiling. The interior has a solid walnut stairway. Out north of town, William B. and Mattie Worthington Caruth are enlarging their estate home that Mrs. Caruth designed patterning it after the Mississippi mansion of her aunt and uncle where she grew up. Completed last year just in time to welcome the couple's second son, William Walter, the grounds now feature a formal garden.

Educational opportunities are also increasing in our area, though not on the scale that is happening in the nation. I was happy to read that some people understand that women have brains and can learn! Sophia Smith used the inheritance from her brother to open Smith College in Northampton, Massachusetts. Established in 1871, it opened its doors for its first class two years ago. At about the same time Wellesley College for Women opened in Wellesley, Massachusetts. It was founded in 1870 by Boston lawyer Henry Durant, who said he used profits he made from business during the Civil War as a way to create good from the evils of that time.

Last year two new colleges were created in our state—Texas University in Austin and Texas Agricultural and Mechanical College on a barren piece of land just south of Bryan. I understand that young women who have outstanding academic qualifications will be admitted along with the boys at the Austin university. But A&M, which is dedicated to business training in agricultural and mechanical endeavors, will not allow girls to enroll. Makes me wonder what they propose to do with someone like me who has excelled in business, improved a farm, built a bridge and heaven only knows what else. Some days I can't remember!

Religious groups are operating several other schools. The Hebrew school created by Rabbi Aaron Sheller three years ago has much enlarged classrooms at the new Temple Emanu-El. Its classes are open to non-Jewish students, and many families are enrolling their children because of its educational excellence. The same is true of Ursuline Academy, the school created by Catholic nuns. A boarding school, it accepts girls from all over the South. Enrollment increases faster than it can expand its facilities.

A number of other schools, most of them private, are operating in the area, but the need is far greater than the available spaces. Last year, in an editorial, the *Herald*, after conducting a survey, said that about fifteen hundred to two thousand children in the Dallas area were enrolled in some sort of school while at least an equal number of boys and girls were not.

Free public education is our next hurdle, though I don't know how long it will take to convince the voters that we must provide education for all children. Recently a city school district was formed and authority for the schools placed under a board of education rather than the city council. The voters balked at providing funding to create the schools after a story in the *Herald* revealed that some $25,000 would be needed in public money to create five schools—one primary school in each of the four city wards plus one girls' high school. I can only assume that the researchers either felt boys did not need a high school education or that their educational requirements were taken care of elsewhere.

I have just about decided to either sell the St. Charles Hotel or convert it to another business, and yet I hesitate to let go of one of the first of my business ventures. It is still profitable. Men who are on the Dallas County Grand Jury always stay at the St. Charles when they are in session, and people from all over the country are our guests. Businessmen from 28 of the 38 states have been our guests during the past year. But I find it even more rewarding that we are considered a family hotel. We registered our first out-of-country guests, Mr. and Mrs. Charles F. Locke from Lima, Peru, on November 16, and we have 29 guests from eight states—Alabama, Arkansas, Illinois, Kentucky, Louisiana, Mississippi, Tennessee and Texas—registered for Christmas Day. I am always surprised that families travel during holidays because I think that Christmas, especially, is such family time when everybody would want to be at home.

And, so, I weigh the good along with the negatives. Since Mr. Thompson left, I have not been able to keep a good manager or staff. Almost daily I am called to intervene in one crisis or another. The expenses of keeping everything functioning may get to be prohibitive. The building needs a new roof. I spent about $10 last year having it patched, but there are still leaks. Last year in February I was out almost a hundred dollars—$95.50 to be exact on supplies and labor. The receipts from O.K. Harry, carpenter and builder, run a full page in my ledger. Everything is rising in costs—$15 alone for new flooring and a whole dollar just to buy nails. The cost of labor is the highest. I paid $3.00 a day for repairmen who worked a total of seven days—$21.00 —just to get everything in working order! And even then, when one thing is fixed, there is a problem somewhere else. I grow weary just trying to keep up with all of the details.

Even more significant than the worry of keeping a good staff and the expense of keeping the building in good repair is that other more opulent hotels are emerging. The LeGrande on the corner of Commerce and Austin opened two years ago. Another, the Windsor on the northeast corner of Main at Austin is under construction and will be ready for occupancy soon.

I no longer hear from any of Alexander's Missouri family, though I understand that Frank keeps up with them. My husband's half-brothers and his sister were helpful when I was seeking a school for the boys, and I shall always be in their debt. But there was a definite cooling between us when I decided to move the boys to Virginia for their schooling. Since none of the family that lived in Missouri ever came to Dallas to see us, I cannot help but believe that they are unaware of what I have accomplished with their brother's inheritance and regard us as poor relations. This is especially true—or maybe it is only my imagination—since both of the men have gained national recognition. Gen. Francis Marion Cockrell was elected to the U. S. Senate from Missouri two years ago and his brother, Col. Jeremiah Vardaman Cockrell was elected to the Texas Senate representing the 16 Congressional District. He now lives in Anson.

Please come to see me or, at least, write to me. I miss you.

Your sister friend,

Sarah Horton Cockrell

December 25, 1890

Mr. Frank M. Cockrell
Kansas City, Missouri

My beloved son,

I miss you so much, but my loneliness is assuaged by the letters from both you and your wife that overflow with your happiness. Alice was such a beautiful bride, and I am absolutely delighted to have her as a new daughter. I was overjoyed that you chose to be married in Dallas and that her mother and other members of her family were able to come here for the ceremony. I doubt that I would have made the trip to Kansas City. In all these years I've never seemed to be able to get away.

Alice's letter expressing her surprise and pleasure at my wedding present to you indicates that she has forgiven me for my initial reluctance at your marriage. You know—and I hope she does—that my reservations had nothing to do with her, but were based solely on my selfishness. When you told me you were getting married and moving to Kansas City, I all but panicked. No one since your father has been so dependable, close and comforting, and I had to adjust to letting you go. I relied on you so much, not only as a devoted son, but also on your business ability and legal advice.

I trust that your association with the law firm in Kansas City will be both satisfying and lucrative, and I am absolutely delighted that you have earned the credentials to practice there. Since laws vary so much from state to state, you doubtless will have a lot to learn. If things do not work out as you hope, you can always come home!

I thought and thought about what I could give you as a wedding present, and it seemed right when I came up with the reservation of a chamber suite and a dining room suite on the train that you took from Dallas to New York. I am eternally grateful for your safe arrival there and that the Normandie Hotel proved every bit as wonderful as you had hoped. Now that you are safely returned to Kansas City, I can breathe easier. Every *Dallas Morning News* has at least one story about a rail disaster. I know that rail transportation will improve, and I am glad that Dallas now has excellent connections to other parts of the country. But I will be so glad when, and if, I feel more assured that travelers will arrive safely at their destination.

Alice's mother and her sister are still here but are eager to go home. I called on them last week. Mrs. Noble said she had received a letter from both you and Alice the day before and expressed great pleasure at having you as a new son. She should! You are pretty special. You may get the big head if I keep telling you how wonderful you are!

As you know, I revised my will in August and am enclosing herewith a copy for your safekeeping. You will remember that I had not updated it since Robert died four years ago, and I wanted to be sure that his children, Clarence Marion and Sarah Louise, are appropriately cared for. It became critical, I thought, when their mother married Wallace Kanady earlier this year. I want to be sure that Clarence and Sarah never forget they are Cockrells. I am happy that Gillie has found someone she can love. She is so young to be a widow, even younger than I was when your father died.

I thought long and hard about the division of the property. The enclosed revision of the will is the result of consultation with both you and your brother and with our lawyers. I trust that the division of my worldly acquisitions is entirely acceptable to all of you and that there will be no rancor among you when I am gone.

I have subscribed to the *News* for you. It's becoming quite an excellent paper, starting as it did on October 1, 1885, with a circulation of 5,000, quickly absorbing the *Herald*, and now only five years later enjoying a circulation that has almost tripled.

Giving up my independence has been very difficult.

Since your father died, I have to be the final authority for both my personal and business decisions and doubtless have become quite set in my ways. When I moved in with Alexander and Ettie, my address changed only a few blocks, from 106 Commerce Street where I lived for more than 30 years to 581 South Lamar. But my life altered dramatically and created changes that are painful. I am having to adjust from running a huge home, always open to anyone who needed sanctuary, to one room in the home of my son and daughter-in-law where I feel like a guest.

Ettie and Alex are marvelous. I haven't a single complaint. They welcomed me into their home and into their hearts and have done everything possible to make my life comfortable. My room, with furniture that is familiar, is cozy and they allow me as much privacy as a busy household can offer. It's the little things I miss—making a cup of tea without thinking that I might be disturbing the routine in someone else's kitchen, knowing when to offer to be of assistance and when to make myself scarce, being sensitive to the needs of my son and daughter-in-law so that they have the privacy they need, being careful not to intrude in the discipline of the children—little things that loom so big when one is making the adjustment to an entirely different way of living.

I knew there would come a time when age would force me to move in with one my children. But I do not feel old! I suppose that nobody recognizes the erosion of years and certainly nobody understands the trauma of giving up independent living until it becomes personal. I try not to let my feelings spill over into their lives.

My two little grandsons, Monroe and Vardeman, help to fill the void left by your absence. Monroe was six and Vard was three both in December. They are delightful children and I cherish them, but I miss seeing Clarence and Sarah Louise since Gillie remarried. I want to be a presence in their lives, but I do not want to intrude on their bonding with their new stepfather. Both of the children are growing up too fast. Clarence is now 10 and Sarah Louise 6. Gillie assures me that she will never let them forget their own father.

I enjoy being a grandmother! For many years I was so busy rearing my own four children and building the business that I did not pause to consider how very much I loved being a mother.

So the joy I felt at the birth of my first grandchild took me totally by surprise. Then, when Sarah Louise, my granddaughter arrived, I was overjoyed and so honored that Bob and Gillie named her for me. I doubtless wore out my welcome being at their house almost every day to check on them. I was especially concerned because Bob and Gillie had lost their first two children, Aurelia Effie in 1877 when she was only 16 days old, and Robert Sidney in 1880 at 2 1/2 . I know what it's like to lose a child. There's always a void for the lost one even when everybody is telling you that you should be grateful for the healthy children you have.

The ascendancy of the Cockrell Clan is now up to you and Alexander since both Aurelia and Robert are no longer with us. Doubtless Alex and Ettie will have other children. I sincerely hope that you and Alice will be blessed with healthy offspring.

The businesses we started together are flourishing. The Dallas Elevator Company we created five years ago is especially profitable. You have such great business sense. I think, of all the boys, you most inherited your father's vision for this town and the ability to make good things happen. Alexander and Mitch Gray are doing a good job of managing our businesses. I doubtless should leave the management of the business entirely to them, but you know how snoopy I am. So, I'm constantly looking at the books and offering not-so-much-wanted advice!

The multi-storied office building we put up at Main and Field is filled to capacity with a waiting list of businesses that wish to office there. See what a successful team we turned out to be! Sometimes I quiver to think that you have turned your back on all this to settle for a start-up practice with the Kansas City law firm—and then I remember that even you, my Paragon Son, have every right to determine your own destiny. I was so fortunate to have you for so long before, at age 37, you married.

Having the city purchase the Iron Bridge and ferry rights eight years ago has allowed us to expand in other significant businesses. I was reluctant to let it go, as you recall, but you were exactly right when you kept gently pressuring me to sell, and Dallas County got a real bargain for its $41,600. The free bridge has helped immeasurably to promote Dallas as a business center.

Other major city improvements have also helped to boost business. The 1890 census counted 67,042 residents in Dallas County with 38,140, more than half of the number, within the city limits. The annexation this year of the town of East Dallas with its 2,000 souls, and 1,500 acres of highly desirable well-developed property is a great boost, especially to our educational and religious community. It is home to several private schools, the new St. Mary's College, Ursuline Academy, and the Terrill School for Boys, and St. Matthews Cathedral not to mention the State Fair Grounds. The addition of these excellent facilities somewhat compensates for the large number of saloons and brothels in downtown Dallas, 189 at last count.

We hope that Oak Cliff will also choose to unite with Dallas. Recently, with a population of 2,500 it was incorporated as a separate town. I have a very tender spot for the area because it's where my family settled when we arrived here from Virginia and where I began my wedded life. The area greatly advanced in esteem in 1887 when John S. Armstrong and Thomas L. Marsalis purchased and began to develop 2,000 acres that included the 640-acre Hord farmstead. They were in the midst of dividing the property into building sites when the partnership unraveled. Mr. Armstrong took over the wholesale grocery part of the business and Mr. Marsalis the real estate division. He is so firmly convinced of the future growth of Oak Cliff that last year he completed a palatial residence on the southwest corner of Colorado at Grand, the name of which was then changed to Marsalis.

Other neighborhoods are developing at a fast pace. North of Dallas, the Oak Lawn area is being touted as a "very desirable place to live." It lies between Lemmon and Turtle Creek and between Maple and Oak Lawn. Near it a section called Highland Park, conceived by John S. Armstrong and developed by Hugh Prather, is being promoted nationally as a prime example of parkway development and an elite residential area. Highland Park and its neighbor, University Park, are both resisting annexation into Dallas. Such a shame!

Other advances in Dallas are also helping. Several of the streets, paved with bois d'arc blocks several years ago—which never proved successful—are now paved with new macadam. This has greatly improved inner city transportation. Several new streetcar lines are in operation in the six years since the Dallas Bell Street Railway Company opened its first line up McKinney Avenue to Thomas Street. This improvement has hastened the development of the Thomas-Colby residential area. We now have a streetcar line operating the entire length of Harwood from McKinney to the new Cedars development in near South Dallas.

Last year the Pearl Street Consolidated Railway used electric power for the first time. Many of us are also lighting our homes with electricity made possible with the continual improvement of the light plant which originally opened in a small wooden building at Carondelet and Austin in 1882.

Telephone service is vastly improved. Alexander and Ettie have a phone in their home as well as in his business office! I cannot believe such luxury. Alex tells me that it will soon be possible for me to talk directly over long distance to you in far off Missouri. The development is exciting, but I am not sure I want to try to use one of the contraptions.

A new courthouse of red brick to replace the one that burned last year is fast going up in the heart of downtown. It will be the sixth edifice to house official Dallas County records. The buildings have gone up in this order: (1) The 10x10 log cabin built by John Neely Bryan in 1846 that served for four years until (2) 1850 when a double log cabin, also built by Mr. Bryan, replaced the smaller building after Dallas became a county. In (3) 1857 a square red brick building replaced the log cabin; it was dismantled in 1871. That year (4) 1871, a gray stone building with bell towers replaced the red brick. The gray stone burned in 1880. (5) In 1881 James Flanders, the reigning architect of the day, designed a white building around the remaining walls of the prior courthouse. It, too, lasted nine years and burned in 1891. (6) Today we are erecting another brick building made of red brick. I wonder how long it will endure?

The Presbyterian Church at the corner of Main and Harwood, termed "an attempt at permanent monumental ecclesiastical architecture" erected eight years ago, is being joined as a religious site by the First Baptist Church located on Patterson Street at Ervay. It will be dedicated next year.

The new Dallas Federal Building, housing the post office and the U.S. Circuit Court, was built six years ago and is already bulging. Located on the northeast corner of Commerce at Ervay, it became far more accessible when macadam street surfacing was laid. Prior to that, when it rained, a sea of mud made it almost impossible to traverse.

The sub-division that Alexander and I began developing on our property between Lamar Street and the Trinity River in 1884 has become quite lucrative and very profitable as industrial sites. When we started the sub-division, Alex wanted very much for the area to become another elite residential neighborhood. His faith was such that he built his own beautiful Eastlake-styled mansion home on a full city block on South Lamar between Arnold and Monroe. I always thought it would better serve as the location for business and industry because of its proximity to the railroad and to the Trinity—if ever that river might become navigable. Also, I remember vividly what happens to homes in the rainy seasons when the river floods and runs out of its banks. Since I have proved to be right, I wonder how much longer Ettie will tolerate being hedged in with heavy industry that is going up just beyond her front door. I know, if I were the mother of young children I would not want them exposed to the atmosphere that prevails here.

A little farther to the east and south of the industrial development, there are marvelous houses being erected in the Cedars where our sub-divided property abuts that which the Browders are developing.

Philip and Alex Sanger, owners of Sanger Brothers Dry Goods Company, are among the first to build palatial homes in the Cedars. Alex Sanger's home is on the northwest corner of South Ervay and Canton. It is extravagantly ornamented with rose silk damask walls, velvet draperies, carved oak and mahogany mantels and crystal and Tiffany chandeliers. Its neighbor and equally lavish home, built by Alex's brother, Philip, is on the northwest corner of South Ervay at St. Louis. In addition to their homes, the brothers have constructed a large building at Elm between Lamar and Austin to house their Sanger Brothers, which, I am told, is the most prof-itable and fashionable business in the entire Southwest.

Your advice to me to get out of the hotel business has proved excel-lent. The St. Charles had been a thorn to me for several years before I sold—and just in time. When the Windsor opened, it pushed me to the decision to sell. Then, the Le Grande opened. Shortly, Col. William E. Hughes bought both hotels and is joining them by a diagonal second story bridge spanning Austin Street. The joined hotels will be called the Grand-Windsor and have a capacity of 300 rooms with rates beginning at the exorbitant rate of $2.00 per day and peaking at $5.00 for the largest and most lavish. I could never have competed with such opulence. Col. Hughes built his home a long way from his Grand-Windsor Hotel—way out east of town on Worth Street between Hall and Adair. It is patterned after the Czarina's home in Belorussia.

Sometimes I think the citizens have lost their minds as they try to outdo each other in such lavish houses. Here is just a sampling: Thomas and Florence Peak Field erected an Eastlake-styled mansion on an entire city block on Peak Street between Gaston and Junius. A little farther out Thomas Jefferson Word built a show-place home on Germania, close enough to manage his several hundred acres of property along upper Ross Avenue. Louis Wagner also built on Germania where it intersects with Bryan. James Moroney was among the first to build in near East Dallas, on the northeast corner of McKinney at Harwood. Captain Walter Caruth chose the very end of Ross Avenue to build a palatial three-story farmhouse-styled estate that his wife has named Bosque Bonita. Along Ross Avenue, the eminent architect, James Flanders has designed homes for some of the most elite Dallas families, the Flippen brothers, Edgar and William; Jules Schneider, William Caruth, Walter's brother, and the

W. H. Gastons in styles ranging from French Chateau, Gothic mansion and Italiante palazzi. All of these are set among spreading shade trees and have manicured gardens tended by numerous servants.

Many other families have chosen to locate nearer downtown. These include the George N. Aldredge family whose new home is on the southwest corner of South Ervay at Corsicana. The Edward Eakins family lives in an enormous Queen Anne-styled three-story house with turrets and gables on South Harwood at Gano. Dallas lawyer James B. Simpson built his two-story home on the southwest corner of Main at South Harwood. Five years ago my own lawyer, John C. McCoy, purchased it. Dr. Jesse M. Pace moved his family into a French-styled townhouse, a replica of New Orleans' French quarter architecture at Young and Browder. And our town's leading social/philanthropist, Amelia Antoine Huvelle and her husband Camile also chose near downtown, at 577 South Ervay.

These are but a smattering of the fabulous homes that are going up all over the city from north to south, from east to west, and across the Trinity farther west in Oak Cliff. Can it be that only a few years ago this place was but a scrubby little village? The dream that Mr. Bryan had of a city here and the vision that my Alex had for this place has more than come to pass.

Educational facilities lag behind business and home building. Most children who attend the free public schools are from working families, the "landed gentry" still choosing to send their children to private schools. It is heartening to have an increasing number of schools, both private and public, where our children can be educated here rather than having to go east to boarding schools. In 1884, when the free public schools opened, the total enrollment was 4,457 students. That number has increased ten-fold. Our most fashionable public school is Cumberland Hill, which opened two years ago to serve children of the wealthy families along Ross Avenue. With parental input, Cumberland Hill is beginning to lure children away from private schools.

The Idlewild Club, which you and your friends organized, continues to introduce its annual array of debutantes. Its sixth annual ball was recently held. I am amused when I remember how hard I tried to discourage you from participating in an organization that termed itself "elitist." Up until that time, the nearest thing that had ever been "High" Society in Dallas was the opening of the St. Nicholas Hotel, and I would never have considered it an exclusive event. We issued an open invitation to the entire state of Texas, and for awhile that evening, I thought everybody had taken us up! When you "boys" decided to create an organization to "present" young ladies at a social event, none of us thought anything would ever come of it. Well, I was wrong again! The five young women you presented at that first ball—Mattie Burford, Minnie Miller, Effie Rauch, Dela Slaughter and Minnie Slaughter—are now all young society matrons, all involved in worthwhile philanthropic endeavors. And the annual Idlewild Club Ball has become THE social event of the year.

Field's Opera House continues to be the cultural center of the city. I recall that soon after Gillie and Robert married, she wrote that she had always considered Dallas lacking in social graces and almost bereft of cultural advantages. Though she was right, it rankled. I suppose when one has been exposed to the finest of music, theater and art in Europe, what we had to offer was vastly inferior. Doubtless it still is. We still lack the educational, cultural and social advantages of the Old World. I sometimes think that all of the monstrous, ostentatious houses are a substitute for the genuine. I don't like to think it will always be thus, that the clamor and competition for *things* will serve as a substitute for more important values. Only time will tell.

Even as I write this, I am both amused and chagrined that the 1890 census listed my occupation as "Capitalist," as if making money has been the most important contribution I have made to this town. It always disturbs me when attention is called to the fact that I am the first millionaire in the city and, arguably, the first millionaire in the State of Texas, as if these are accolades I value. I don't.

I still consider myself the least likely of all people in the world to have "made it." I have been lucky. I have had health and stamina and sometimes courage. I was lucky to have been married for 10 years to a man with vision and perseverance. Inside, I am still the same shy, untutored, wistful young woman of yore who came to this untamed country 36 years ago. And if I have contributed anything of value to the expansion of this land, I owe it all to others for I measure my value in my faith in God, and the love of my family and my friends.

Whatever you do, my dear son, may you, too, measure your worth in terms of contribution rather than acquisition.

Your loving mother,

Sarah Horton Cockrell

Epilogue

January 1, 2004

As unobtrusively as she had lived, Sarah Horton Cockrell died quietly in the home of her son and daughter-in-law, Alexander II and Ettie Fulkerson Cockrell at 581 South Lamar Street on April 26, 1892, at the age of 73 years, three months and 13 days. Family legend has it that she simply closed her eyes in her sleep and was no more.

Family legend is wrong.

Sarah's presence walks among us. Today. And always.

An enigma to her contemporaries, who could not comprehend that a mere woman would shape the destiny of Dallas for all generations to come, she was most loved and most honored by the humble and the disenfranchised of her day, those who she most cared about and supported. Just as she is today more than a century later.

Her obituary, buried on an inside page of the *Dallas Herald* on April 27, 1892, reads:

A PIONEER GONE
Death of Mrs. S. H. Cockrell in
This City Yesterday

At 1:10 yesterday afternoon there died at the residence of her son, Alex Cockrell, on South Lamar street, Mrs. S. H. Cockrell, an old landmark of the early settlement of this county, she having settled near Eagle Ford in 1844. She was the third daughter of Enoch Horton, a Virginian, and the widow of Alex Cockrell, a Missourian, who settled in Dallas one year after the time that the aforementioned Mr. Cockrell came to this county. She was an honored member of the Dallas County Pioneer Association and was well known for her good old time hospitality. Frank M. Cockrell and Alex Cockrell, both well-known and prominent business men of this city, are her only surviving children, one brother and one sister having died.

Mrs. Cockrell leaves a magnificent estate, embracing large farms and some of the best business property in the city.

The funeral will take place tomorrow afternoon at 2:15 from the Commerce Street Methodist Church. Rev. C. O. Jones will preach the funeral service.

Such a travesty, the obituary. Every business in the city closed its doors for Sarah's funeral, and it took almost an hour for the slow-moving cortege to wend its way from Commerce Street to Trinity Cemetery.

And such a travesty that she would be recalled in the final story about her only as a daughter, a wife and a mother. True, she was all of those things, the daughter of Enoch Horton, but why no mention of her beloved mother, Martha Stinson Horton, who left a comfortable life in Virginia to follow her adventuresome husband to the unsettled frontier of Texas? True, she died as the widow of Alexander Cockrell, but she had been married to him for only 10 years when he died. She outlived him for a third of a century, reared their four children as a single mother while successfully completing all of his business ventures and initiating countless ones of her own. True, she was the mother of two surviving sons, but "the one brother and one sister having died" referred to in the story were, instead, her daughter, Aurelia, and her son, Robert. There is no mention of Logan, her cherished first-born.

Most of all, the story is a travesty because there is no mention of her outstanding contributions:

> What she gave away—property for two railroads, for a church, for a college, uniforms for military men who signed up from Dallas County to fight in the Civil War;

> What she created—the first iron bridge across the Trinity River linking Dallas and Oak Cliff, the first opulent hotel, the first flour mill and the first downtown office building. She was also the first woman to speak before the Texas State legislature;

> What she accomplished as a business woman—secretary, confidante and partner-in-business to Dallas' first business visionary, entrepreneur in her own right of early Dallas; the area's first millionaire and, perhaps, the first millionaire in the State of Texas.

> Who she was as a woman—matriarch and protector of women, children and families in early Dallas and successful single mother of four children.

Sarah is buried in the lot she had purchased in Trinity Cemetery beside her husband, across a pathway from her daughter, and in the community of other family members. The cemetery, renamed Greenwood after it fell into bankruptcy as Trinity, is in the heart of downtown Dallas at 3020 Oak Grove. The Cockrell plot is on Grace Street between Peace and Freedom.

Sarah Horton, at left, at age 29,
in the wedding dress she made,
and, below, in her last photograph
made in 1890 when she was 71.
Photo at Dallas Historical Society.

Sarah's first Dallas home
was at 106 Commerce
where Commerce ended
on the banks of the
Trinity River.
– Dallas Historical Society.

*NOTE: All photographs were
among the Cockrell papers.
Credits are to places where
pictures are now located.*

Enoch Horton
3-22-1776 to 3-21-1851

⇩

Mary	Jane	John	James	Sarah	Enoch, Jr.
11-18-1810	9-3-1812	6-3-1814 to 1848	8-4-1816 to 4-24-1876	1-13-1819 to 4-26-1892	1-8-1821 to 11-23-1874
Married Marlin Thompson	Married William Bradshaw	Married Margaret Hopkins	Married 1851 Jane Phillips	Married 9-9-1847 Alexander Cockrell 6-8-1820 to 4-3-1858	Married 1. Nancy Reed 2. Lucy Latimer

⇩

⇩

Logan	Aurelia Effie	Robert Benjamin
9-9-1848 to 1-25-1849	5-25-1850 to 2-28-1872	1-16-1852 to 5-21-1886
	Married 5-11-1871 Mitch Gray	Married 1-26-1876 Guillelmine Jones

⇩

⇩

Aurelia Effie	Robert Sidney	Clarence Marion
12-25-1876 to 1-10-1877	4-13-1878 to 11-4-1880	10-18-1880 to 10-10-1946
(died at age 16 days)	(died at age 2 yrs. 7 mos.)	Married 7-25-1907 Alice Naomi Mounts

⇩

Ruth Elizabeth	Sarah Louise	Joseph Elmore
7-21-1908 to 8-5-1982	7-25-1911	1-12-1913 to 9-18-1987
Married 9-28-1929 James M. Wilson	Married 4-18-1941 Richard Stevens, M.D.	Married 7-16-1941 Allene Fay Mays

⇩　　　⇩　　　⇩

Children		Children		Children	
1. Wynant Stone	10-19-1930	1. Chari Louise	8-29-42	1. Marilyn Kay	7-25-43
2. Ruth Elinor	12-6-1934	2. Mary Alice	10-17-43	2. Nancy Carolyn	12-9-47
3. Alice Naomi	2-7-1947	3. Richard John, Jr.	3-2-45	3. Joseph Elmore, Jr.	4-6-51
		4. Ralph Albert	4-9-47	4. Janis Allene	6-5-53
		5. Johanna	7-20-49		
		6. Robert Cockrell	8-16-53		
		7. Randall Clarence	8-10-54		

enerations in Dallas

ed

1797   Martha Stinson
9-19-1788 to 4-7-1850

Robert	Martha	Lucy	Rachel	Emmarine
-28-1823 to 1849	7-3-1825	5-17-1828	6-7-1831 to 1848	7-19-1833
Died Single	Married William Horton	Married A.B. Lanier	Died Single	Married Joseph C. Reed

Francis Marion	Alexander II
8-29-1854 to 11-22-1935	9-6-1856 to 2-24-1919
Married 11-19-1890 Alice Gertrude Nobel	Married 5-13-1884 Ettie Fulkerson (see chart below)

Children
1. **Monroe Fulkerson**
   Married Nadine Steele 11-2-1910
2. **Alexander Vardeman 12-10-1877 to 12-19-1943**
   Married Mary Cockrell (cousin) 1-15-1916
3. **Aurelia Ettie 6-3-1891**
   Married (1) Robert Lee Kurth (2) Davis Spangler
4. **Sarah Elizabeth**
   Married Abram A. Green 4-7-1891 to 11-11-1946
5. **Francis Nicholas III 7-18-1895 to ?**
   Married (1) Clyde Holley 7-13-1914 to 1-6-1919
   (2) Modene Sarver 9-12-1937

Sarah Louise
5-30-1884 to 12-9-1900
(died at 16 yrs.)

Clarence Marion, Jr.	Mary Alice (Mackie)	Robert Benjamin
1-4-1916 to 12-3-2003	7-30-1918	1-21-1921 to 6-14-1979
Married 4-14-1951 Patsy Dean Reeves	Married 2-2-1943 W. Allen Dealey (divorced)	Married 1. 8-14-1945 Willene Hinchliffe 2. 10-8-1954 Martha Austin Hughston

Children	**Children**	**Children**
1. Sara 10-22-51		No children by Wife (1)
2. Linda 3-2-53	1. John Carpenter 2-28-48	1. Kathryn 7-23-56
3. Tom Alexander 1-10-55	2. Norman Cockrell 9-25-52	2. Frank Austin 11-23-59
4. Chris Mounts 12-19-56	3. George Bannerman II 7-23-60	3. Adopted Gerald Lee, bn. 11-7-44
		4. Adopted Jana Kay, bn. 6-23-47

SIXTH GENERATION OF COCKRELL FAMILY

I. Children of Ruth Cockrell Wilson

1. Wynant Stone Wilson

  (1). Joseph Carlton Wilson
  (2). Derrick Stone Wilson
  (3). Wesley Jones Wilson

2. Ruth Elinor Wilson Melton

  (1). Pamela Ann
  (2). James Wilson
  (3). Roberta Louise
  (4). Lance Paschal

3. Naomi Wilson Burke

[handwritten: Alice]

  (1). Warren Porteus
  (2). Pamela Ruth
  (3). Joseph Martland Wilson
  (4). ~~Edwin~~ McIlhenny Perry

[handwritten: Edmund]

II. Children of Dr. Sarah Louise Cockrell Stevens

1. Chari Louise Stevens Singleton

  (1). Maria Louise Hellberg Orr
  (2). Jeffrey Wallace Hellberg, Jr.

2. Ralph Albert Stevens, M.D.

  (1). Whitney Wyatt Stevens

3. Johanna Stevens Holswade

  (1). Sarah Louise Holswade
  (2). James Frederick (Jesse) Holswade IV

4. Randall Clarence Stevens

  (1). Joshua Paul Stevens
  (2). Jonathan Peter Stevens
  (3). Jeremiah Phillip Stevens

III. Children of Joseph E. Cockrell

1. Marilyn Kay (Katie) Cockrell Wadle
  (1). Scott Wadle
  (2). David Wadle

2. Joseph Elmore Cockrell, Jr.
  (1). Michael Bertram Cockrell
  (2). Robert Joseph Cockrell

[handwritten: 3. Nancy Carolyn 4. Janis Allene]

IV. Children of Clarence Cockrell Jr.

1. Linda Cockrell Wright
  (1). Scott DeSanders
  (2). Spencer James Wright

V. Children of Mackie Cockrell Dealey

1. John Carpenter Dealey

  (1). John Carpenter Dealey Jr.
  (2). Georgia Dusseau Dealey

2. Norman Cockrell Dealey

  (1). Tellericia Dealey
  (2). Isaac Dealey

Dallas Dallas Co Texas
July 23rd 1870

Miss ~~Amelia~~ Cockrell
           My Darling child
this morning finds me very sad
your an Robert both absent the
death of your aunt ~~Jane Cocs.~~ Jane is
enough To make me feel very
Sad I receive Roberts letter I was
so glad To hear from you Mag
Hanks called to See me I was
gone to your uncle Jims he called
again that night I was tired
gone To bed did not See him he
Told Lou that you was well
an in good Spirits gave her your
keys I do hope you will stay well
come home well your aunt Jane
died just as her father died it
was what the ~~Drs~~ called the
conception of the Bowels She
eat verry hasty dinner of roasting
~~ears cucumbers~~ an potatoe

Mother S H Cockrell

THE MEN IN SARAH'S LIFE

The Rev. James A. Smith
who proposed to Sarah
by letter.
*- Photo, First Methodist Church,
Dallas.*

Alexander Cockrell in a
photo Sarah had made
after his death.

Col. George W. Guess,
Sarah's lawyer, friend and,
perhaps, a new love.
- Cockrell Papers Photo.

PRINCIPAL DALLAS AREA LANDMARKS
WHEN SARAH AND ALEXANDER WERE MARRIED

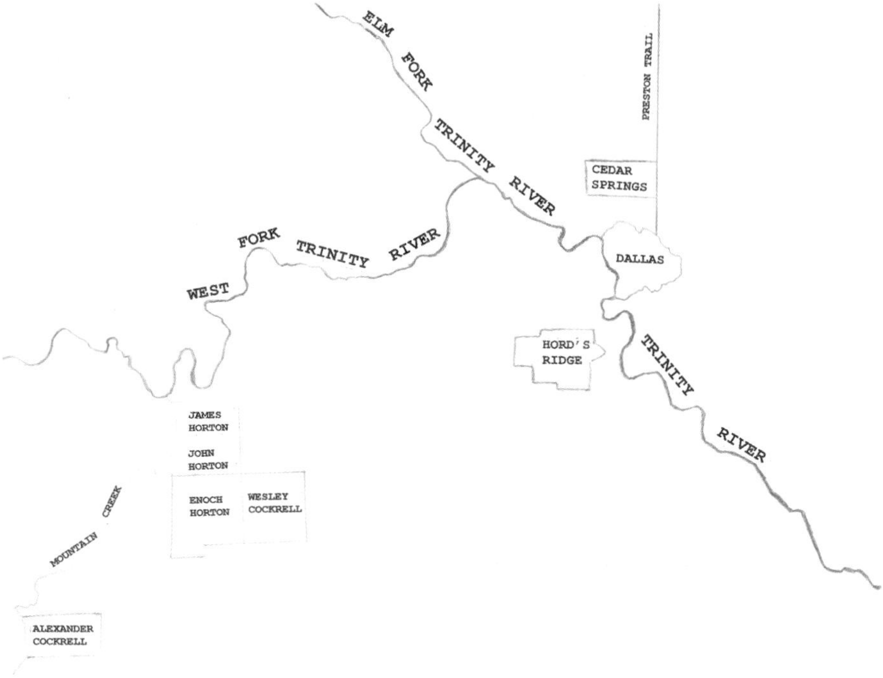

John Neely Bryan,

Dallas' founder, and

Margaret Beeman Bryan

were Cockrell

friends.

*- Photos among Cockrell
personal papers.*

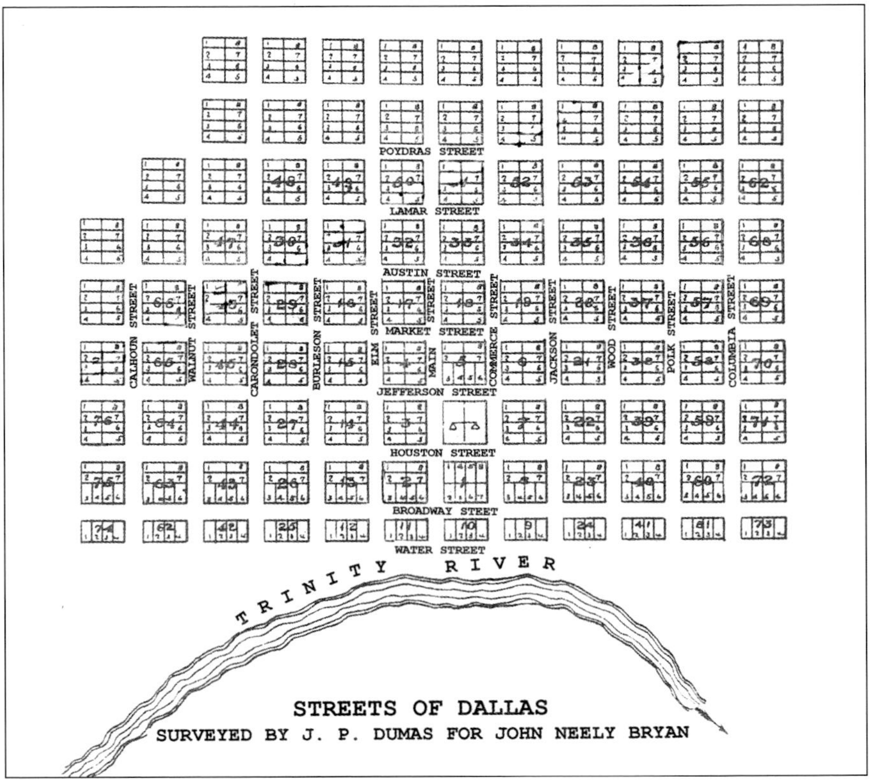

Sarah's children and children-in-law, top, left to right, Aurelia, Robert and Frank. Left, Alexander II, and right, Mitch Gray, Aurelia's husband. Bottom, left to right, Guillelmine, Robert's wife; Alice, Frank's wife and Ettie, Alexander II's wife.

- The Gray Photo courtesy Mitch Gray and Lee Gilbert. All others Cockrell Papers.

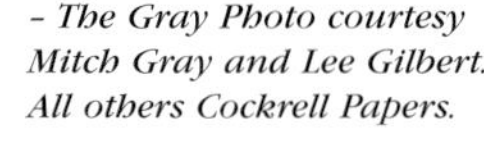

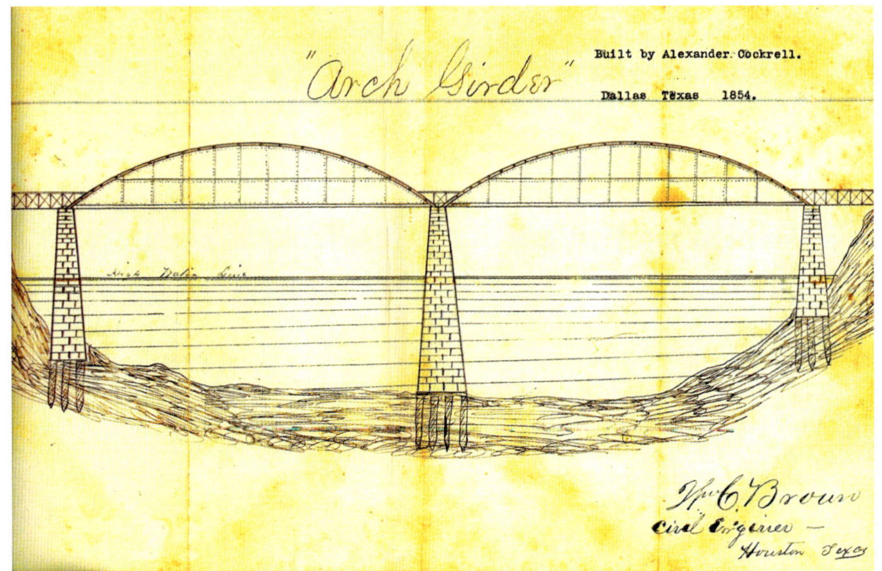

The Arch Girder Bridge, sketch above and photo at left, built by Alexander Cockrell that opened in 1854. Below, Sarah's Iron Bridge opened in 1872.
- Bridge photos from Collection of the Texas/Dallas History and Archives Division, Dallas Public Library.

The St. Nicholas, Dallas' first opulent hotel, opened with a grand ball in 1859 and was destroyed when almost everything in the town burned on July 8, 1860.

This trunk served as Sarah's bank and the respository for her important documents.
Trunk at Dallas Historical Society.

Robert Cockrell and Guillelmine Jones, above, in their wedding picture. Below, the gift card Sarah left on the train as her wedding present for Frank and Alice Noble Cockrell.

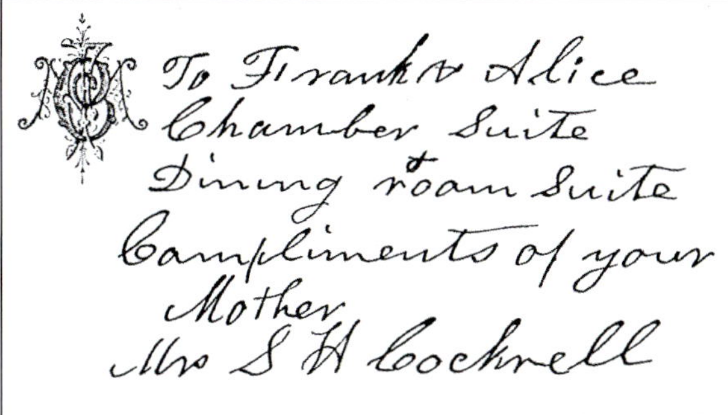

Todd Mills, right, was the area's first flour mill. Above, Sarah's letter giving one-fourth of the mill to her son, Frank.

Sarah Louise and Clarence Cockrell.

Clarence with his mother, Guillelmine Jones Cockrell.

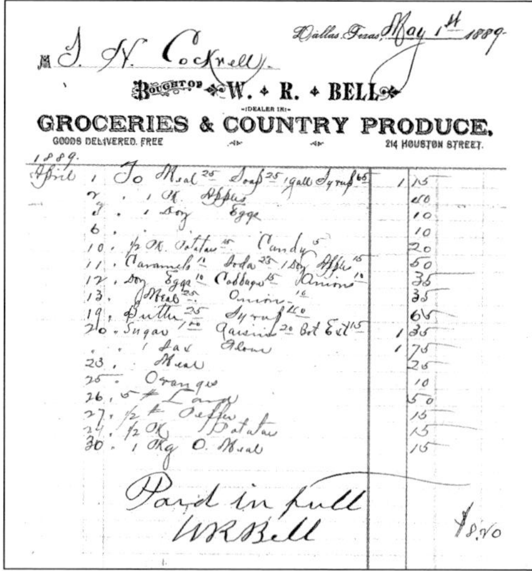

Sarah's food bill for April 1889 shortly before she moved into the home of her son, Alexander II at 581 South Lamar.

Sarah Cockrell,
circa 1860.

Mary Alice, Clarence and Sarah Louise Cockrell are descended through two early Dallas families, the Hortons who moved from Virginia to Dallas in 1844, and the Dusseaus, who came from Europe and settled at LaReunion in 1855.

Louise Dussea,
from a painting.

Alexander II Married Ettie Fulkerson 2-13-1854

Children

1. **Monroe Fulkerson**
   Married Nadine Steele 11-2-1910
2. **Alexander Vardeman 12-10-1877 to 12-19-1943**
   Married Mary Cockrell (cousin) 1-15-1916
3. **Aurelia Ettie 6-3-1891**
   Married (1) Robert Lee Kurth (2) Davis Spangler
4. **Sarah Elizabeth**
   Married Abram A. Green 4-7-1891 to 11-11-1946
5. **Francis Nicholas III 7-18-1895 to ?**
   Married (1) Clyde Holley 7-13-1914 to 1-6-1919
   (2) Modene Sarver 9-12-1937

Above, children of Alexander II and Ettie Cockrell with their care-taker, William Winn. Left to right, front row, Sarah, Old Bill, Aurelia. Back row, Monroe Frank and Vardeman.

At left, the home of Alexander and Ettie Cockrell, 581 South Lamar, where Sarah spent the last two years of her life.

Cockrell children, Ruth, Louise, Joe, Clarence Jr. and Mackie on running board of 1920 Franklin.

Alice Mounts Cockrell with her six children, Ruth and Louise to her left and right, and front row, Joe Mackie, Bob and Clarence Jr. when she graduated from SMU.

Mary Alice (Mackie) Cockrell Dealey, Clarence Cockrell Jr., and Dr. Sarah Louise Cockrell Stevens.
- Photo by Linda Cockrell Wright.

Dr. Sarah Louise Cockrell, right, above, with her fiance, Dr. Richard Stevens, behind her, when she brought him to introduce to her family, left to right, Joseph Wilson, Ruth Wilson, Clarence Cockrell Sr., Joe Cockrell, Alice Mounts Cockrell, and Allene Cockrell.

The Stevens family, left to right, Marjorie holding Joshua; Randy; Chari Singleton; Jeffrey Hellberg; Stevie; bride and groom, Robert and Anne; Dr. Sarah Louise; Mary Alice; Johanna; Jill, and Dr. Ralph.

THE FIFTH GENERATION

The Wilson-Cockrell descendants, left to right, Alice Naomi Wilson Burke, Wynant Stone Wilson and Ruth Elinor Wilson Melton.

Descendants of Joseph E. Cockrell, Joseph Elmore Jr., Janis Allene, Marilyn Kay Wadle, and Nancy Carolyn, seated.

The Dealey-Cockrell descendants, John Carpenter Dealey, Norman Cockrell Dealey and George Bannerman Dealey.

Descendants of Robert Benjamin Cockrell, Kathryn Cockrell Bollinger and Frank Austin Cockrell.

Clarence Cockrell Jr's descendants, Tom Alexander Cockrell, Linda Cockrell Wright, Sara Cockrell and Chris Mounts Cockrell.

HONOUR
THE
PAST

CHERISH THE FUTURE

Maria Hellberg Orr

The Drs. Stevens –
Sarah Louise and Richard

Joe Burke with son,
Owen Alan Breaux Burke

Pam Burke

Katie Wadle's sons, David
Edward and Scott Allen

Johanna Stevens Holswade, second
from right, with family, James Frederick
and Sarah Louise and husband, Jim.

Dr. Ralph Stevens with daughter,
Whitney and wife, Jill.

Mackie Dealey's grandchildren,
John Carpenter Dealey, II, left, and Georgia Dusseau Dealey, right.

Jeffrey W. Hellberg Jr. with wife
Mandy, and daughter, Hope.

Isaac Dealey's descendants, Alexandra,
Calli and Nicholas.

Roberta Wilson Tidwell's children,
Taylor James, left, and Zachary Arthur.

Maria Hellberg Orr's children,
Gabrielle, Caswell and Elizabeth.

Appendix

PETERS' COLONY

On the 4th day of February, 1841, the Texas Congress passed an act to attract attention, and be an inducement to Emigrants to come and populate this then uncivilized country.

"Be it enacted...that every head of a family who has emigrated to this Republic since the first of January, one thousand eight hundred and forty, or who may emigrate before the first day of January, one thousand eight hundred and forty-two, with his family, and who is (a) free white person, shall be entitled to six hundred and forty acres of land provided he settle and actually reside on the same for the term of three years, and cultivate an amount of the same not less than ten acres and further, provided, he shall have his land surveyed and plainly marked so as to include his improvements.

That each single man over the age of seventeen, who has or may emigrate as provided in the first section of this act, shall be entitled to three hundred and twenty acres of land, upon the same conditions and restrictions as the heads of families.

The contract was made between Sam Houston, president of the Republic of Texas, and Samuel Browning, attorney for a company composed of Joseph Carroll, Henry Peters, et al, on the 30th day of August 1841.

The colony would be known as Peters' Colony and should include the northern portion of the state. It covered the southern border of the Red River to a line as far south as Ellis County.

THE KING IRON TUBULAR ARCH BRIDGE OVER THE TRINITY RIVER AT DALLAS

(Story in the Dallas Herald, Saturday, March 2, 1872, page 2, cols. 2 and 3)

Today we are informed this bridge which has been in progress of erection for several months past, at this place, will be completed and ready for use, and in making the announcement we desire to give a brief history of the enterprise from its inception.

The Dallas Bridge Company was first chartered by the Legislature of Texas, July 20th, 1870, under the name of the "Dallas Wire Suspension Bridge Company." A supplemental and amendatory Act passed and was approved March 2, 1872, with the following Incorporators, viz: J. K. P. Record, T. C. Jordan, W. H. Gaston, Sarah H. Cockrell, J. W. Haynes and J. W. Crowdus. Active measures were at once inaugurated for building the bridge—books of subscription were opened, and stock to the amount of about $85,000, specie, taken in a few days. On the 10th of April last, the company was fully organized by the election of a Board of Directors, and the necessary officers; a preliminary survey of several crossings were made—one at the foot of Main street, one at the foot of Commerce street, and a third between the two streets named. These three surveys were made and estimates of costs furnished by Capt. W. H. WENTWORTH, C. E. whose was employed as engineer of the bridge.

The stockholders, by a vote, decided to locate the bridge at the foot of Commerce street, the site of the old bridge and ferry. Fifteen per cent of the capitol stock was called for and collected, and work commenced at once. A contract for the stone work of the three piers of abutments required was entered into with Messrs. BRENNAN & DONEGAN which were to be completed by the 1st of October, 1871. In the mean time, the company had been in correspondence with several Iron Bridge builders, and finally, about the 1st of July entered into a contract with Col. W. W. H. LAWRENCE, Agent of the "King Iron Bridge Company," Iola, Kansas, for a wrought iron tubular arch bridge, with two spans—one 160 feet and the other 140 feet in length, making 300 feet in all. The contract was, that the bridge should be completed and ready for use by the 1st of October, provided the foundation or piers were ready to receive it; but delays of various kinds occurred both in the building of the piers and in the transportation of the iron work, the latter not reaching here until about the 1st of January.

At this time, Capt. CHAS. N. POINTS arrived here to superintend the erection of the bridge, and commenced operations, assisted by ED. H. GIBBS, Esq., both of whom have been in the employ of the King Bridge Company for a number of years. These gentlemen, we feel pleasure in saying, have worked energetically and constantly during the past two months, with many and unforeseen disadvantages, but always with a hearty good will toward the completion of this bridge. At one time a high rise in the river threatened the entire destruction of their temporary trestle work over the river—the work of a large gang of men for several weeks—and did carry away a portion of it; but by dint of hard work and untiring energy, all obstacles were overcome, and today, our citizens will see the noble structure complete in all its fair proportions and ready for use. CAPT. POINTS tells us that the erection of this bridge—that is, the placing of the iron work on the pier—has cost more than any bridge of the same length . . . that the King Company have ever put up. This has been caused by various reasons, not necessary to enumerate here. We can say, however, as we do on the word of those thoroughly experienced in such matters, that Dallas now possesses the best bridge to be found in the State of Texas, not even excepting the famous Wire Suspension Bridge at Waco.

As to the capacity of the bridge, that can hardly be estimated by us, and we do not know that it will be tested before being received by the Company. We are satisfied that it will bear up any weight that will ever be placed upon it, and that is sufficient. One of these bridges recently erected at Waverly, Iowa, as we learn from the Nebraska City Chronicle, was subjected to the following test: 30,000 lbs. weight was placed on each side, after which a boiler weighing 5,000 lbs. Hauled by four horses driven in a trot, passed over without showing the least sign of weakness in the bridge. Such testimonials are held by the company in large numbers, from points in the Northwest, and we are quite sure that the Dallas bridge will prove equally strong. The masonry is pronounced A No. 1 by experienced men, and all the other parts of the structure are equally well made.

In connection with the bridge, under the charter, is macadamized roadway through the bottom to the high ground on the West of the River. This was made during last summer, and is now an excellent road, but it will be greatly improved hereafter by the Company. The approach from Commerce street to the first pier is graveled, and will also be improved hereafter—this approach is 150 feet in length; then comes the first iron span of 140 feet, next, the second span of 160 feet, then the trestle work on the West 160 feet, then the earth work, of 124 feet, and last the graveled roadway through the bottom of 1224 yards, or nearly three quarters of a mile. The total length of the bridge and its approaches, is 734 feet. The arches are respectively 14 and 16 feet in height; height of floor from low water mark, 56 feet; height of floor from the highest known high water mark, two feet.

We get the above figures from the gentlemanly Secretary of the Dallas Bridge Company, Capt. GEO. M. SWINK, who also furnishes us with the following table of the cost of the different portions of the structure, and total cost.

Cost of Iron Bridge	$18,000.00
Cost of Roadway through bottoms	4,671.96
Cost of Trestle work on West approach	2,500.00
Cost of Wing fills and filling East approach	3,500.00
Gate keeper's house	800.00
Pay of Engineer Superintendent and Incidentals	3,000.00
Cost of two piers and abutments	24,524.04
Total Cost	**55,000.00**

The trestle work and approach on the West end has a descent one foot in ten, to bring it down to the roadway, which is not made above high-water mark. It is the intention of the Company, however, to keep a good, substantial boat to facilitate travel whenever the water is over the roadway, which does not occur more than two or three times a year, and sometimes not at all.

At the Eastern of town end of the bridge, the Company have erected a handsome brick toll house, where the gate-keeper will always be found. This appointment has, we learn, been given to Mr. SAMUEL GALLEHER, a good and worthy selection.

The following are the rates of toll which the charter allows the Company to charge, and which we presume will be adhered to:

For each wagon, cart, carriage, or other vehicle drawn by more than two horses, 20 cents for each wheel and five cents for each animal, by which the same is drawn and where there are two animals, or less, ten cents a wheel, and five cents for each animal, by which the vehicle is drawn.

For each animal and driver..10 cents

For each loose horse, hog (or other animal) ....5 cents

For each foot passenger..5 cents

For loose animals of the cattle kind ....5 cents

For each sheep, hog or goat ....2 cents

And for citizens of Dallas county, one-half the above rates.

The following are the officers of the Company at present:

    J. W. CROWDUS, President

    GEO. M. SWINK, Secretary

    JNO B. BRYAN, Treasurer

    DIRECTORS: J. W. Crowdus, Geo. M. Swink,. Jno. N. Bryan, A. C. Camp, C. H. Beauchamp, W. H. Prather and E. P. Bryan.

We cannot close this article without tendering our congratulations to the Company on the completion of their labors, and we wish also to award to the gentlemanly representatives of the King Bridge Company, Col. W. W. H. LAWRENCE, the general agent, and Capt. CHARLES N. POINTS and E. H. GIBBS, Esq, our mead of praise for their uniform courtesy and energy. They are all the right men in the right places, and we take pleasure in commending them to the people of Texas wherever they may go.

AURELIA COCKRELL'S ACCOUNTING

(Expenses from Baxter Springs to Uncle Rubin's)

Railroad Passage from Baxter Springs to Kansas City$10.00

Supper en route to Kansas City..1.00

Hotel bill in Kansas City, Breakfast and Dinner..............4.00

Drayage from one depot to another in Kansas City........2.00

Railroad passage from Kansas City to Kingsville..............1.50

Hotel bill in Kingsville, one night and breakfast..............1.00

Conveyance from Kingsville to Uncle Rubes, 7 miles......1.50

TOTAL (note: total is off 50 cents)................................$22.50

Robert's expenses since arrival in Missouri

Hat *$2.00*
1 pair kid gloves...*1.75*
Coat, pants, vest...*18.00*
Collars...*50*
1 pair boots *6.00*
2 pairs drawers...*1.80*
4 pairs socks,woolen *1.70*
Cravat...*50*
4 pocket handkerchiefs....................................*1.00*
1 pair gloves, fleecelined................................*2.50*
Overcoat...*11.00*
Pocket knife *1.25*
Ink & inkstand..*25*
Pens, penstaff, rubber.......................................*20*
Paper *25*
Stamps...*1.00*
Envelopes *30*
14 pictures *1.75*
Box of 100 collars *1.75*
6 song books..*60*

Railroad passage from Kingsville
*   to Warrensburg, 3 trips*...............................*2.55*
Railroad passage from
*   Warrensburg to Kingsville, 2 trips*............*1.70*
Railroad fare from here en route
*   to Kansas City and McGee College*............*2.90*
Omnibus ticket and breakfast in Kansas City....*1.00*
Railroad fare from Kansas City to Jacksonville.............*6.45*
Hauling brother & trunk from last depot, 6 miles...........*1.00*
Room and board for Robert at McGee College,
*   paid to Col. Sharp* *150.00*
Robert's spending money while here with me.................*14.00*
Washing & ironing Robert's clothes for college.................*1.00*
My railroad expenses accompanying Brother.................*2.55*
TOTAL *$238.95*

Mama, I paid all of this out of the money you gave me, also paid for everything we used on the road out of mine, for Brother would get nothing. As to what he did with the ten dollars he left home with and the ten you sent him I can't tell.

SAMUEL S. JONES'S LETTER TO HIS DAUGHTER GUILLELMINE
*(From the family papers of Joseph M. Wilson,
unpublished manuscript. Permission granted)*

May 7th, 1893

Dear Gillie:

Thinking that you will feel some interest in what follows, I write for you.

In the beginning of the year 1855 I was a clerk in the mercantile establishment of Gold & Donaldson, then the largest in the town of Dallas. They were doing business in a large two story wooden building situated on Main Street on the southeast corner of the block north of the court house square.

A little before that time a colony of French people was established on the bluff west of the town of Dallas about 3 1/2 or 4 miles distance; among whom was a man named Pierre Dusseau, his daughter Louise and son-in-law G. Poitvin and wife.

They all moved to Dallas where Poitvin opened up a restaurant as they could find nothing to do in the colony. None of them could speak a word of English and it was therefore difficult for them to proceed with the business in a little american town such as Dallas at that time.

Miss Louise being very intelligent, vivacious, sprightly and of prepossessing appearance, became at once the leader of the little band in all business transactions. This brought her to the store of G. &D. to purchase supplies, where by accident I waited upon her, and thereby formed her acquaintance.

By some incomprehensible power two hearts were drawn toward each other. She became my french teacher and I her english teacher.

We progressed rapidly in the two languages, especially in those words expressing love and passion. Time passed, and in a few months we could talk a little french, a little english blended together, so as to understand each other dimly.

Now I had determined to ask her hand in holy wedlock: But I was all at sea for language in which to express the question in french, and I was not certain that she would fully comprehend my meaning in english. I was not long however in devising ways and means. I found an old frenchman who could talk some english. He penned the following line which I presented in due time. "Voulex Vou, Vou Marria Aavec Moi?" The response was a gentle "Yes" So you can imagine my happiness.

After our engagement became known to her brother-in-law, Poitvin, and he seeing that he was going to lose his main stay in business, drove her and her father from his house without a cent upon which to live. Her father was old and infirm, not knowing a word of English. They went to an old leaky log cabin with all the cracks unchinked and undaubed, where I supported them during our engagement. I even furnished her the means to purchase her wedding trousseau.

On the night of the first day of November 1855 we were married by A. M. Dean a christian preacher, in the Methodist Church, under the old Masonic Hall. My happiness was then complete. Her brother-in-law relented and gave us a wedding supper.

I had rented a small cabin on the block north of the store which we occupied for a short time, until I bought a lot on the north side of Elm & East side of Jefferson Strts., upon which stood an old carpenter shop constructed out of round sided slabs set on end. I canvassed this with brown domestic and we moved into it.

There a daughter was born and your dear Mother named her Guillelmine in honor of your deceased grandmother. I afterward built a house on the northend of the lot where we lived, nothing occurring to mar our happiness until the breaking out of the rebellion. I not willing to serve the confederacy left the country and went to Mexico with your mother and you.

On our return we were flat, having spent our last cent except $150 which mexican brigands relieved me of.

By the indomitable energy of your dear mother and by the accident of my obtaining the county clerkship we were again enabled to move on in life.

Not long after this time your grandpa died giving your mother many pangs of sorrow. We all loved him but she was deeply attached to him.

S. S. Jones